THE ART
of
USING YOUR WHOLE BRAIN

I. KATHERINE BENZIGER & ANNE SOHN

KBA Publishing
Advanced Strategies for Personal Growth

Box 116, Rockwall, Texas 75087 USA

This book is dedicated to the Tradition of Thinking about Thinking, most especially to The Native American Medicine Wheel and to Carl Jung;

to Isabel Hamilton Rey
Katherine's maternal grandmother, who studied with Jung in Switzerland in 1932-33, establishing a family commitment to personal growth;

to Patricia Rey Benziger
for her enthusiastic carrying forward of this commitment; and

to James Benziger
for his encouragement, critical contributions and editorial assistance.

Additionaly Books, Profiling and Workshops on this subject are available in many parts of the United States. For the licensee closest to you, contact KBA or the Licensee identifed below:

Your Local Licensee:

Additional appreciation is extended to: Tom Nutt-Powell for his encouragement and invaluable support throughout; Jeff Vasbinder, Anne's husband, for being patient, understanding and keeping the home fires burning while Anne was in Texas writing; Mindy Klein and Elizabeth Myers for the long hours of editing and proof-reading given in friendship; Keith Simmons for his inspiration and assistance with illustrations; and Lori Polin and Doyle Sherman without whose loving friendship the completion of this book would have been more difficult.

TABLE OF CONTENTS

INTRODUCTION

Simply stated, the Benziger Model is an explanation of how and why human beings think the way they do; why they don't all think alike; and why some of them are better at certain types of thinking than others. If you have ever wondered why you think the way you do, why you just can't understand a certain subject or can't seem to pay attention when a particular person is talking, or why you have difficulty making yourself understood by others, or even what type of job or career would best suit you, this book will give you some of the answers.

The book draws upon the lives and professional experience of both authors. In particular, it synthesizes Katherine's work since 1978 in the area of maximizing human potential by understanding human differences. She began using the work of Carl Jung, the Thomas-Kilman Conflict Assessment, and Bernard Haldane's model for identifying individual, transferable "dependable strengths" to assist individuals and organizations to make change and manage differences. In 1981, Katherine began to explore the relationship between her own work and that of Ned Herrmann. Shortly thereafter, she began collaborating with Herrmann and using his assessment, along with the others she was already using, to gather and study data on her client groups. As time passed, Katherine became convinced that although each of the tools she was using had value, all of them were lacking in the ability to identify the areas within the brain responsible for each specialized mode as well as to explain the physiological difference between preference and competence. In 1984, therefore, believing that such information would be critical to the model's usefulness to both business and education, and at the suggestion of several physician clients, Katherine began to dig more deeply. In 1985, Dr. Karl Pribram, gave Katherine a suggestion along with a couple of missing pieces to the puzzle, which enabled her to build a new, more accurate and powerful model. Finally, by 1986, her on-going reading on the brain's physiology and discussions with Dr. Frank Farley had convinced her to begin to present her own model.

As a theory, the Benziger Model links current "hard" scientific knowledge about the brain, its structure and physiology with a "softer" body of psychological knowledge about thinking and learning styles. As such, it is rapidly becoming a powerful tool for management consultants, communications specialists and psychologists.

Until now, however, this model and assessment, the BTSA or Benziger Thinking Styles Assessment, have been available only through corporate and organizational workshops. Even people attending these programs had no way of sharing the information. Thus, The Art of Using Your Whole Brain was originally written for workshop participants who wanted something they could take home or back to the office to give to friends and colleagues.

To assist you in mastering the content, the book is divided into four parts: an overview of the model and four modes, a discussion of how it affects our work life, a discussion of how it affects our personal life, and guidelines and strategies for expanding your access. As well, we have included application exercises. The first of these exercises is a Self-Assessment, included in Chapter 1, which will help you to identify your personal thinking pattern or brain dominance. Although not as comprehensive as the instrument used in our workshops, this assessment can be self-administered, making it possible for you to immediately apply it. The remainder of the application exercises are in Appendix E: Your Whole Brain Workbook. Some of these are from our workshops, others have been designed specifically for this book. In either case, their purpose is to assist you in developing a visceral understanding of the model through its step-by-step application to your own life.

As authors and individuals committed to human growth, we hope you will enjoy reading the book, as well as doing and learning from the exercises. If after reading it, you would like to order additional copies of the book or arrange a workshop for your company or organization, you may contact us by writing **KBA *THE HUMAN RESOURCE TECHNOLOGY COMPANY* BOX 116, ROCKWALL, TEXAS 75087** or phoning **214-771-3991**.

PART I.

THE MODEL

ABOUT MODELS:

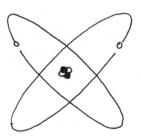

Look at the above picture. What do you see? If you're like most people you "see" an atom. Of course, technically speaking, what you see is not a "real" atom, but rather Neil Bohr's <u>model</u> or representation of an atom. Significantly, the purpose of such intellectual models is to enable us to work with and understand the structure of systems we cannot directly or completely experience.

Now, in the course of reading this book, you will learn about another, equally significant model--the Benziger Model of human thinking. This model is comparable to Bohr's model in several ways. Both models seek to explain something extremely complex and as yet largely unknown. Just as the atom has been unknowable because it is too small, the human brain has been unknowable because it is too complex. Moreover, both models have the same three elements which characterize most useful scientific models:

1. **an identification of the system's key physical elements**
2. **a set of laws describing the model's internal dynamics** (e.g., how the various elements of the atom/brain interact); and,
3. **a set of laws describing the model's external dynamics** (e.g., how the atom/brain interacts with its environment).

Finally, in the same way that Neil Bohr's model has proven to be a useful tool for physicists seeking to understand creation, the Benziger Model is proving to be a useful tool for business executives, educators, psychologists and parents seeking to understand, predict and manage human behavior. Notwithstanding, it would be a good idea to remember that all models are <u>abstractions</u> of reality and, like caricatures, tend to exaggerate specific unique or key features while simultaneously de-emphasizing or ignoring other features.

We'll begin with a brief overview of the three elements which comprise the Benziger Whole Brain Thinking model.

1. THE KEY PHYSICAL ELEMENTS OF YOUR BRAIN: ITS FOUR CORE MODES

In seeking to understand where and how different types of thinking are managed it is helpful to begin by looking at the complete human brain. The human brain, sometimes called the triune brain, is a single, unified, highly adaptive system comprised of three subsystems: the reptilian core, limbic system, and cerebral cortex. Together, these three systems manage, or enable us to manage, ourselves and our lives:

- The reptilian system[1] manages our **energy level**, our wakefulness, sleep cycles, heart rate and breathing.
- The limbic system manages our **emotional responses** and the

---

[1]For a more complete understanding of how each of these systems functions, see Appendix B: The Physiological Bases for the Model.

storage and retrieval of memories, as well as our blood pressure, body temperature, sex drive and appetite.

• And, the cerebral cortex manages our **thinking**.

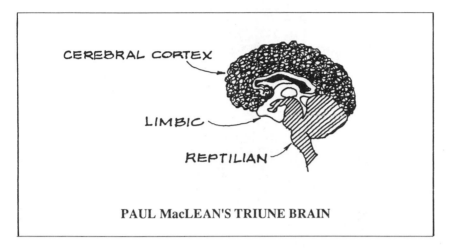

CEREBRAL CORTEX

LIMBIC

REPTILIAN

PAUL MacLEAN'S TRIUNE BRAIN

Importantly, although each subsystem has its own unique contribution or specialty, it is also true that to some extent all three work together and are interdependent. Thus, although "thinking" per se is largely a function of our cerebral cortex, thinking would be impossible without the involvement of our reptilian and limbic brains. For one thing, much of our thinking involves processing new information about our environment and this new information is brought to our awareness by our reptilian brain, which is the central conduit through which all sensations about our external world pass en route to the cortex.

In the same way that our reptilian brain serves to provide us with information about our present environment, recent discoveries have demonstrated that a portion of the limbic brain provides our cortex with the means for accessing memories, themselves stored in the cortex. When damage occurs to the part of our limbic system involved in accessing our memories, as happens in the case of Alzheimer's disease, the person can no longer retrieve or process long-term memories, even though the memories themselves are still intact in the cortex. Thus, in the truest sense the three major subdivisions or subsystems within our brain--our cortex, our limbic system and our reptilian core--are interactive.

Even so, "thinking" is primarily a cerebral process. Our cerebral brain or cortex "thinks" about the past, present and future utilizing the capabilities of the limbic and reptilian brains to supply it with data and to carry its thinking into action.

To truly understand the process of thinking, therefore, we must focus our attention on the cortex. When we do this, several things become immediately apparent. First, we notice that the cortex is broken down into four key components or areas by two intersecting fissures: the central fissure and the longitudinal fissure.

THE CEREBRAL CORTEX'S FOUR COMPONENT AREAS

central
fissure

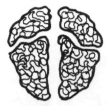

central
fissure

longitudinal fissure

Additionally, we see that each of these four areas has a generalized mode of accessing and processing information, based on its unique structure and physiology, as indicated in the following chart.

CEREBRAL CORTEX'S FOUR MODES OF THINKING[2]

region	mode
BASAL LEFT	Sequential
BASAL RIGHT	Feeling
FRONTAL RIGHT	Internal Imaging
FRONTAL LEFT	Analytical

---

[2]Additionally, your body's movements are controlled by the motor cortex, which spans the posterior region of both frontal lobes, as well as by the brain's reptilian area. However, as yet we have insufficient data to comment more on this fact; it does suggest several intriguing possibilities concerning the potential intelligence of true athletes on the one hand, and an innovative approach to developing intelligence on the other.

If we explore further, we find that the basal left and right areas are both repositories for sensed information, although the manner in which each processes information causes them to attend, in very different ways, to quite different information. The basal left senses information in a linear, step-by-step way. This sequential processing is most easily understood as the ability to learn and perform an established sequence of movements -- a procedure or routine. By contrast, the basal right senses information in a felt or rhythmic manner which leads it to specialize in recognizing and processing nonverbal information and vocal tones, sensing and enjoying musical rhythm, picking up and storing emotional signals and memories, and attributing "meaning" to spiritual experiences.

Compared to the immediacy of the basal focus, the focus of the frontal lobes often appears removed and conceptual. In fact, one understanding of the frontal lobes has been that they "think" (e.g., conceptualize) about what has been sensed by the basal lobes. And, although it now appears that the frontal lobes do receive sensory information directly, this generalization is not a bad way to begin to understand how the frontal lobes work. To go a step further, it seems that the left frontal lobe prefers mathematical, logical and structural analysis while the frontal right, by virtue of its ability to generate and manipulate internal images, prefers abstracted or complex spatial and metaphoric thinking. Thus, the frontal left excels at "breaking things down," "weighing all the variables" and "prioritizing," and, the frontal right excels at imaginative and "holistic" systems thinking. Moreover, research has recently confirmed that what we call "expressiveness" is housed in the frontal right lobe. Additionally, both frontal lobes are hard wired to a powerful energy source in the reptilian core which energizes their thinking. We might perceive the left frontal's analytic mode as driving and the right frontal's imaging mode as charismatic or inspiring. Combining this new image of the cortex with a more in-depth information about how each of the four areas thinks, we can create the model of our cerebral brain shown on the next page.

Importantly, although each of the four key regions of our cortex has its own specialty, the individual modes were not designed to function alone, but in concert with the others as part of a **unified brain system**. In fact, only by working together can they accomplish their shared purpose: **to insure man's survival, growth and evolution.** For, although each area has a specialized function and each is of equal importance, human life as we know it would not be possible if any one of the four modes were absent. Given this, one might assume that every human being is born with equal access to all four modes. Paradoxically, when we explore the second element of the Benziger Model, the Law of Dominance, which describes the model's internal dynamics, we find the contrary to be true.

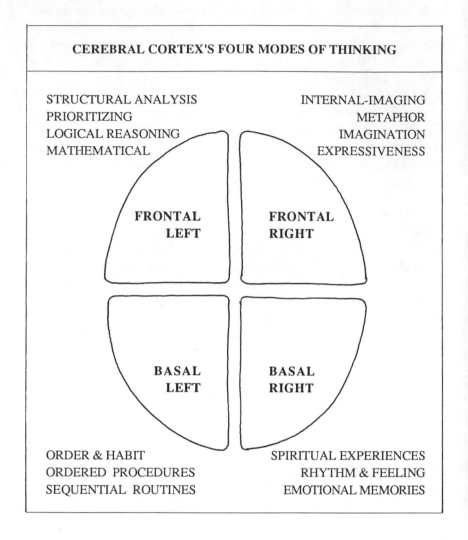

CEREBRAL CORTEX'S FOUR MODES OF THINKING

STRUCTURAL ANALYSIS
PRIORITIZING
LOGICAL REASONING
MATHEMATICAL

INTERNAL-IMAGING
METAPHOR
IMAGINATION
EXPRESSIVENESS

FRONTAL LEFT

FRONTAL RIGHT

BASAL LEFT

BASAL RIGHT

ORDER & HABIT
ORDERED PROCEDURES
SEQUENTIAL ROUTINES

SPIRITUAL EXPERIENCES
RHYTHM & FEELING
EMOTIONAL MEMORIES

2. LAWS GOVERNING YOUR BRAIN'S INTERNAL DYNAMICS

Far from being born with four equally available and equally strong modes, most of us are born with one or two clearly "preferred" modes, in which we have a tremendous natural adeptness, and one, two or three "nonpreferred" modes which do not come as naturally to us.

This tendency was noted earlier in this century by the Swiss psychologist Carl Jung, who observed that there were four basic functions which characterized human behavior and thought. Jung further believed that each person was born with a natural preference for one of these, which he labeled their lead function, which shaped their way of being and life. Although he popularized this idea of dominance Jung was not its originator. For centuries, perhaps millenia, it had been noticed and accepted by a variety of peoples, most notably, the Native Americans, whose traditional belief in a medicine wheel says that we are each born in a specific position on the wheel of life and always carry with us the perspective inherent in that location.[3]

What is important to pick up on here is that physiologically speaking, dominance is natural and normal. As a matter of fact, dominance governs much of our physiology. And yet, as natural as dominance is, it is generally not understood or accepted as valid, and its implications are often ignored. In fact, this lack of understanding for how dominance affects us is the source of many chronic problems which block those seeking to live a joyous and effective life from achieving their goals.

Additional laws which govern your brain's internal dynamics and to which we refer later in this book concern <u>simultaneity</u> and <u>introversion-extraversion.</u> Simultaneity describes the brain's ability to unconsciously continue processing one idea while consciously processing another. Introversion and extraversion refer to the direction of our mental focus -- whether outward or inward.

3. LAWS GOVERNING YOUR BRAIN'S INTERACTION WITH ITS ENVIRONMENT: RULES OF THUMB INSURE SUCCESS

Once you have gained a full appreciation for the model's first two elements-- principally the Four Core Modes of human thinking and the Law of Dominance-- we will assist you in parts two, three and four of this book to understand the effects of dominance in your life and to master the Two Rules of Thumb which tell you how to guide and control the effect dominance has in your life for maximum success and effectiveness. Some of the effects described will seem obvious, such as your tendency to procrastinate tasks which require the use of your weakest or least dominant mode. Other effects are less obvious, such as the connection between a person's dominance and their self-esteem, mid-life and marital difficulties. Whether obvious or not, you will also learn how all these effects can be predicted and managed by using these Two Rules of Thumb.

    1.   To develop or nurture your self-esteem, as well as insure your immediate effectiveness and success, select activities which match your dominance.

---

[3]For additional information about these and other models describing human thinking see Appendix A: The Tradition of Thinking About Thinking

2. To assure your survival, as well as guarantee your long-term effectiveness and success, manage activities and people not matching your dominance by enlisting assistance from complementary brains.

Now, before exploring any further, you will need to have an idea of your own brain dominance -- that is, which and how many of the modes you prefer, and which if any you avoid. The following self-assessment[4] will help you do this.

BRAIN DOMINANCE: A SELF-ASSESSMENT:

General Directions: This assessment is in four sections, one for each mode. In each section you will find a descriptive paragraph followed by 15 statements designed to assist you in evaluating your strength in that mode exclusively. As you read, keep in mind two things:

1. Dominance is **normal** and **natural**. Do not expect or try to score high on all four modes. Most people will (and should) have high scores in only one or two areas.

2. There is an important difference between Preference and Competency. Therefore, we do not want you to identify what you can do; we want you to **identify what you like to do** and **what you do easily** and **effortlessly**.

For these reasons, as you read through the assessment, consider how you think and act **at work and at home**. Read slowly, and notice the degree of real **comfort, familiarity, and identification you have with the specific words and phrases** used for each particular mode. Be sensitive to the fact that you may have developed some competencies or mental skills in areas which you do not necessarily prefer, just as a child born left-handed may have developed a competency in using his or her right hand. If you do something well, but do not feel comfort, ease, satisfaction, and delight in it as you do it, your ability may not be a preference.

Lastly, the more comfort you feel applying these specific words and phrases to yourself, the more likely it is that you actually think in that mode, so **DO NOT PARAPHRASE.**

[4]This self-assessment will assist most of you to identify your strongest and weakest modes. However, due to the tendency of many people to adapt--that is to develop and identify with competencies in their non-preferred modes in order to survive or fit in where their dominance is not accepted or rewarded--the results of this short and simple assessment are not always accurate. For a more accurate 22-page analysis of your profile, your patterns of adaption and introversion-extroversion tendencies, we recommend you order the Benziger Thinking Styles Assessment (BTSA) which we use with our clients and in our workshops.

MODE I

Mode I thinking is ordered and procedural, distinguished by the ability to <u>repeat an action consistently and accurately over time</u>. True mode I thinkers derive satisfaction and a sense of accomplishment from following <u>established routines and procedures</u>. They are masters at attending to the details. Loyal, <u>dependable</u> and <u>reliable,</u> they may remain with the same company for years, where they are valued for the <u>consistency</u> of their work and the <u>thoroughness</u> with which they complete tasks. Naturally <u>conservative</u>, they appreciate <u>traditional</u> values and prefer to approach tasks and solve problems in a step-by-step manner.

Now, on a scale of 0 (not at all) to 5 (completely), how comfortable are you with this paragraph as a description of yourself? Write that number here: Part I:_4_ .

Next, read through the following 15 statements, putting a checkmark next to those which are <u>very descriptive</u> of you. Leave blank any that don't apply or are only somewhat descriptive of you.

1. I excel at keeping things organized. ____✓____
2. I like working with details. ____✓____
3. I am very productive, reliable, & self-disciplined. _____
4. I enjoy doing sorting, filing, planning & making labels. ____✓____
5. I think rules are important & should be followed. ____✓____
6. I prefer to have specific instructions & procedures to work by. ____✓____
7. I consider myself to be conservative & traditional. _____
8. Both at work and home, I like to have specific places for everything. ____✓____
9. I use a step-by-step method for solving problems & approaching tasks. ____✓____
10. I actively dislike ambiguity, uncertainty & unpredictability. _____
11. I complete assignments on time & in an orderly way. _____
12. I prefer to associate with & most highly approve of people who have their emotions under control & behave appropriately. _____
13. I always read the directions completely before beginning a project. ____✓____
14. I enjoy having regular routines & following them. _____
15. I prefer to schedule both my personal & professional life & am upset when I have to deviate from that schedule. _____

To calculate your score for Part II, count the number of checkmarks above, and give yourself one (1) point for each. Write your total here: Part II: ___8___ .

Now, add the numbers from Part I & Part II and write the total below:

TOTAL MODE I SCORE:___12___ .

MODE II

Mode II thinking is spiritual, symbolic and feeling-based. It picks up the subtleties and shifts in others' moods, emotions and nonverbal signals. Strong mode II thinkers are often highly expressive, instinctively reaching out to comfort, encourage or connect with others through words and gestures. Naturally caring, they believe that how someone feels is of utmost importance and they bring this concern for compassion, relationship and interpersonal harmony to both their personal and professional lives. Given their ability to relate positively and empathetically, Mode II thinkers also excel at motivating others to "join in," by sharing their own excitement, enthusiasm and support.

Now, on a scale of 0 (not at all) to 5 (completely), how comfortable are you with this paragraph as a description of yourself? Write that number here: Part I:_3_.

Next, read through the following 15 statements, putting a checkmark next to those which are very descriptive of you. Leave blank any that don't apply or are only somewhat descriptive of you.

1. I pay particular attention to & am skilled at understanding body-language & nonverbal communication.   ✓
2. I believe feelings are truer & more important than thoughts.   _____
3. I enjoy verbally "connecting" with others, listening to their problem & sharing their feelings.   ✓
4. I consider myself a highly spiritual person.   _____
5. I relate to others empathetically & find it easy to feel what they feel.   ✓
6. I excel at creating enthusiasm & positively motivating others.   _____
7. I often spontaneously touch others in nurturing & encouraging ways.   ✓
8. I automatically watch someone's face when talking with them.   ✓
9. I love to sing, dance & listen to music.   ✓
10. I believe personal growth & development are extremely important.   ✓
11. I define success by the quality of the experience.   ✓
12. I consider my relationships to be the most important part of my life. ✓
13. I feel uneasy in conflict situations.   _____
14. I consider cooperation & harmony the most important human values.   _____
15. I always want to know how people feel & how they are relating.   ✓

To calculate your score for Part II, count the number of checkmarks above, and give yourself one (1) point for each. Write your total here: Part II: __10__.

Now, add the numbers from Part I & Part II and write the total below:

TOTAL MODE II SCORE:___13___

MODE III

Mode III thinking is <u>visual, spatial</u> and <u>nonverbal</u>. It is <u>metaphoric</u> and conceptual, expressing itself as <u>internal "pictures" or "movies"</u> which the Mode III thinker delights in viewing and which naturally makes them masters of <u>integration, innovation</u> and <u>imagination</u>. Easily bored, they constantly <u>seek the stimulation of new concepts</u>, new information and new adventures. They are readily identified by their visual "filing system" which stores material in stacks or piles around their home/office; and their quirky, sometimes "off the wall" sense of humor. . As "<u>conceptual humanitarians</u>" they are interested in humanity and its evolution, even though they may not be especially adept at relating one on one.

Now, on a scale of 0 (not at all) to 5 (completely), how comfortable are you with this paragraph as a description of yourself? Write that number here: Part I:_ /_ .

Next, read through the following 15 statements, putting a checkmark next to those which are <u>very descriptive</u> of you. Leave blank any that don't apply or are only somewhat descriptive of you.

1. I focus more on the "Big Picture" than "titchy" details, such as spelling.____
2. I regularly come up with innovative ideas & creative solutions. _____
3. I am recognized as a highly energetic & expressive person. _____
4. I actively dislike & get quickly bored with routine tasks or activities. _____
5. I excel at synthesizing disparate ideas or items into new "wholes." _____
6. I prefer to work simultaneously, processing lots of ideas & tasks
   at the same time. _____
7. I consider <u>novelty, originality</u> & <u>evolution</u> the most important values. _____
8. I find information easily in the stacks I use to organize my home/office._____
9. I use metaphors & visual analogies to explain my thinking to others. _____
10. I get excited by others' novel or "off the wall" ideas. __✓__
11. I rely on hunches & my intuition when solving problems. _____
12. I have a sense of humor that's gotten me in trouble for not behaving
    appropriately. _____
13. I get some of my best ideas while doing "nothing in particular." _____
14. I have well developed spatial skills, can easily "see" how to re-arrange
    a room, re-pack a suitcase or car so everything fits in. _____
15. I have artistic talent. _____

To calculate your score for Part II, count the number of checkmarks above, and give yourself one (1) point for each. Write your total here: Part II: _____ .

Now, add the numbers from Part I & Part II and write the total below:

TOTAL MODE III SCORE:__ 2 __ .

MODE IV

Mode IV thinking is <u>logical</u> and <u>mathematical</u>, excelling at <u>critical analysis,</u> <u>diagnostic problem solving</u> and in the use of <u>tools</u> and machines. Mode IV thinkers have well defined goals and the ability to <u>calculate</u> the most direct, efficient and <u>cost-effective strategies</u> for any situation. This leads them towards positions of <u>leadership</u> in which they can control <u>key decisions and manipulate</u> <u>circumstances</u> into alignment with their desired results. Given their ability to be critical and precise, it is not surprising they prefer technical, mechanical, or financial work.

Now, on a scale of 0 (not at all) to 5 (completely), how comfortable are you with this paragraph as a description of yourself? Write that number here: Part I:_/_.

Next, read through the following 15 statements, putting a checkmark next to those which are <u>very descriptive</u> of you. Leave blank any that don't apply or are only somewhat descriptive of you.

1. I prefer to work with technical or financial matters. _____
2. I like doing critical & analytic thinking. _____
3. I have good diagnostic & technical problem solving skills. _____
4. I excel at studying science, finance, math or logic. _____
5. I find I enjoy & am energized by verbal argumentation or debate. _____
6. I excel at understanding machines& enjoy using tools & building or fixing things. _____
7. I prefer to have the final responsibility for making decisions & setting priorities. _____
8. I consider thinking <u>significantly</u> more important than feeling. _____
9. I excel at making investments & in managing and leveraging key resources such as time & money. _____
10. I consider myself a primarily logical thinker. _√_____
11. I excel at delegating & giving orders. _√_____
12. I regularly organize material into key points & operational principles. _√_____
13. I evaluate my success by the actual results I produce & by the bottom line. _____
14. I consider myself a powerful, decisive & effective leader. _____
15. I value <u>effectiveness</u> & <u>rationality</u> above all else. _____

To calculate your score for Part II, count the number of checkmarks above, and give yourself one (1) point for each. Write your total here: Part II: _____.

Now, add the numbers from Part I & Part II and write the total below:

TOTAL MODE IV SCORE:_?_____.

INTERPRETING YOUR SCORES:

Now, in order to get a complete picture of your brain, transfer all four of your scores to the spaces below.

MODE I	MODE II	MODE III	MODE IV
basal left	basal right	frontal right	frontal left
12	13	2	3

By looking at your scores for each of the four modes all at once, you can begin to get a sense of how you are using your brain. You can see immediately whether one or perhaps two of your scores are noticeably higher than the others.

Significantly, most of us only have <u>one natural preference</u> which we can use alone or in conjunction with non-preferred competencies in one or more of our three non-preferred modes. If we are living true to our natural preference, using our brain as it was designed to be used, leading with our natural lead; our scores show our natural preference as highest and our greatest natural weakness - located diagonally across the brain from our natural preference - as lowest. The other two modes, called auxiliaries, may be minimally to strongly developed. When you are using your brain most effectively, however, neither auxiliary is equal to or greater than your natural lead. In this situation:

20 +: a very high score indicates a **Commitment** to one's preference. If you scored this high, it means you emphatically prefer to think in this way, believe it is the "best way to think," and possibly believe that everyone else should think this way.

13 to 19: a high score indicates a **Preference** or very highly developed non-preferred competency in an auxiliary - something that is part of your "bag of tricks" and the way you most often want to do things.

6 to 12: a moderate score indicates non-preferred, developed **Competencies** in an auxiliary. You will generally find that you can access and use such a mode <u>at will</u> and with the conscious choice to do so, especially <u>when what you want it to do serves a greater purpose more aligned with your preferred mode</u>. Continued focus in this area, however, will take effort and, over time, will drain you.

0 to 5: a low score indicates a lack of preference for and often an actual **Avoidance** in a mode. Situations requiring you to perform in this area may evoke a strong sense of resistance in you, induce you to immediate anger, or motivate you simply to leave, procrastinate, day-dream, doodle or make lists of what you really want to do.

Again, these 'meanings' apply if you are living over center, leading with your natural lead.

For many of us the meaning differs somewhat. Our data accurately identifies how we are currently using our brain, but not our natural preference. This is because we have had to adapt or falsify type to survive, fit in, belong or be rewarded. Significantly, persons who've been adapting heavily report experiencing frequent anxiety, exhaustion and/or an increasing number of health problems. If you experience these problems or if your memory of yourself as a child differs significantly from how you are today, read Chapters 1-5 and 7 of this book and then retake this self test or arrange to take the BTSA itself to gain a deeper understanding of your natural preferences. (see pp. 301-302)

For now, continue by developing an appreciation for how you are currently using your brain by listing below those modes (i.e. Frontal Left, Basal Right...) in which you have a score of 13 or more.

My primary modes are: *basal left   basal right*   .

If you wrote one mode in this space, you are a **Quarter Brain Specialist**, operating out of that one mode.

If you wrote two modes in the space you are a **Half Brainer**, operating out of those two modes.

If you wrote three modes in the space, you are a **Triple Brainer**, or **Translator,** operating out of those three modes. As a triple translator you probably need a variety of activities in order to use/satisfy each of your developed modes and you may frequently find yourself "translating" between them as you explain to one person what another person is saying.

If you wrote all four modes in the space, you are a **Whole Brain Thinker**, interested and satisfied by almost any task, as long as it doesn't last too long. As such, you are also capable of <u>understanding</u> and getting along with almost anyone.

DESCRIBING YOUR DOMINANCE:

In describing people's patterns, it can be useful to use phrases which give a dynamic picture of the person's pattern. Thus:

Quarter-brainers are described by affixing the phrase "quarter-brain" to the preferred or primary mode (i.e., a "quarter brain frontal left;" or a "quarter brain basal right").

Half-brainers are described as being: "double right" (someone with primaries in both right modes), "double frontal" (someone with primaries in both frontal modes), "double left" (someone with a primaries in the frontal and basal left), "double basal" (someone with a primaries in both the right and left basal modes) and "diagonal" (someone who has a primaries in the basal left and frontal right, or alternately, the frontal left and basal right).

Triple-brainers or Translators are described by indicating the person's area of weakness, such as: "A triple translator with a weakness in the basal left," or a "triple translator with a weakness in the frontal left."

Finally, whole brain patterns are simply referred to as "whole brained."

Using the above information, describe your own pattern in the space below:

My pattern is: _____ *double basal* _____.

One final point we wish to make is that very often to communicate a person's dominance, a graph of the actual scores is drawn. The purpose of this is two-fold. First, such graphs often convey more effectively the dynamic energy which accompanies each pattern. Secondly, graphs, which are linear abstractions of a score, like caricatures and models, communicate best with the frontal right brain which really doesn't understand words and numbers very well.

For this reason, we will conclude the chapter on You, Your Brain and Your Dominance with a series of typical graphs. Spend a few moments studying them: Do some appear to be more balanced and even? Some more skewed? Some more uplifting? Some more weighty? Some almost like arrows pointing towards a specific direction? How would you describe each of these people?

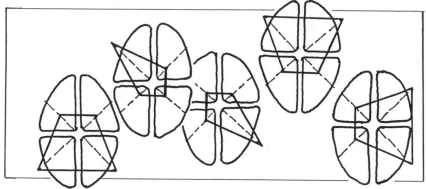

Given what you already know about each of the four modes, which ones identify people who would be likely to attend to details and deadlines? To how you are feeling and whether or not you are feeling welcome? Which would be likely to be artistic? To be analysing the mechanical or technical cause of an accident?

For those wishing to graph their own profile, a blank profile graph with instructions on how to use it is in the portion of Your Whole Brain Workbook (Appendix E) corresponding to this chapter.

CHAPTER 2
DOMINANCE IS NATURAL

In chapter three we will explore each of the four modes in depth, giving multiple examples of how each functions. Before doing this, however, it is important that we explore the concept of "Dominance" more fully. You'll recall that dominance, the principal law governing the our brain's internal dynamics, controls which modes within your brain are naturally strong and which are naturally weak. As such, your dominance determines how easily you use each of the four processing modes, as well as how these modes interact to guide your behavior and your decisions. In other words, your dominance structures your thinking.

What's more, dominance, as we use it here, refers to a physiological principle which governs most systems within our body and is both normal and natural. This is an important point so we'll repeat it: Dominance is completely normal and natural. In fact, many, including Carl Jung, believe dominance to also be desirable.

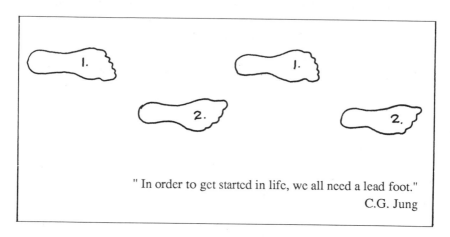

" In order to get started in life, we all need a lead foot."

C.G. Jung

Even so, in working with several thousand people we have noticed that many people have difficulty with the concept of dominance. These people associate it with the word "dominating," an unfortunate association which suggests controlling, limiting and overbearing behavior.

Actually, in scientific terms, dominance simply means that within a given system, comprised of discrete elements, **one part of the system leads while the others follow**--an organizing scheme which is found in countless natural and man-made systems.

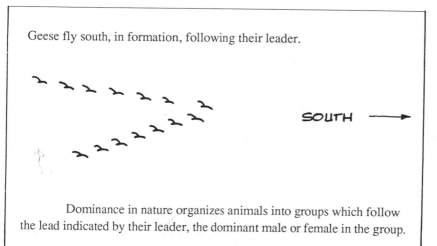

Geese fly south, in formation, following their leader.

SOUTH ⟶

Dominance in nature organizes animals into groups which follow the lead indicated by their leader, the dominant male or female in the group.

We even apply this structure to how we, as humans, co-function or collaborate:

When two people dance together, one usually leads, while the other follows.
When an orchestra performs, its members follow the lead of the conductor.
When the violin section plays, its members follow the lead of the 1st violinist.
A scouting party follows the pack leader, who sets the direction.
Employees work under the direction of their supervisor or manager.

What's more, dominance in thinking is just one of the many ways in which
dominance governs our bodies and behavior. We all experience dominance
within our own bodies most immediately through our handedness. We are also:
armed, footed, legged, eyed and often eared. In other words, one arm is
naturally stronger, one foot generally leads, one leg is naturally stronger, one eye
does most of our focusing, and one ear may hear slightly better.

Moreover, if we take time to consider what we know to be true about
handedness, we can anticipate some of the truths of brainedness. For example,
dominance in our hands is so much the natural state of affairs that over 95% of us
have a clear handedness. Thus, it should not surprise us that by far the majority
of people have a clear dominance pattern in their brain.

In considering handedness as an example of "dominance in action," it is important
to notice that "handedness" does not limit us to the use of only one hand or
minimize the importance of the nondominant hand. Rather, it defines the role of
the nondominant or "minor" hand as that of a follower or supporter.

Consider what happens when you write a letter. Naturally you do the actual
writing with your dominant hand. In order to keep the paper from moving, and
perhaps to get the cap off the pen in the first place, you will, however, invariably
need and use your nondominant hand. Your two hands work together, one
leading, one supporting, to successfully complete the task. When we consider
brainedness, then, we might anticipate that, for most of us, having a lead in one
or two modes does not necessarily render useless or unimportant our other
modes.

Finally, by looking at what we already know about handedness, we see that when
our environment matches our dominance, we are able to perform naturally and
easily; when our dominance does not fit the environment in which we find
ourselves, with all its opportunities and limitations, we are uncomfortable and
often function poorly. Two examples with which we are all familiar are: the left-
handed person who has only right-handed scissors for cutting; and the left-
handed person sitting immediately to the right of a right-handed person at the
dinner table. And so again, it would be natural for us to anticipate that as we find
ourselves in an environment which matches our brainedness, we will be mentally

on top, and when we are in an environment which does not match the natural abilities of our mental preferences, we will have problems.

Once you understand that brain dominance is as common and as natural as handedness, it becomes easy to understand how and why two people with similar backgrounds, even within the same family, can think very differently about the same idea, topic or event. In fact, you may even begin to see how many interpersonal conflicts and miscommunications have their roots in people's differing pattterns of dominance.

In summary, the second element of our model, the law of Dominance, is normal, natural, desirable and pervasive, and it governs our ability to use and develop the model's first element, the Four Core Modes.

QUESTIONS AND ANSWERS ABOUT DOMINANCE:

What is the difference between a preference and dominance?

Our innate neurochemically-based preference for 1 mode over the other 4 does not change, and is identical to our <u>natural dominance</u>. Practically speaking, however, our life experience can lead us to develop and use one of our 3 non-preferred modes more than our natural preference. When this happens how we are using our brain, our <u>effective</u> or <u>practical dominance</u>, will reflect these changes rather than our true preference or <u>natural</u> dominance.

How many different patterns of mental dominance are there?

There are only four patterns of <u>natural dominance</u>. These are the four "1/4 brained" patterns in which only 1 mode is dominant and that mode is also the person's natural preference.

By contrast there are fifteen patterns of <u>practical</u> or <u>effective dominance</u> that can occur as a result of a person developing and using non-preferred competencies. These are: four "1/4 brained" patterns in which only 1 mode is dominant, and that mode is not the person's natural preference; six "1/2 brained" patterns in which two of the four modes are dominant; (one of which may be the person's natural preference); four patterns in which all but one mode is dominant (one of which may be the person's natural preference); and one pattern in which all four modes are dominant (one of which is the person's natural preference).

In general, a person is healthiest and most effective when their natural preference is included in their <u>practical dominance</u> pattern and is their most developed or strongest mode. Problems are more likely to occur when a person's natural preference is not included in their practical dominance; and/or when their practical dominance scores indicate that their greatest natural weakness (diagonally opposite their natural preference) is being used more than the person's natural preference or auxiliaries.

Which pattern is the most common?

Statistically speaking, the most frequent pattern is the one with two leads. This pattern is also called "dual-dominance." Approximately 55% of the population have dual-dominance. What's more, half-brainers come in several forms. They might be double frontal, double basal, double left, double right, or even a diagonal combination of the basal left and frontal right. This insight with respect to the range and variety of patterns is particularly important as some people in the early 1960's and 1970's were hypothesizing that we were all either "Left Brained" (e.g. double lefts) or "Right Brained" (e.g. double rights).

What is the approximate frequency of the other patterns given?

Approximately 25% of the population have only <u>one mode</u> which is dominant. When these persons are in a situation which demands the expertise of their natural lead, they tend to come across as "experts." When the context shifts and the necessary skills are outside their single area of strength, however, these same persons may be seen as "too narrowly focused," or "narrow minded." An example of such context-dependent labeling is the strong frontal left thinker who is respected for his analytic skill in structuring contracts yet is seen as a "dud" the same evening at a cocktail party.

In contrast to these quarter brains, the 55% of the population with <u>dual dominance</u> is seen as more flexible and "broad-minded." Nonetheless, even these persons can be seen by others as distinctly skewed. This seems to be most obvious when the person in question is a double left or a double right thinker.

Tri-modal thinkers are far rarer, making up only about 15% of the population. These individuals, with their flexible strength in <u>three</u> out of the four modes, are often referred to as "triple translators" as they find themselves being asked to assist people with differing and narrower patterns to understand each other. Although many people look at triple translators with a sense of envy or admiration, the pattern is not without its disadvantages, one of which is difficulty in decision making. With three equally developed modes all vying for control, it is not uncommon for tri-modals to feel confused or terribly at odds with themselves.

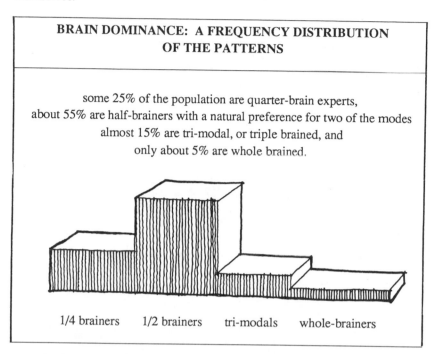

BRAIN DOMINANCE: A FREQUENCY DISTRIBUTION OF THE PATTERNS

some 25% of the population are quarter-brain experts,
about 55% are half-brainers with a natural preference for two of the modes
almost 15% are tri-modal, or triple brained, and
only about 5% are whole brained.

1/4 brainers   1/2 brainers   tri-modals   whole-brainers

The last of the general patterns in which all <u>four</u> of the modes are strongly developed, might be termed "omni-brainedness." More often it is referred to as simply whole brained. The pattern is found in only a small portion of the population, approximately 5%, and is noted for either its high degree of flexibility or its indecisiveness, depending on the context.

What is important to keep in mind, however, is that all patterns are equally valid and equally useful in life. The energy and drive which the quarter-brain expert focuses in one mode enable him or her to devote countless hours and concentrated effort to accomplishing things for which a more "broad-minded" person would not sit still. At the same time, the breadth and holistic understanding of the more whole-brained person enable him/her to communicate more readily and effectively with a wide range of persons, a task which would confound and exhaust the narrowly-focused brain.

CHAPTER 3
TWO HANDS, FOUR BRAINS

As you know from Chapter 1, each of our brain's four core modes has its own unique way of processing information and its own "point-of-view" toward the world. Now, as we explore each mode in more depth, you will begin to see how each of these modes is actually a **specialist**, particularly adept at those tasks which are best and most easily accomplished by its own unique way of processing. The underlying purpose of this division of labor within our thinking brain is to insure that we will have the maximum capacity to adapt and survive. By having four thinking modes, each an expert at dealing with a particular aspect of reality, we vastly increase the amount of variety and flexibility we can achieve as a total system. We also guarantee that what needs to be looked after will be looked after and that all our survival bases will be covered. In this way, the four specialized systems definitely provide us with a whole greater than the sum of its parts.

So what is the specific value, function, and purpose of each of the four expert systems? Let's begin with the Basal Left and take a look.

As you read these in-depth descriptions and characterizations, keep in mind how strong you are in each mode. If you are reading about a mode which is one of your strengths, ask yourself: What positive things have occurred in my life as a result of my strength in this mode? What rewards or accomplishments? And what, if any, negative things have come about as a result of that same strength? Similarly, when you are reading about one of your areas of weakness, ask yourself: "What are some of the obvious, important effects of my not being strong here? What limiting, unpleasant or negative effects do I know of? And What if any positive effects occur to me?"

THE BASAL LEFT, SEQUENTIAL MODE:

This mode of thinking processes by following a preestablished or programmed order:

> It alphabetizes a set of files.
> It orders a set of documents chronologically.
> It carries out tasks in a step-by-step manner.

We often describe this kind of activity as "routine" and it is **routine work** or routine thinking that is the province of the Basal Left brain. As a mode, it is structured to be detailed and procedural and to focus on the successful execution of routine tasks.

**SEQUENTIAL ORGANIZING SYSTEMS
FOR MANAGING DATA, SCHEDULES, PROCEDURES**

A, B, C, D, E, F, G, H, I, J, K, L, M,
N,O,P,Q,R,S,T,U,V,W,X,Y,Z
1,2,3,4,5,6,7,8,9,10
1900, 1901, 1902, 1903, 1904, 1905, 1906
I, II, III, IV, V, VI, VII, VIII, IX, X
1:00, 1:15, 1:30, 1:45, 2:00, 2:15, 2:30

Although some of us use this brain a great deal more than others, everyone has and uses this mode. A good way to see how this type of thinking operates in your own life is to observe your "morning routine." What do you do between the time you awaken and the time you go to work? Do you exercise? Bathe? Dress? Make coffee? Prepare and eat breakfast? Feed the children? How about the cat? If your work is outside the home, do you leave at a particular time? By a particular mode of transportation?

What constitutes a **routine** is that you do the <u>same things</u> every day, in the <u>same order</u>, in approximately the <u>same amount of time</u>. Some people have only three or four steps in their routine, while others have as many as fifteen or twenty steps. For some people one "step" such as "bathing," can be broken down into an entire sub-routine like: start the hot water running, make sure the soap , shampoo and wash cloth are within reach, adjust the water to the desired temperature, turn on the shower, remove robe and hang it on the hook, get in the shower, wet hair and wash it with shampoo, rinse hair, put conditioner on hair, wash body with soap, rinse off conditioner, turn off shower, reach for the towels, put one towel on hair, dry body with second towel, get out of bath tub, hang wet towels over the shower rod, etc. In other words, although at first glance a given routine, such as your own morning routine, might have just a few simple steps, when examined more closely, this same routine may well be found to have tens or even hundreds of discrete, detailed steps arranged in a pre-established sequence.

Understanding that whenever you perform routine activities, you are using this Basal Left, sequential mode of thinking is an important first step. Seeing the value of this mode as part of the entire system and appreciating its contribution are necessary next steps.

The first value of routine thinking is that it is **efficient**; it allows you to accomplish a great deal in a short amount of time. Compare if you will the days on which you follow your morning routine (work days) with the days you don't (weekends). Following the routine you are able to get yourself up, dressed, and moving in a short period of time. By contrast , on the weekends, it may take you hours to get through many of the same steps (if you get through them at all!). Routines help you to accomplish these tasks efficiently by locking in a given set of decisions or acceptable choices, thereby making it unnecessary to re-decide every day/time what needs to be done in order to get ready. Not having to decide,

> "Should I exercise or not?'
> "Should I jog around two blocks or three this morning?"
> "Should I take a bath or a shower?"
> "Should I eat cereal or make time to cook pancakes?"

keeps you from wasting time in the process of prioritizing and deciding. Another way to view this is that routine enables you to predict and control the amount of time it takes you to do something. This characteristic of routine thinking is a tremendous benefit not only because it allows you to roll over for another five minutes of doze-time in the morning, but also because it enables parents to know how much time they need to allow to get to work (given they have to dress the kids first), as well as making it possible for companies to know how many people to hire to accomplish a certain amount of contracted work, and supervisors to manage and set their expectations of employee performance.

Another value of routine thinking is that it **frees your mind** to think about other things which may need your attention. Look again at yourself and what goes on as you move through your morning routine. Do you actually, actively think about each of the things you do? If you're like most of us, the answer is "No, of course not." You're functioning "on automatic," letting your Basal Left mode manage the routine activity while the rest of you thinks about something else, often totally unrelated. This unrelated, second thinking process may be passive or active. You may simply be enjoying memories of a recent pleasurable event, such as a date the night before, or, you may be actively strategizing about the best way to approach your boss at an upcoming staff meeting. Either way, routine thinking allows you to have "two thinks for the price of one." And once again the Basal Left sequential mode is found to be efficient at saving you time and energy.

The third value of routine processing is that it is **dependable**, even under stress. Have you ever gotten to work and suddenly wondered: "Did I turn off the tea kettle?" or "Did I remember to lock the house?" and either called a neighbor or driven home yourself to check, only to discover that there had been no cause for alarm. Everything was as it should be: the kettle off and the house locked. This type of occurrence usually happens when we are either heavily preoccupied ourselves or accidentally interrupted during the course of carrying out a routine. At these times, the semi-conscious monitoring, which we might otherwise do to insure that the routine is run completely and correctly, is forgotten. Nonetheless, because our Basal Left mode operates as dependably as a computer, programmed to complete any set of routines it begins, we generally find that even when we have been distracted, everything in our routine has been accomplished.

Bringing all these positive traits together, a fitting motto for the Basal Left mode might be: "Count on me for: Double Efficiency With Dependability."

A point which might be best made here is that while the Basal Left mode functions in an ordered, step-by-step manner, the Basal Left Thinker is no happier working on a production line, doing an isolated task, which in and of itself completes nothing. Indeed, by definition, a procedure moves in a step-by-step way towards a goal.

Of course, there are drawbacks to using the routine mode. For one thing, it does not handle interruptions easily. By its very nature, sequential thinking adheres to a specified format which does not vary or change. Thus, when a change or interruption occurs, it reacts like a computer whose data has been entered incorrectly. It registers confusion and sends up the "Does not Compute" flag. And, if there are too many interruptions or irregularities in the schedule or environment, this mode may actually need to close down while a more active, decision-making mode comes in to sort out the problem.

Another point worth mentioning is that although our total brain/thinking system is designed to function on an "appropriateness" model, passing control to whichever area can best handle the issue or task at hand, in practice, each mode tends to be resist giving up control. Hence, the Basal Left might respond to an interruption by saying: "We don't need to change the way we do this. It works just fine. It's been working just fine for forty years."

And yet, despite these drawbacks, the Basal Left continues to be an extremely valuable mode for all of us. Viewed from a systems perspective, this mode performs the **meta-function** of **building and maintaining orderly foundations** in our lives. With its ever-present attention to detail, its dependability and its efficiency, it keeps us organized both at work and at home. And because it is at work, or "on" so much of the time, insuring a strong foundation, it frees us to learn, explore, enjoy and grow.

BASAL LEFT FOUNDATION-BUILDING TASKS:
A Partial Listing

Buying Groceries	Purchasing Supplies
Keeping Supplies Orderly	Filling Orders
Paying Bills or Taxes	Balancing Your Check Book
Invoicing Clients	Writing Pay Checks
Preparing Monthly Statements	Keeping Financial Records Straight
Washing Clothes or Dishes	Folding Clothes
Routine Cleaning	Preparing Routine Meals

Assembling a toy , piece of furniture, or stereo
system according to the instructions provided

Creativity and innovation are wonderous things, but constantly having to re-invent the wheel takes unnecessary time, energy and attention. Thus, we can see how procedural and knowledge-based foundations are necessary for individual life, family life and corporate life: A tree grows only as tall as its roots allow. A building can only climb as high as its foundation can support. And the best logical argument is no stronger or better than the data base it is using.

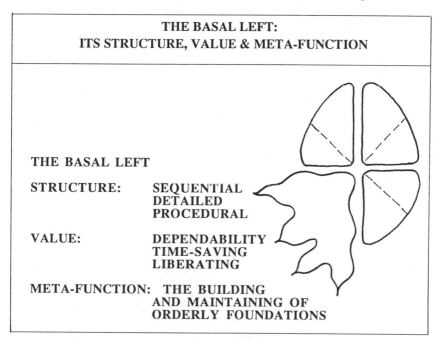

THE BASAL LEFT: ITS STRUCTURE, VALUE & META-FUNCTION

THE BASAL LEFT

STRUCTURE: SEQUENTIAL
DETAILED
PROCEDURAL

VALUE: DEPENDABILITY
TIME-SAVING
LIBERATING

META-FUNCTION: THE BUILDING
AND MAINTAINING OF
ORDERLY FOUNDATIONS

This then is the meta-function of our Basal Left Sequential Thinking Mode. As life and human civilization continue to evolve, the strong orderly foundations it provides are what ultimately enable us to live broader and more expansive lives.

In order to review what you have just read, as well as check to see what you might have missed, take a moment to look at the above chart. Then, read through the next chart on the Basal Left Thinker, asking yourself as you go, who do I know who thinks this way? Myself? my mother or father? my child? my friend? my spouse? When someone comes to mind, ask yourself in what way they have provided you with foundations?

THE BASAL LEFT THINKER

ARCHETYPES: The Adding Machine
                          or Plow Horse

SYMBOL: An Anchor

MOST ATTENTIVE TO: Following the instructions.
                          Matching action to the prescribed routine or
                          procedure.
                          Doing things by the book.

VALUES LEARNING: Procedural applications which have an
                          immediate & clear use, and which are presented
                          to them in an organized, pre-digested or step-
                          by-step manner.

INTERNAL LANGUAGE: Data in, data out. The sequential
                          play-back of previously experienced or learned
                          events, rules or procedures such as:
                          "Always put the cart before the horse."
                          "Always file your IRS return by April 15."

USES LANGUAGE TO: Communicate the prescribed order, or to
                          communicate that something is wrong, that is,
                          something is out of order.

FAVORED MODE OF COMMUNICATION: Written forms which
                          maximize efficiency by requiring or enabling
                          check marks.

PATTERN OR RHYTHM OF SPEECH: Slow and even or steady.
                          Often they only talk to verbalize existing
                          expectations, or report what is wrong & the
                          sequence of events leading to the moment in
                          time the problem was discovered.

CHARACTERISTIC THOUGHT PATTERN: Is visceral more than conceptual, preferring to work with things rather than ideas. Also prefers to work with things rather than people.

TYPICAL PHRASES: "Just tell me what to do & I'll do it."
"Let's play it safe..."
"the importance of establishing good habits is that..."
"Remember the importance of self- discipline is that..."
"The law is," "The rule-book says..."
"We do it this way here..."
"Good fences make good neighbors..."

SELF-PERCEPTION: A highly productive worker.

AS SEEN BY OTHERS: Boring, non-imaginative, stick in the mud, with not an original bone in their body; a work-horse who grinds out the task.

THE BASAL RIGHT, FEELING MODE:

The second of our cerebral brain's four key modes of thinking is the Basal Right Feeling mode, which is located in the basal lobes of the right cerebral hemisphere. This mode is particularly sensitive to **rhythm** and **harmony**. It is the part of our brain which enjoys listening to music (paying particular attention to the "rhythm section") and which, when talking to another person monitors and responds most directly to **nonverbal communications**. Its sensitivity to the subtleties of nonverbal cues often result in what others might describe as "mind-reading" or a "strong intuitive sense about people."

Strong Basal Right thinkers not only read others' cues easily, they also tend to match the nonverbal messages they pick up, mirroring them back with their own body language. As such, they become openly enthusiastic when they sense another's excitement and demonstrably sad as they sense another's sadness. Perhaps, because they are so naturally expressive themselves and so "smart" at nonverbal communication, it is also true that they prefer to spend time with people who, like themselves, are openly expressive. Whatever the case, their mood matching response to others transcends words, tending as it does to include the full repertoire of nonverbal gestures: smiles, frowns, pats, hugs.

Programmed specifically to monitor harmony, this mode is particularly sensitive to disharmony or discord. When it senses that someone is upset or uncomfortable, it rapidly and single-mindedly begins providing the soft words and caring touch needed to reestablish harmony. People who have strong access to this Basal Right mode frequently amaze others with their revealing post-meeting or post-party observations about other people's emotional states: "What do you suppose has Mary so upset?" or "I wonder what was bothering John. He certainly was preoccupied with something." Furthermore, committed as they are to reestablishing a state of harmony, they appear to have no hesitation about intervening in what might be considered a person's private life: "I think I'll go talk with John. Perhaps I can help." Or, "I think I'll ask Mary if she'd like to have a cup of coffee. I'll bet she needs to talk with someone."

Although people without a lot of Basal Right access find this ability to read other people's feelings "strange" and "mysterious," there is really nothing odd about it. The feeling brain has a special sensitivity to facial expressions, tones of voice, and subtle body movements. In fact, there is evidence that it is the Basal Right region of our cerebral brain that actually <u>recognizes faces</u> and differentiates one person from another. As astounding as this may seem to you, it is nonetheless true that despite all the sensory information and the mental capabilities available to us, we recognize the faces of those we know and love almost exclusively through the efforts of this single, limited, specialized area in our brains. And, if this specialized area in our own brains were damaged, we would be unable to distinguish even those we have known well for years. (see: The Man Who Mistook His Wife for a Hat by Oliver Sacks, 1986).

Certainly this is an important skill, but inasmuch as even the weakest Basal Right thinker still recognizes his friends and relatives, what is it that is so important about this area's broader skills in nonverbal communication? A partial answer can be found in the work and writings of Dr. Albert Morabian. In his landmark analysis of the human communication, Dr. Morabian demonstrated that as much as 55% of any message conveyed by one person to another through speech is contained in the speaker's nonverbal signals and cues (facial expressions and body language), 35% in their vocals (voice tone and rhythm) and only 10% in the actual words and their meanings. Thus, although the feeling mode may not be able to make sense of specific words, especially those dealing with precision or measurement, it can and does understand the bulk of what any given person is communicating because it reads faces and listens to bodies in the same way the left brain reads books and listens to the spoken word.

If you listen closely to someone with a strong preference for this mode, you'll notice that they are particularly fascinated with eyes. These individuals watch eyes closely. If a person's eyes appear dull and cloudy, the sensitive feeling thinker knows that what he has been saying has not connected with his listener. When he finally does say or do something which reaches the other, he knows it by the light which comes on in the other person's eyes. One strong Basal Right thinker of our acquaintance used to rate men by the "twinkle" in their eyes. We don't know how valid her ratings were, but her approach was clearly Basal Right.

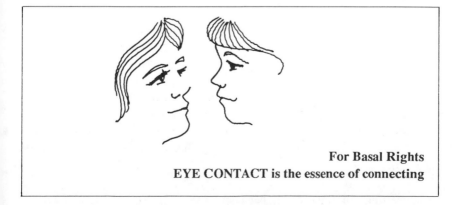

For Basal Rights
EYE CONTACT is the essence of connecting

The mouth is also an important source of data for the Basal Right thinker and they also monitor it for nonverbal messages. Is it smiling? Is the smile broad, full and generous? Are the lips relaxed, tense, twitching? All of this is grist for the nonverbal processing mill.

Given their druthers, Basal Rights prefer to have a lot of human interaction, preferably face to face (so they can monitor the eyes and the mouth). Obviously, people are important to them and so are <u>smiles</u>. Strong feeling types not only doodle smiling faces all over their notes, they are also buy and use "Smiley Face" stickers.

**FACIAL EXPRESSIONS are given more meaning and value
than words.**

Another characteristic, and perhaps the most interesting and visible behavior pattern typifying people with a strong feeling mode, is their use of language. Left brainers use speech (spoken language) in the same manner they use other tools, to accomplish the tasks for which it was designed: to communicate to another person the results of a decision, an expectation, a goal, or a set of instructions. In contrast, people with a strong preference for the harmony-focussed feeling mode talk with others in order to <u>connect.</u>

Constant hugging and touching, both of which strongly appeal to Basal Rights as techniques for "coming together" and increasing harmony, are not fully sanctioned behaviors in our culture. They are permitted between lovers, as well as between parents and children, but discouraged heavily between men and between employees. Perhaps in response to these taboos, Basal Rights seem to use language to make up for the deficit they sense in communication by touching. This specialized use of language might even be called **"verbal hugs,"** a term created by Katherine, which many Basal Rights have responded to with enthusiasm.

An interesting point about this behavior is that since Basal Rights like and apparently need to touch a lot, they also like and apparently need to talk a lot, most especially when they are in an environment in which touching is taboo.

These same people are the ones who regularly reach out and touch someone over the phone, or through greeting cards, or by sending a special smile or a questioning frown across a crowded room. And, when they do these things, it is to connect or communicate intimacy and acceptance, not to pass along instructions or decisions. The Basal Right use of language is about relating and relationships, not information.

This aspect of relatedness is key to how the Basal Right processes data. It does not see or experience things in isolation. There is no harmony when you hear only one note. Only by progression, only by providing an immediate context does the harmony appear.

Taking this one step further, Basal Rights seem to be particularly sensitive to harmony on all the sensory levels. They might pick up the visual harmony which exists between certain colors and remark: "That dress looks good on her. It goes well with her coloring." They might just as easily notice the olfactory harmony between two scents: "That perfume didn't go well on me (with my body's natural odor), but it smells wonderful on you (with your body's natural odor)." And, of course, they are particularly sensitive to auditory harmony, in both vocal and musical tones. Late in his life, the composer, Maurice Ravel, suffered from Wernicke's Aphasia, a disease which damages the left temporal lobe of the brain. As a result he was no longer able to either compose or perform. And yet, with his Basal Right mode still intact, he was fully able to listen to and enjoy music.

One final aspect of the Basal Right is its specialized ability to orchestrate the dressing and un-dressing of the body. Given the chance, even very young Basal Rights will play dressup or simply change clothes several times a day. Later, adolescent and adult Basal Rights will elect to spend their leisure time "shopping" -- their word for trying on clothes to see what looks good, feels right or fits the occasion.

To understand the **meta-function** of this mode, consider what the feeling mode is trying to accomplish. By reaching out to connect, this sensitive brain is attempting to bridge the gap which exists between people and to create peace and unity. This brain's ability to sense so clearly what others are thinking or feeling and to capture that awareness in a gesture or with words, is our most powerful tool for experiencing and reaffirming our human connectedness.

Significant research in the area of successful, long-term relationships and collaboration done by L.K. Steil[1], suggests that one of the foundations for "A mutual, predictable problem-solving capability" (the ability to work things through without recourse to violence) is a "phatic bond." This bond is nothing more or less than seeing in another person something of yourself. If Steil is correct, then those with the strongest natural ability to see what connects them to others at the deepest level are the natural collaborators and champions of peaceful relations.

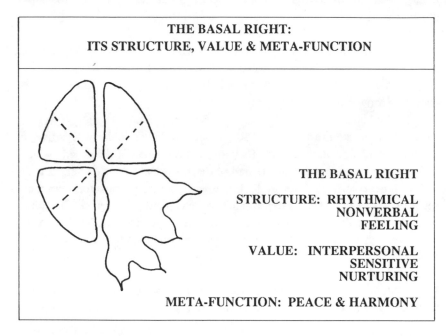

THE BASAL RIGHT:
ITS STRUCTURE, VALUE & META-FUNCTION

THE BASAL RIGHT

STRUCTURE: RHYTHMICAL
NONVERBAL
FEELING

VALUE: INTERPERSONAL
SENSITIVE
NURTURING

META-FUNCTION: PEACE & HARMONY

Life itself is created only through the connection of one person to another. This Basal or basal portion of the right cortex is designed to insure those connections. It helps us bond and motivates us to nurture each other. It fosters our awareness that we are "all one" and that to do harm to any of us is to do harm to all. In recent years the megatrend of High Tech/High Touch seems to be suggesting that the success and intensity of our technological development is naturally giving birth to a period in which the opportunities for the Basal Right to contribute to the evolution of life will be immense.

Indeed, the internally prestructured drive for peace and harmony of the Basal Right mode is designed to insure survival of the species. By constantly striving to bridge the gap between itself and others, by constantly monitoring hurt feelings

---

[1]This information was presented by Professor Steils in a workshop sponsored by IBM in Seattle in 1981, which Katherine attended.

and sadness, and by exuding a passion for enthusiasm and connection, this mode actively works to bring about the peace which is necessary for our survival. As such, we acknowledge this mode as the guardian of vitality, peace and harmony, and it becomes clear why its motto must be: "United we stand, divided we fall."

So, take a moment now to review what you have read about the Basal Right mode of thinking. Once you have reminded yourself of all the key characteristics of the mode itself, look at the following chart on The Basal Right Thinker, asking yourself as you read: Who do I know who thinks this way? Myself? My mother or father? My child? A Friend? My lover or spouse? And, when you think of someone who seems to you to be naturally strong in this mode, ask yourself, "In what ways has this person contributed to the building and or maintaining of peaceful and harmonious foundations in my life?"

THE BASAL RIGHT THINKER

ARCHETYPES: Earth Mother, Mother Theresa
A Jewish Mother, the Shaman,
Florence Nightingale, and
The Reverend Jesse Jackson.

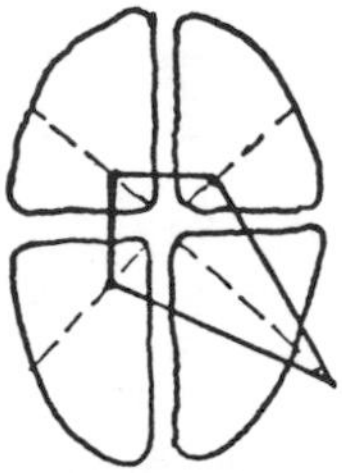

SYMBOL: An egg, a smiling face,
A bouquet of mixed flowers,
A pregnant woman's belly.

MOST ATTENTIVE TO: Relationships and people.

VALUES LEARNING: How to harmonize and information which "proves" the underlying unity or equality of all people/life; or which enables them to connect with god and god's creation (e.g., meditation & prayer), other people (e.g.active listening & empathy training).

INTERNAL LANGUAGE: Feelings

USES LANGUAGE TO: Express or share their own feelings, to "reach out and touch someone" or to harmonize the environment.

FAVORED MODES OF COMMUNICATION: Singing, dancing, speaking with the eyes, and touching.

PATTERN OR RHYTHM OF SPEECH: sometimes slow, often flowing or modulated. Clearly louder and more pronounced if angry and in sync with whatever they're feeling in the present moment.

CHARACTERISTIC THOUGHT PATTERN: Visceral more than conceptual, sometimes to the point of being earthy.

Jumps quickly to a level of enthusiasm which may seem almost child-like in response to good news (such as the news that someone special is coming to visit).

TYPICAL PHRASES: "I care about you."
"I empathize with you."
"Tell me what you feel."
"Let's do something together."
"Oh, it will be fun, we can share."
"Teamwork" and "Participation."
"When life gives you lemons, make lemonade"
"Personal growth"

SELF-PERCEPTION: A caring person.

AS SEEN BY OTHERS: Touchy-feely, a soft touch, a non-stop talker, a chatter-box, "fluff," Little Goody Two Shoes.

THE FRONTAL RIGHT,
INTERNAL IMAGE-GENERATING MODE

Our brain's third mode is the **spatial, internal image generating** Frontal Right, which is located in the frontal lobe of the cerebral cortex's right hemisphere.

One of the easiest places to notice this brain's <u>spatial</u> skill in action is while we are moving furniture. Although many pieces require only brute strength, others require a special spatial sensitivity. Most of us have been in this situation. We have a large, heavy piece of furniture, perhaps a dining room table, which we want to move through a doorway. Despite the concerted effort of two or three persons, we are unable to accomplish the task. In fact, after fifteen or twenty minutes, if not longer, all we have managed to do is scratch the table, chip the door jam and exhaust ourselves. Then, just when we are about to give up, concluding from our experience that the table simply will not fit through the door, a passerby stops and casually suggests a new angle. Following this person's suggestion, we meet with success.

How did he do it? How does spatial sensitivity work? Actually it's all quite simple for someone with strong access to the Frontal Right mode. First, you capture both the image (the table) and the shape (the doorway) on this lobe's internal "screen." Then you rotate the two forms until the needed position becomes clear. It is nothing more or less than the ability to manipulate images spatially.

Another behavior common to all Frontal Right thinkers which also stems from their spatial sensitivity is **visual filing or stacking**. The system is a simple one. Incoming and working documents are arranged in piles. And, over time, these piles grow into stacks, which cover the desk, the shelves, the chairs and even, eventually, much of the floor area. Although to a non-stacker such a system appears messy, to the strong Frontal Right, the consistent and stable visual stimulation it provides is essential for success. A more traditional organizing system, using filing cabinets and drawers (Basal Left), removes the files and information from the field of vision, and hence make it likely they will be totally forgotten by the spatial thinker. In fact, it occurs to us that the saying "Out of sight, out of mind," must have been developed to describe the Frontal Right propensity for losing track of things that have been stored in filing cabinets, even when the files in the cabinet are carefully marked.

An important advantage of 'visual filing' for the Frontal Right thinker is that it is generally 'label free,' thereby enabling the storage of many bits of information whose precise category or relationship to the problem is as yet unclear. More traditional systems which are grounded in labels would make storing such "vague" data impossible. When we relate this to the Frontal Right's general purpose (innovation and adaptive behavior), the value of this flexible storage pattern becomes even clearer.

Another characteristic of 'visual filing' is that the specific spatial location or <u>context</u> of each file, relative to other files or objects is significant in the mind of the Frontal Right thinker. This of course is fine, unless a helpful relative or clerical worker is moved to "straighten up" your office.

Frontal Rights prefer to store their information in STACKS.

Katherine is a typical stacker. And, despite nice furniture, her personal office often resembles a paper-recycling plant, especially if she's in the process of creating something new. When Katherine first hired a full-time secretary, problems naturally arose due to her Frontal Right approach to filing. Since the only key to the order in Katherine's stacks was inextricably stored in Katherine's spatial brain, it became necessary on occasion for her secretary to phone her long distance for instructions.

"Where is the CMC file? Oh, yes, it's there. Go to the desk, stand facing the west window. Put out your left hand. Move three stacks over to the left. Go down about half way. It's under a purple file and has a small piece of torn lime green paper clipped to the front with a phone number."

As you might imagine, this procedure fostered resentment on the part of the secretary, whose efficiency and productivity were interrupted whenever she needed something Katherine had been using, especially as reaching Katherine on the road can involve many calls.

In the end, the problem was resolved by giving the files which had to do with program administration and the daily operations of the business to the secretary to organize into a system she (and anyone else) could work with in the outer offices, while those files related to new product designs, which were rarely needed by anyone other than Katherine herself, were left in Katherine's inner sanctum. Such a division appears normal and natural, but in the day-to-day running of a business, what seems rational is not always what feels right. Even with the new system, when Katherine needs to write or call a client, she is likely to take the file for that client to her office, where it will sit as a <u>visual reminder</u> until she gets it done.

Not surprisingly, many research scientists, a group which tends to have a substantial amount of Frontal Right access, have to work out the same sort of "boundaries" with their technical assistants, as well as with some of their other coworkers, including their managers. In fact, one of our favorite Frontal Right stories involves Dr. Richard Feynman[2], the nobel prize-winning physicist, in just such a situation.

During the second World War, Feynman was asked to join the team of scientists working at Los Alamos. From the moment he set to work, his style of thinking was apparent. As he thought and doodled and listened and doodled, the papers relevant to the project began to amass. Feynman understood from his own past experience working on difficult problems that his ability to work comfortably, as well as successfully, was linked to his notes and papers being left out and undisturbed. Unfortunately, those in charge of security for the project thought that his work was a matter of national security and should, therefore, be locked up nightly in an office vault. You can imagine, knowing what you now know, the amount of frustration such a requirement would engender in a spatial thinker. As Feynman put it: "You asked me to leave my job and to move three thousand miles to help you because you need my brain, and yet you insist on handicapping it."

This would be a good, illustrative Frontal Right story if it ended here. What makes it an even better one is what Feynman did to deal with the handicap. Over the years, as a hobby, he had learned how to break into safes. This turned out to be just the skill he needed now. At night when his papers were locked safely away, Feynman broke into the compound, eluded both guards and guard dogs, entered the building (picking locks along the way) and finally broke into the safe

---

[2]For those interested in other stories about Feynman, his own autobiography is excellent and enlightening reading: <u>Surely You're Joking Mr. Feynman, Adventures of a Curious Character,</u> released in 1985 , just a few years prior to his death, by W.W. Norton & Co.

in which his papers were "securely stored" to leave a note attached to them which said: "Feynman was here."

As predicted by Feynman, his "prank" evoked both anger and frustration. And yet, had anyone there understood brain dominance, all of his behavior might have been both anticipated and accepted. As a Frontal Right with a strong preference for change, innovation and mental risk, Feynman had little use for procedural rules or "securing" things. Additionally, Frontal Rights frequently report getting a kick out of breaking rules simply to see what happens. Although this behavior appears counterproductive to most people, it is only counterproductive when the goal is "to keep things as they are." If your goal is to create new solutions or engender change, testing or challenging the boundaries may actually be necessary.

Yet another aspect to this tale is Feynman's bizarre and quirky sense of humor. Another person angered by having his hands tied might well have behaved more brutally or destructively. Yet, for Feynman, the kick was in demonstrating that the other side was not "right" and then leaving a flippant note. With a natural gift for imaging, it must have been easy for Feynman to picture the project manager opening the safe, and for him to imagine the anger, confusion and helplessness the manager would feel as he read Feynman's note and realized that Feynman had broken through his trusted security system.

We learned of an interesting follow-on to this story recently while Katherine was working with a client who needed to foster creative thinking within his company. Inasmuch as our data indicated that the company's existing "brainpower" included several people with primary Frontal Right access, she suggested he consider that the problem lay in the company's climate. She then related the above Feynman tale to illustrate how legitimate company policies can inadvertently curb creative thinkers. As she recalls, the chief executive's face began to break into a smile as she talked, as if a light bulb had gone on inside his head. He had, it seems, been attached to the military defense industry for some time, and recalled working on a project where all the "creative types" had had the same spatial stacking habits/needs as Feynman. Although at the time he thought it was simply their generally recalcitrant natures, he also recalled that the project manager took the need very seriously. So seriously in fact that he had a "safe-room" constructed so that when these people arrived in the morning they could enter it, work to their heart's and mind's content all day and finally leave with everything still out and intact -- because the entire room was a locked safe. Bizarre? Only if one doesn't understand the value of undisturbed stacks and papers to a spatially-sensitive thinker.

Yet another odd behavior which characterizes most Frontal Right thinkers is their tendency to laugh when no one else is laughing. This behavior, when unexplained, confuses others and raises their suspicions as to the sanity of their Frontal Right colleagues or relatives. In point of fact, the explanation is both simple and rational. As we have noted, in order to think at all, the Frontal Right brain must translate everything it sees and experiences into pictures. This translating is most relevant and valuable when the person is attempting to solve a complex problem creatively. It does, however, go on intermittently all the time, which means that while the Frontal Right thinker is listening to or watching anything, some of what he is experiencing will automatically be translated into pictorial form so that his preferred mode can process what's happening. These translations are often bizarre and humorous. If the speaker is loud and forceful, for example, the Frontal Right thinker might "unthinkingly" observe a picture floating across his mind of the speaker transformed into a bull elephant. Or, if the speaker is going over detailed notes which to the Frontal Right seem unnecessarily time consuming, the Frontal Right might look at the speaker and see a turtle in a business suit. No wonder that these people laugh. Wouldn't anyone who saw those pictures?

Thus, there are many behaviors typical of Frontal Rights which, while appearing quirky to the world, are the necessary and instinctual result of their strong spatial sensitivity. But to say or think that spatial thinking is all that this brain does would be a mistake.

The Frontal Right mode is also structured to **perceive broad stroke patterns**. As such it is the part of our brain which draws and recognizes **caricatures** as well as **models**. It does not process all the rhythms and details of a person's face as does the Basal Right. Instead, it sees key lines and captures the **overall effect**. It is interesting to note that if an individual damages his Basal Right brain to the extent that he is no longer able to recognize the photograph or face of a friend or loved one, he will still be able to recognize a caricature of the person, providing his Frontal Right is undamaged.

Often, while listening or talking, Frontal Rights capture the force and direction of what is being said in "doodles." Although such doodles have not been seen as valuable until fairly recently, we now understand that they are a dynamic map of what the Frontal Right is "picturing," and when properly decoded, often hold valuable insights about the problem or issue being discussed.

Although this may seem a bit too simplistic, it is an important reminder that as a mode the Frontal Right is totally visual. Technically, you might say it is both "dumb" and "mute" for it neither understands nor expresses itself in words or numbers. In order for it to learn or think, everything it sees in the world around it must be translated into internal images. As it takes in more information and translates it into more and more pictures, patterns begin to emerge. The phenomenon is that simple. And yet, describing the patterns it perceives can be very difficult. For one thing, the degree of complexity and the multiple relationships conveyed by an image exceed anything that can be captured in simple verbal reporting. Hence the old adage: a picture is worth a thousand words.

Add to this fact that the pictures being viewed internally by the Frontal Right thinker are frequently dynamic and moving, rather than still, and you can begin to grasp the magnitude of the problem. Imagine that you are looking at a still image and trying to describe what you see to someone who cannot see the photograph. Then imagine that every 15 seconds the image shifts noticeably. What would happen if you continued to attempt to describe the images aloud? First, your speech might become very rapid as you attempt to describe all of what you see (and how the various parts relate). Then, as the images begin to outpace you, you might find yourself dropping an idea mid-sentence in an effort to keep up. You might also give up attempting to capture the shifting details in an effort to describe fully the result. Or, you might lapse into long periods of silence as you get absorbed in watching everything that's happening. All of these--rapid speech, dropped ideas, non-sequential reporting and lapses into silence--are typical speech patterns for strong visual thinkers.

This confused communication pattern is exacerbated when the Frontal Right thinker is attempting to solve a problem and talk at the same time. When the mode is actively being used to solve a problem, the speed of the pictures increases. By the time a few words have been spoken, ten pictures have moved across their internal screen and, no matter how hard they try, they can't keep up with their pictorial brain. The best they can do is annotate the film inside their head with captions much like those used in silent movies. The only problem is that the listener in this case has only the captions of the film (which is going on inside the speaker's head).

So now we know that there are people who think in internally generated film strips. So what? Why create a mode which works exclusively with silent moving pictures? One clue lies in the role it plays with furniture moving in which this ability was the key to success. Another clue comes to us from the chronicles of Nickolaus Tessela, an inventor par excellence, who consciously used this ability to design and test new machines "in his head." Both examples suggest that the **meta-function** of this mode is to be the part of our brain which can envision a different way of doing things. Thus, just as we have a part of our brain which focuses on keeping things stable and anchored, we have a part devoted to making **changes**, to **adaption**. You might say the Frontal Right is a kind of cost-effective research and development lab: no salaries, no costly supplies or machines, plus the ability to do rapid, low risk experimentation.

Unfortunately, although we are beginning to understand how much we owe to this part of our brain, we are, as yet, only beginners at consciously accessing its assistance. Some of the ways that are currently under development include the conscious use of guided visualization, a technique based on the Frontal Right's internal image generating skills, to assist in wellness and behavior change.

In this area the Carl Simonton's cancer treatment center has demonstrated that when people repeatedly vividly imagine, or visualize, their own white blood cells destroying the cancer cells in their body, they increase the actual rate and strength of this natural disease fighting mechanism, sometimes to the extent of actual recovery. The breakthrough made by the Simontons was the discovery that for those persons for whom **visualization** was difficult (e.g., they had difficulty in seeing any pictures at all, in creating images which were specific and recognizable, and in manipulating the images so that the dynamic aspect of the white cells destroying the cancerous cells was clear), a film/video showing the desired images and action functioned as an effective training aid, increasing the success of the process.

A similar approach has been designed by Sybervision, under the guidance of Dr. Karl Pribram, then head of Stanford's Behavioral Research Lab. Here, in a program to improve one's tennis game, videotaped, broad-stroke drawings of the desired muscle and movement patterns are used to seed the user's imagination.

In both of the above examples, there is no actual creativity involved, as the specific desired future is known: the white cells must attack and destroy the cancer cells and the muscles must coordinate in a specific known manner. Nonetheless, the abilities of this Frontal Right mode appear to be useful in manifesting, or actualizing, the pre-known vision. In other companies such as Pillsbury, Apple Computer, DuPont, General Electric, Shell Oil, and Proctor & Gamble, people are hiring creativity consultants, such as ourselves, to go one step further and to consciously develop Frontal Right thinking in order to increase their creative abilities to solve problems and invent solutions. It is easy to see how this latter use of our Frontal Right internal image-generating abilities, not being seed-able (as the desired outcomes are by definition as yet unknown) is a more advanced, and perhaps more difficult, application. Nonetheless it is the direction of the future.

THE FRONTAL RIGHT:
ITS STRUCTURE, VALUE & META-FUNCTION

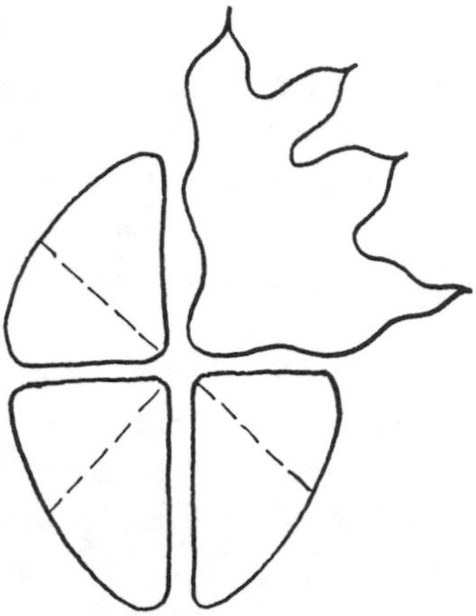

FRONTAL RIGHT

STRUCTURE: INTERNAL IMAGES
NONVERBAL
SPATIAL
DYNAMIC

VALUE: INNOVATIVE
AMUSEMENT

META-FUNCTION: GROWTH
& ADAPTION

In summary, then, the Frontal Right mode is one which processes by generating and manipulating internal images. Although less well understood for years, the **meta-function** or contribution of this mode is now clearly understood to be adaptation. As such, it is this mode that helps us change, whether in response to our own internal need to learn and grow (a need which Abraham Maslow felt was so strong in humankind that it should be categorized as an instinct), or in response to the external demands of a changing environment.

Characteristics of this mode's internal structure are that it needs to work with information spatially and will create stacks wherever it goes; that it frequently laughs at the visual representations it creates; and that it tends to break rules and procedures as a matter of course. Most of these behaviors tend to alienate others. Nonetheless, it seems to be true that because these internal images are often transferred into cartoons and jokes, the Frontal Right mode could also be called the Guardian of our **Amusement & Humor**.

So, again, take time to review what you have learned about this mode of thinking, comparing and contrasting it with the others already identified, as well as relating it to any existing understanding you might have about "intuitive types." When you have completed you review, then begin exploring the following chart on The Frontal Right Thinker, asking yourself as you read who you know who thinks this way. And, as before, when you identify the Frontal Rights in your life, ask yourself: "In what way do these people contribute to life, especially to my ability to be adaptive and flexible.?"

THE FRONTAL RIGHT THINKER

ARCHETYPES: The Mad Scientist: Richard Feynman
The Dreamer: Martin Luther King "I have a Dream"
John F. Kennedy[3] "Ask not what your country can do for you, but what you can do for your country."
The Grand Architect: Buckminster Fuller

SYMBOL: Rainbows, Butterflies, the Eagle Wings and Sails.

MOST ATTENTIVE TO: New Ideas

VALUES LEARNING: New Concepts.

INTERNAL LANGUAGE: Images.

USES LANGUAGE TO: Think out loud, to think out a problem or idea they have been looking at inside in symbolic or imaged form.

FAVORED MODE OF COMMUNICATION: Metaphoric or symbolic images or "word-pictures" such as, " I hit a log jam."

PATTERN OR RHYTHM OF SPEECH: Rapid, trying to capture the picture that's worth "2000 words." Punctuated at times with silences when they have gone within to look more closely at something, and they are "lost to the world."

---

[3]Although John F.Kennedy is best known for his visionary leadership, he was also very analytical with a keen sense of strategy , which tends to come most easily to double frontal thinkers.

CHARACTERISTIC THOUGHT PATTERN: Metaphoric and pictorial. Very conceptual, sometimes to the point of "losing touch with reality."

TYPICAL PHRASES: "Wing it."
"When all else fails, read the instructions."
"Let's play with that idea."
"Take an idea and run with it."
"New," or "being at the cutting edge."
"Linkages" or "synergistic."
"Getting the big picture."
"Using a wide angle lens."

SELF-PERCEPTION: A visionary leader of people, a lighthouse. .

AS SEEN BY OTHERS: A space cadet, a dreamer, someone who can't focus, or who has his/her head in the clouds.

THE FRONTAL LEFT, ANALYTIC MODE:

We now have three of the four key thinking modes in place: one to build strong, stable foundations in our lives, one to insure that we live in peace and harmony with others, and one to assist us in adapting and making change. All that we lack is the analytic ability to monitor our environment and decide which of the modes is best suited to handle the situations in which we find ourselves. Not surprisingly, this is precisely the task of the Frontal Left lobe of our cerebral cortex.

To say that Frontal Left thinking is analytic is to say, according to Webster, that it is capable of "separating a whole into its component parts." A key ability of this mode is **critical analysis**, the ability to "chunk" or group items into significant categories or components without the use of preestablished guidelines. This ability to divide and classify, without preexisting rules or direction, is an important function of the Frontal Left. Also important is the Frontal Left's ability to create and use signs. Indeed, because of this ability, this chunking may be done symbolically, as is the case with mathematics.

A key application of this skill is the act of labeling or **naming**. The Basal Left may store a piece of information from a sensory experience, but unless that experience or key component of it is labeled, it will be difficult to retrieve the memory. Recent research on memory retention suggests that this is precisely the reason many of us have so much difficulty retrieving our early childhood memories; with no well-developed labeling system in play at the time, we did not classify them in ways we can now easily access and recall.

Obviously the ability to "name" is strongly tied to the ability to develop a growing body of knowledge. A word or concept once named may be stored and retrieved. It also may be explained to or discussed by others. All of us have this ability to name and use labels but it is the analytic brain which excels in the area of creating new names and classification systems. Thus, it is the Frontal Left which is responsible for the division of experience and information into functional parts with discrete meanings and applications.

Frontal Lefts excel at **symbolic logic**, but the Frontal Left is not a symbolic brain. This apparent contradiction is explained by the fact that symbolic logic does not actually use symbols. It, in fact, uses signs (which are a specialty of the Frontal Left). A **sign** is something which has, at a any moment in time, one and only one set of meanings. As such, signs are specific and exclusive.

"SIGNS"	AND ....THEIR MEANINGS
chair	any of a variety of pieces of furniture designed to be sat on
$F(X)=Y$	F stands for a specific function X stands for a specific set of variables Y stands for the specific set of solutions generated when the specified function is applied to each variable in the referenced set, X.
$C=\pi r^2$	π is a sign for the value 3.14159265 r is a sign for the length of the radius, C is a sign for the circumference of a given circle generated by its radius.

By way of contrast, <u>true symbols,</u> which are processed by either or both of the right brain modes, have <u>layers of meaning</u> and are more generalized and all-inclusive than signs. Consider the symbol "circle." It may describe a closed, unified system like a prayer circle, a healing circle, or a sewing circle. It can also signify unity or a stable cycle of repetition. Another point about symbols is that they often include an emotional element lacking in signs. The symbol "birth," for example, which can signify any number of new beginnings, also carries with it a good deal of emotional content, like"positive and hopeful." Contrast this to the sign for radius (r) which has no emotional over- or under-tones.

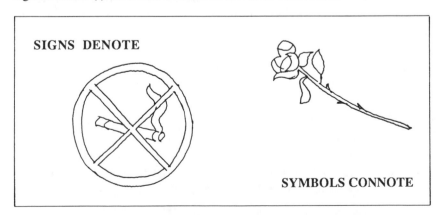

SIGNS DENOTE

SYMBOLS CONNOTE

This differentiation is important because the Frontal Left has none of the emotion we associate with symbols. Skilled in the use of "sign" language, it is most adept at cool, logical, non-emotional decision-making. In fact, you might say that part of the value of this mode is that it is **nonemotional.**

When this cool, analytic mode applies itself to an external, physical reality (such as a machine), its key concern is to identify the object's significant parts and their functional relationships. This type of processing,which focuses on seeing <u>cause</u> and <u>effect</u> is called <u>diagnostic thinking</u>. Frontal Left thinkers excel not only at discovering what is wrong with and repairing broken machines, but also at analyzing and diagnosing the cause of illness in a sick body.

Not surprisingly, when this same Frontal Left <u>analytic</u> approach applies itself to an idea or concept, much the same process takes place. For example, if a strongly Frontal Left manager is given a proposal for a new program, he is likely to see the proposal as a single component in his total operation and to try to understand how it will affect the other components and the structure of the whole system. If, "after due analysis," he determines that the overall effectiveness of the operation will be enhanced by the new program, he is likely to approve it. If he doesn't see how it fits in <u>functionally</u>, he is likely to turn it down.

Not surprisingly, this mode also excels at **comparing differing realities in order to make a recommendation or decision.** For example, if you wanted to compare apples, oranges, celery and veal, although you might have a difficult time getting a meaningful answer from the other modes, the analytic brain would have no trouble whatsoever. It would immediately sort out the information and establish that there are many possible answers depending on the intended <u>purpose</u> or <u>use</u>. In other words, it would seek a basis for the comparison. Depending on the basis, the above items might be compared by their cost, weight, protein value, calories, vitamin A content, regional availability, or income value to produce. Thus, the analytic thinker begins processing by asking you: "What is the purpose of this comparison and what are you trying to find out?" Once the purpose is known, it identifies appropriate <u>criteria</u> and the desired <u>comparison</u> becomes a matter of mere <u>calculation</u>.

Another frequently used application of this Frontal Left skill is the act of **prioritizing.** For prioritizing, whether applied to tasks at work or a child's requests for Christmas gifts, involves the comparison of disparate things. Although everyone manages in some way or another to prioritize, many of us feel we muddle through the task. For a strong Frontal Left thinker, however, any and every task which involves the setting of priorities is a welcome opportunity to analyze, categorize, chunk and evaluate.

Another characteristic of analytic thinkers is that they are exceptionally good at staying "on track." They are adept at looking at and evaluating various chunks or components with one eye, while simultaneously keeping their other eye on the ultimate purpose of their actions and the direction they want things to go. In other words, they are not only excellent at goal setting, they are also equally adept at goal achievement. This skill tends to lead them to manipulate the variables in a given situation in order to bring them into alignment with their chosen direction. Perhaps for these reasons, many of us sense capable Frontal Lefts to be very **goal directed**.

Perhaps because machines tend to embody analytic thinking in its purest form--that is, they have specific, precisely defined components each of which has a contributing function--Frontal Lefts often show a liking for and comfort with machines. Sometimes this liking shows up in an unexpected interest in personally assessing a new office machine or appliance. Often it shows up in their tendency to acquire tools and machines which they assemble into a "workshop." Most often, this particular affinity is observable in their characteristic use of mechanical metaphors to describe and understand other less mechanical things. An analytic thinker, for example, may talk about "getting a mechanical advantage" in a difficult situation or about managing to get "leverage." They also "nail things down" and "put the screws" to someone or some organization. And, when referring to a collection of personal skills, they describe them as "my tool kit." This "machine talk" reflects the way they think about things. They are not usually using it to be poetic or colorful, but simply because it is the most natural way for them to think.

Yet another characteristic behavior of Frontal Left thinkers is **verbal fencing.** Because critical analysis is their most valued personal "tool," and because one's ability to use a tool well is derived from frequent practice, analytic thinkers often play with this skill for the pure pleasure they derive from doing so. Thus, when you observe two lawyers or two physicians in what appears to be a heated argument, you may not be seeing a fight, but rather two adept mental swordsmen practicing the art of mental fencing in order to hone and polish their most valued tool. That they are getting as much fun out of doing so as an NBA player gets shooting a few baskets while crossing a gym floor may be difficult for some of us to understand, but it is, nonetheless, true. **Verbal argumentation** or **debate** is actually energizing for Frontal Lefts and they seek out opportunities to engage in it. They simply don't perceive it as fighting, even if others around them do.

In summary, we might say that the Frontal Left, with its ability to compare disparate realities and to analyze complex situations, is the mode which enables us to be the <u>responsive</u> and <u>responsible</u> managers of our own lives and the lives of others. In the final analysis, it is this mode which is intended to direct the operations of the total system, making sure each of the modes contributes in a useful and appropriate way to the success of the whole.

Now, read through the following chart on the Frontal Left Mode. As you read, see if you can explain each word on the chart and give an example of how it typifies this mode.

THE FRONTAL LEFT:
ITS STRUCTURE, VALUE & META-FUNCTION

FRONTAL LEFT

STRUCTURE: USES 'SIGN' LANGUAGE
ANALYTICAL
LOGICAL

VALUE: NON-EMOTIONAL
NAMING
DECISION-MAKING

**META-
FUNCTION:** MANAGEMENT

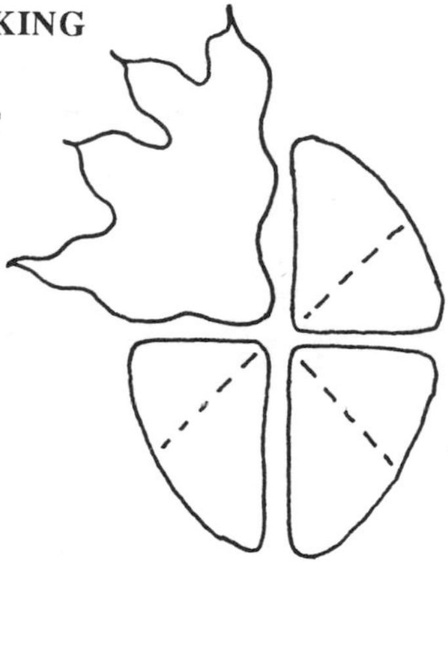

And now, continue to develop your understanding and mastery of the model by reading the chart below on The Frontal Left Thinker. As with the other modes, as you read the chart, ask yourself, "Who do I know who thinks this way?" When you have identified a couple of people, then stop to consider how or in what way these people contribute to your ability to make difficult decisions, to remain goal-directed when it's important. What specifically have they done to assist you?

THE FRONTAL LEFT THINKER

ARCHETYPES: The King, King Solomon
                     The Judge

SYMBOLS: A Scepter
                     Scales
                     Gavel

MOST ATTENTIVE TO: Operational Principles which enable the
                        efficient use of resources and facilitate technical
                        problem-solving and decision-making.

VALUES LEARNING: General Operational Principles

INTERNAL LANGUAGE: Logic

USES LANGUAGE TO: Communicate the results of their thinking,
                       frequently a decision they have made.

FAVORED MODE OF COMMUNICATION: The half-page
                       summary and verbal debate, "verbal fencing."

PATTERN OR RHYTHM OF SPEECH: Short, crisp, chopped,
                       dry.

CHARACTERISTIC THOUGHT PATTERNS: More conceptual
                       than visceral, often preferring to weigh the
                       variables, make a decision and then delegate the
                       doing of the task to another person.

                       Records information by chunks or key
                       concepts, allowing for easier transfer and
                       application of an idea from one area or field of
                       study to another because in each situation the
                       same operating principle is found.

TYPICAL PHRASES: "What's the bottom line."
"According to my calculations..."
"See if you can get some leverage for us."
"Weigh all the variables."
"Look at the penalty clause."
"Break it down," "Take it apart."
"Do a critical analysis."
"What's it worth to us?"
"Fundamentally speaking,..."
"A key point to be reckoned with is..."
"How do we strengthen our position?"

SELF-PERCEPTION: A strong leader and competent decision maker

AS SEEN BY OTHERS: Powerful, but often also uncaring,
unfeeling, overly critical and calculating in a
manipulative manner.

FOUR BRAINS, ONE SYSTEM:

Now that you have had a chance to consider each of the brain's four modes as separate entities, take a few minutes to look at the charts on the following pages. They have been designed with a eye towards whimsy, to assist you in locking in your understanding of how differently these four modes see the world around them. Scanning them will help you to integrate your understanding of the four separate modes into one "whole brain" model. When you have finished looking at the charts, continue with the question and answer section of this chapter.

OTHER WAYS TO SEE THE MODES CLEARLY:

Because the foregoing descriptions of each mode have depended heavily on words, they have in effect been communicating most directly to the double left reader. For this reason, the next few pages will seek to "explain" each mode using playful and symbolic images that speak more to the right modes, and "mathematical symbols" that speak more to our analytical frontal left.

A SYMBOLIC GRAPHIC PERSPECTIVE, or
A FRONTAL RIGHT SUMMARY OF THE MODEL

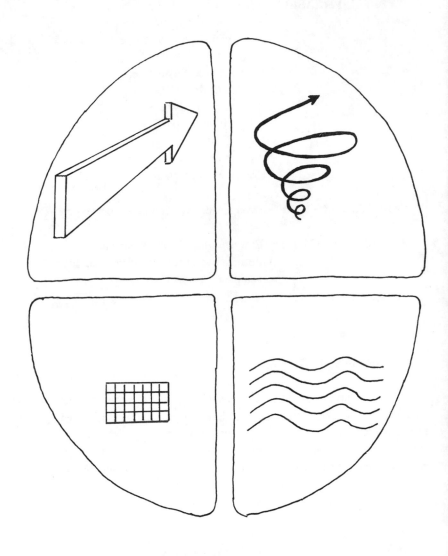

The Basal Left pigeon-holes everything in a **GRID**.

The Basal Right goes with the flow, like a **WAVE**.

The Frontal Right **SPIRALS** high, playing with an idea.

The Frontal Left focuses in on the target, like an **ARROW**.

A PLAYFUL PERSPECTIVE IN PICTURES
or, YET ANOTHER RIGHT-BRAINED PERSPECTIVE

The Basal Left **sustains order** by having a place for everything
and everything in its place.
The Basal Right **fosters peace and unity** by
harmonizing with others.
The Frontal Right **accomplishes the impossible** by using visionary guidance
to leap over tall buildings and broad canyons in a single bound.
The Frontal Left **makes difficult decisions** by using logic
to compare seemingly dissimilar options.

FOUR PERSPECTIVES ON ARTISTIC COMPOSITION:

Given that:
The Frontal Lobes are conceptual and idea-driven;
The Basal Lobes are visceral and sensory;
The Left Lobes are parts focussed;
The Right Lobes experience the gestalt;

It can be said that:
The Basal Left focuses on sensed pieces or tangible objects.
The Basal Right focuses on the sensed connection or relationship.
The Frontal Right focuses on abstracted totality or a unifying symbolic picture.
The Frontal Left focuses on abstracted pieces or key concepts.

Thus,
Frost's *The Road Not Taken* might be viewed from these four perspectives:

The Basal Left notices and values the words, the written poem.

The Basal Right notices and values the feeling of discomfort and sadness
which is commonly felt by people reflecting about a lost opportunity.

The Frontal Right notices and values the unifying symbolic image
of the fork in a road as a time of both opportunity and decision.

The Frontal Left notices and values the meter, measure and form
used to structure this well-known "great" poem.

And similarly,
Beethoven's *Ninth Symphony* might be viewed from these four perspectives:

The Basal Left notices and values the notes, the written score and possibly any
theme which is repeated over and over.

The Basal Right notices and values the feeling of harmony or discord conveyed
by the relationship of each note to those around it as well as by the tonals --
loudness, softness, increases or decreases in speed, silences.

The Frontal Right notices and values the unifying symbolic image
of lightening and storm clouds.

The Frontal Left notices and values the tools which were used to create the
masterpiece, such as meter and percussion instruments.

HOW EACH MODE THINKS: A SYMBOLIC SUMMARY

A = A: The Basal Left remembers definitions. To it, what is is.

:   The Basal Right picks up the "emotional tone" in the communication or situation. What is is not as important as how we feel about it.

A = B: The Frontal Right, unable to access and use words directly, generally captures the essence of experiences and data using pictoral, metaphoric analogies. What is, is seen as something else.

A = A: The Frontal Left, with its focus on using sensed data to made decisions, uses logical functions to convert the raw data into useful data. What is is analyzed to generate new information.

QUESTIONS AND ANSWERS:

You've spent a good deal of time describing and detailing the positive aspects of each mode. What are some of the "negative" behaviors which we might encounter or experience with each?

The Basal Left sequential thinker, while highly productive and necessary can at the same time be a "drag" in situations when change is needed. Their increased sense of stress at these times can cause them to sabotage others' efforts or to become rigid in their adherence to "what is." It is also true that when in conflict with another person, strong Basal Lefts tend to resort to rules and <u>procedures</u> for mediating the conflict, rather than try to process the feelings involved. This approach, particularly if used in family and personal relations, can cause unresolved bad feelings to remain even after the crisis has been "solved."

The Basal Right feeling-focused thinker, while excellent at nurturing and bridge-building, may have difficulty in making and presenting unpopular decisions. Their fear of causing upsets can lead them to avoid "the realities of life."

The Frontal Right adaptive thinker, while unparalleled in the ability to respond creatively, may nonetheless cause problems for others because he cannot "let well enough alone." He will make unnecessary changes simply because adhering to sameness is counter to his internal nature. As well, many Frontal Rights, although "committed" to a positive and humanitarian vision, may inadvertently walk on people or offend them, simply because the frontal right pays little attention to their needs, feelings and non-verbal signals.

And finally, the Frontal Left analytic thinker, while perhaps most adept at setting and attaining goals, can become too easily attached to a win-lose scenario in which he intends to win and thus sets others up as losers. In addition, many Frontal Lefts have a weakness in the feeling mode which means that, like the Frontal Right, they may walk on others and offend them without realizing it and without even seeing the inherent "wrongness" in doing such a thing.

The negative behaviors that characterize any given person are a complex matter which arises from the individual's self-esteem and general psychological make up as well as his brain dominance. We can, however, note that, at least in part, our characteristic "negative behaviors" are determined by how many strengths we have. A half-brainer who is a strong Basal Left and a strong Basal Right will probably not engender as many "bad feelings" in the process of resolving conflicts as either the quarter-brain Basal Left or the half-brain double left, both of whom lack strength in the feeling, bonding, peace engendering mode.

According to your model, the only real "logical" thinker is the Frontal Left. And yet, many people I know, who are clearly not Frontal Lefts, consider themselves to be very logical. Can you explain this?

Actually, your experience is not as unusual as you might think. As a society we value logic so much that everyone wanting to "fit in" seeks to be logical. It is also true, according to our own research, that many many people simply do not understand what the term "logical" really means.

Indeed, once logic is truly understood, it becomes easy for most people to see whether they are or are not logical. When some difficulty arises it usually comes from one of two sources. The first is the strong Basal Left thinker who adheres assiduously to routines and procedures originally established by logical thinking. Such an individual may well confuse his <u>adherence</u> to a logically-derived procedure with being logical. The way to assist such a person to realize his confusion is to point out that when a true Frontal Left thinker engages in any procedure, he is likely to stop first to ask: What, if anything, has changed? What, if anything, is different? Their purpose in doing this is to determine whether the logical in the present situation. If he determines everything is the same, he will "follow the procedure." If he determines, however, that there is a significant difference in some aspect of the situation, he will first, by logically analyzing what has happened, adjust the procedure so that he has a revised procedure to use. In contrast, the purely Basal Left person tends to simply plunge forward into the procedure regardless of the change in circumstances.

The other source of confusion comes from Basal Rights who see themselves as "rational" because their behavior and decisions are based on "reasons". Our society has lost sight of Jung's understanding that feeling-based decisions are based on reasons and are, as such, "rational." Moreover, because we tend to equate rational with logical, many Basal Rights confuse these two terms, asserting to themselves and others that they are indeed "rational and logical"-- when in point of fact they are rational, but not logical. In such cases, a person can be helped to understand their misperception of themselves most easily if they are validated and recognized as rational, and their feeling-based information is recognized, valued and used in problem solving and decision making.

I understand the concept that people with differing mental preferences might see the same reality quite differently, yet I'm having trouble translating this conceptual understanding into concrete examples. Are there some common examples which specifically illustrate these differences in perspective?

The following seven questions, which cover a wide range of everyday issues and concerns, should help develop your understanding of the <u>differences in point of view</u> of the various modes.

Take time to read through these examples slowly. As you do so, consider how you would answer each question. Which answer is most comfortable for you? Which answer is most uncomfortable, or unlike you? How do your answers match up with your dominance.

HOW THE BRAIN'S SPECIALIZED MODES
SEE THE SAME WORLD DIFFERENTLY

Question #1:   How do you manage your income?

Basal Left: I budget my income: 20% for housing, 30% food, 10% clothing, 5% car payment; 5% insurance premiums, 5% entertainment and 5% towards my annual vacation. The remaining 20% goes to the bank into a savings account..

Basal Right: I go easy at the end of the month.

Frontal Right: I don't know. Managing money is a detail in life. I can't seem to focus on it. But I'm lucky, and things generally turn out all right.

Frontal Left: I get my money to work for me.

Question # 2: How did you select your last car?

Basal Left: I decided how much I could afford to spend based on my savings and income. And I read*Consumers Guide* to determine which of the bigger, safe cars had the best performance rating.

Basal Right: I talked with several friends and decided to get the kind my best friend has. Oh, except that I wanted a blue car. Hers is red.

Frontal Right: I like cars that are different. Fast. Generally I buy foreign cars.

Frontal Left: The car I own must have a powerful engine & precision handling so that it holds the road.

Question #3:   Are you presently successful?

Basal Left: "Yes, we are successful because we have a daily goal of processing fifty people, and today we processed fifty people. Yesterday was not a good day because we only saw forty people."

Basal Right: "Some of the staff are not very happy about what's been happening around here. But I think it's going to change. I noticed the boss had a twinkle in her eye when she came back from the board meeting."

Frontal Right: "We're really doing well. Batting a hundred. Yesterday didn't look like such a good day at first, but in the last inning we hit one out of the ball park."

Frontal Left: "We had a successful day today because we have a goal of processing fifty people a day, and today we saw sixty. On the other hand, yesterday was also a good day, despite the fact that we only saw forty people, because one of the persons we saw gave us a contract worth eight times one of our normal sales."

Question #4:   Why do you do what you're doing in that way?

Basal Left: "This is how we do it because we have a procedures manual which says to do it this way."

Basal Right: "I feel comfortable doing it this way."

Frontal Right: "Our department is a war zone. Most of the time I try to stay in the trenches."

Frontal Left: "This is how we do it because, despite what the manual states, we have found that things work faster and are safer when we do it this way."

Question #5:   If someone came to you with a new way of doing your job, how would you respond?

Basal Left: I'd be very cautious. A lot of new ideas are hair-brained. Trying them just wastes time and money.

Basal Right: If they seemed to care about me, I'd be appreciative and enthusiastic.

Frontal Right: I'd probably listen to what they had to say. New ideas are like a fresh breeze, they stir your imagination. Perhaps later I'd play with the idea to see how it might relate to some of my own ideas.

Frontal Left: I'd test its feasibility: Can it be done? Can it be done cost effectively? Will it sell?

Question #6: If you were standing at a <u>cross-roads</u> at a place <u>unknown </u>to you, how would you decide which direction to go in?

Basal Left: I probably go along the most well-worn path.

Basal Right: I go where there were people & something 'happening.'

Frontal Right: Ah yes, 'Two roads diverged in a yellow wood....' Well, naturally I'd take the road less travelled, to seek adventure and excitement.

Frontal Left: I'd go where I could accomplish something, where there was a phone, a bank, or a car rental agency.

Question #7: What's wrong with the world?

Basal Left: There's not enough food, and people don't respect law and order anymore.

Basal Right: There's not enough love. People don't care enough or give enough.

Frontal Right: The human race is like a pack of turtles. People are too slow to change. Even now, when we understand the planet's total ecological system and how our past and current behavior is endangering the balance in that system--even to the extent that our own lives are in jeopardy. We need to learn to live as part of the total synergistic system.

Frontal Left: Distribution is the principle problem. 80% of the food is produced by countries with only 30% of the population.

The above examples focus specifically on the points of view most

often taken by people with only one lead mode. How can we begin to recognize and understand the more complex patterns?

Just as yellow and red blend to make orange, and blue and yellow blend to make green, the four core modes blend together to create new and specialized perspectives. Learning to recognize and relate to these takes time and practice Even so, they will become more familiar to you as you read the remaining chapters in the book

Additionally, you may recall that in Chapter 1, we mentioned that the Benziger Model has three components or elements:

1. a physical component, that is, an updated, physiologically-grounded picture of the four core modes of human thinking;

2. a set of laws, principally dominance, but also including simultaneity and introversion/extraversion, governing the internal dynamics which exist between the modes themselves within our brain; and

3. a set of two laws or rules of thumb governing the external dynamics between one brain and another or between one brain and its environment.

Thus far, you have read about the model's first two elements: the four modes and the law of dominance. In the remaining sections and chapters of the book, we will explore the model's third element--The Two Rules of Thumb. To set the stage, we'll restate them now:

1. To develop or nurture your self-esteem, as well as insure your immediate effectiveness and success, select activities (and people) which match your dominance.

2. To assure your survival, as well as guarantee your long-term effectiveness and success, manage activities (and people) not matching your dominance by enlisting assistance from complementary brains.

How these two rules have already shaped your life will be revealed to you as you read Parts II and III of this book. Then, once you have the picture, Part IV: The Art of Using Your Whole Brain, will help you to learn how to consciously use the two rules of thumb to shape your own life, to insure the personal satisfaction, success and the sense of well-being which you deserve.

PART II.

USING WHOLE BRAIN THINKING TO INCREASE YOUR EFFECTIVENESS & SUCCESS ON THE JOB

Rule #1: To develop or nurture your self-esteem,
as well as insure your immediate effectiveness and success,
select activities which match your dominance

CHAPTER 4
WORKING RIGHT, WORKING EASY

CAREER SELECTION & SUCCESS: THE BASIC PRINCIPLE

Why do people select the careers they do? Why did you decide to become whatever it is you are? These questions have been asked and answered in a multitude of ways ranging from in-depth statistical analyses to Studs Turkel's rambling, anecdotal masterpiece, Working: People Talk About What They Do All Day and How They Feel About What They Do. And yet, our fascination with the subject continues. Obviously, our choice of life work is very much a part of "what makes us tick" on some essential level.

Traditional approaches to the subject tend to focus on role models, socio-economic status, learned skills and competencies and our access to, or the availability of, higher education as the key factors in that choice. And although we will be focusing on brain dominance as a determining force in our selection of the kind of work that "will work for us," we do not dispute the importance of each of these other factors in the career selection process. All of us know of an individual who attributes his selection of a specific profession to the family role models: "My dad and granddad were both lawyers. I'm just carrying on the family tradition," or, "There's always been a doctor in our family. I simply didn't consider becoming anything else," or, "Smith Brothers is a family business. It was just assumed that after college, I'd go to work in the family store." We also know of certain underlying career "guidelines" or assumptions which are generally seen as "true" and "appropriate" by many people: upper class kids don't drive trucks for a living; minority kids from lower income families aren't likely to become stock brokers; if you're a girl from a lower-middle class family, you probably should plan on being a teacher, a secretary, a nurse or a nun. Not surprisingly, these cultural assumptions have had a major impact on many people's choice of career.

Nonetheless, for every child who buys into a cultural stereotype or who follows a parental role model, there is another who actively chooses to "march to the beat of a different drummer" and make his own choice of career. In fact, it is not uncommon for a child to actively reject the path his parents want or expect him to take because "it's just not right for me." We often hear stories like:

"My dad is a physician and he wanted me to be one too. But, I just couldn't do it. I'm an architect which is what I wanted to be."

"Dad's an executive with a Standard Oil. He always tried to get me interested in business, but it's just not my thing. I'm an artist and a painter."

"Dad was a colonel in the Air Force and he sent me to military school hoping it would motivate me to join up. Well, I guess I'm a real disappointment to him since I was never interested. I was a monk for nine years and now I'm a free-lance photographer. This way I get to travel around the world taking pictures and helping people wherever I can. I did actually co-found a travel agency a few years ago, but I turned it over to my partner last year. I need to move around more, have adventures and help humanity."

So, what made these people choose the work they chose? What made certain kinds of work "right for them" and other kinds not an acceptable fit? Why do they prefer one job over another?

The answer would appear to be that given the choice we choose work that relies on our developed natural preferences, or as the grandfather of life-work planning Bernard Haldane says our "dependable strengths".   Moreover, how we feel about ourselves and our work, on a day-to-day basis, depends largely on how well that work matches our brain dominance.   When our work matches our preferences, we feel positively reinforced--we feel smart and energized.   When there is a mismatch, when our work draws heavily on areas outside our preferred modes, we are negatively reinforced.   We have difficulty concentrating, feel fatigued at the end of the day, and often in the course of trying to learn and do our work feel dumb.   Subsequently, **as people naturally want to feel smart and energized, they gravitate more towards work which they believe matches their dominance.**

This key principle, the Smart-Dumb Rule, can be is very important.   Whether consciously or unconsciously, this rule guides many of our work-related decisions.   We are more attracted to jobs that we sense depend heavily on our greatest natural strength.   We tend to avoid jobs which would require frequent use of our greatest weakness.   Once in a job, we seek advancement opportunities which we sense are even more in tune with who we really are.   And, if once we start a job experience tells us it is going to rely heavily on our greatest weaknesses, we often will find or create reasons for quitting.

Thus, by making career and job decisions in alignment with this natural principle, you will indeed be following the first rule of thumb for insuring your own success and effectiveness at work.   To assist you, in using the information about brain dominance to select an appropriate career, or to understand and relate more successfully to someone else in a particular profession, we have prepared several examples which demonstrate the variety of ways in which people are made smart by the "right" career choice.   Since it would be impossible to discuss each and every career area, we have elected to give you several examples from each of four general categories: business, health care, the arts and leadership.

These examples are by no means comprehensive, but rather reflect the window of opportunity we have had to gather data.   And so, if your own profession is not described here, we hope that the examples we do provide will stimulate your thinking and give you some direction which, combined with the workbook exercises for this chapter, will enable you to apply the model to your own career. As you read through these examples, it may be helpful to begin with the general area which is closest to your own.   Feel free to do so since there is no correct order here.   As you read each example, however, think of someone you know in that profession.   How well does the information you are reading describe them?

BRAIN DOMINANCE AND THE BUSINESS COMMUNITY

PEOPLE DOING FINANCIAL PROBLEM SOLVING, ANALYSIS AND DECISION-MAKING: including, but not limited to MBAs, CPAs, accountants and financial vice presidents, all of whom focus on how to leverage money, that is, how to make money make money.

Most of these people have a strong preference for both left brain modes, that is, they are analytic-sequential thinkers, with a lead preference in the Frontal Left analytic mode.

This type of thinker enjoys working with data, particularly numbers. And using the Frontal Left mode, they particularly enjoy analyzing those numbers to determine "Am I better or worse off than last month? Better or worse off than last year at this time? Given what is happening in the national and local economy, in this sector and in others, do these numbers represent a gain or a loss?" This type of analysis is what accounting is all about. In their own way, accountants are like physicians for both of these groups gather and analyze a body of data about a system. And, when the diagnosis indicates poor health, both prescribe new and different courses of action to take to fix the problem.

Profiles typical of people holding such positions, therefore, would resemble these profiles belonging to three of our clients.

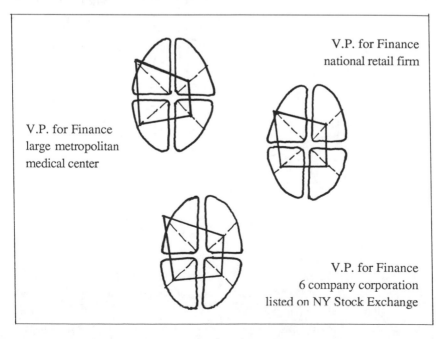

V.P. for Finance
national retail firm

V.P. for Finance
large metropolitan
medical center

V.P. for Finance
6 company corporation
listed on NY Stock Exchange

PEOPLE RESPONSIBLE FOR MAINTAINING ORDERED OR SEQUENCED INFORMATION IN AN ORGANIZED, CORRECT AND TIMELY MANNER: including, but not limited to, file clerks, records clerks, forms processors, bookkeepers, all of whom attend to seeing that the information necessary for the day-to-day operation of the business is kept current and correct.

Although these people often work with the same information as the above group, the diagnostic and prescriptive work done by the MBA's does not interest them. They strongly prefer the Basal Left sequential mode, and are often quarter brain experts, deriving satisfaction from keeping files current and correct, balancing the books, preparing monthly statements. Careful and correct in their work, they have no difficulty in performing the routine tasks which provide the MBA or accountant with the data he analyzes. In fact, they get satisfaction from having and following "standard bookkeeping (or recordkeeping) procedures" consistently and according to a schedule over time.

As such, the following sample profiles taken from a few of our clients are typical of people attracted to and energized by work in this field. Note that to the extent that the job also involves being a receptionist, as in many secretarial positions, the profiles indicate additional access in the Basal Right.

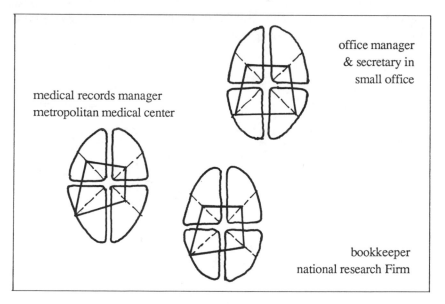

office manager
& secretary in
small office

medical records manager
metropolitan medical center

bookkeeper
national research Firm

PEOPLE RESPONSIBLE FOR SUPERVISING OTHERS DOING ROUTINE AND PROCEDURAL WORK: including, but not limited to, line supervisors and lower to middle management personnel, who are expected to hold the line, meet deadlines, see that performance, service and production are all up to established standards.

Persons attracted to the lower levels of management as a lifetime job tend to naturally focus on and attend to <u>maintaining</u> the status quo more than to problem solving and issues of growth or expansion. As such, they generally have a strong preference for the foundation-building, procedural mode. Historically, these people have been given the mandate to keep the business moving; keep the assembly line up and operational and keep the workers on task and on schedule. Such a mandate not only requires that the individual excel at working with routines, it also requires that they make the execution of those routines their highest priority. This means they must be able to stay focused on the procedures and not get distracted by "people issues" or by trying to make improvements in the system. All of which comes quite naturally for a Basal Left thinker.

By way of contrast, people with more Frontal access, especially Frontal Left thinkers, with more analytic access, view lower and middle management not as goal in its own right, but as a passageway. As such, these natural negotiators spend only a short time in the middle ranks, moving higher and faster up the organizational ladder as their inherent ability to compare "apples and oranges" puts them in demand for upper management positions. Similarly, right brain people filling lower or middle management positions will tend to be frustrated with all the procedure, which they find inherently difficult to attend to, and will either spend time chatting with others to keep in touch with what's happening (Basal Right feeling/connecting thinkers), or developing new ideas for how to do things differently, whether or not the current system needs improvement (Frontal Right, adaptive thinkers). Thus, in environments in which consistent productivity is the desired goal, Basal Left middle managers are both a logical choice and a natural fit.

ENTREPRENEURS:

If, however, the person has a Double Frontal configuration, which combines the spatial Frontal Right with the analytic Frontal Left, his options for a satisfying career in business are substantial. Such a person might well turn out to be a company president. Or, if his preference for the Frontal Right is significantly stronger than their preference for the Frontal Left, he might become an entrepreneur. By contrast, Double Frontals who are more introverted will be happier as research scientists working in a corporate lab. Regardless, what characterizes this brain configuration is a fascination with new ways of doing things and an ability to visualize goals so clearly that they seem already accomplished.

Thus, the profiles illustrated of entrepreneurs with whom we have worked, tend to be typical of **entrepreneurs**. Knowing that entrepreneurs have this very, very strong access to the Frontal Right, we can begin to hypothesize why they take the <u>risk</u> they're known for and are willing to bet every cent they have on a new idea or business. Simply put, given their brain dominance, they are able to picture the successful outcome so clearly and vividly that <u>they may be virtually unaware of the risks involved</u>.

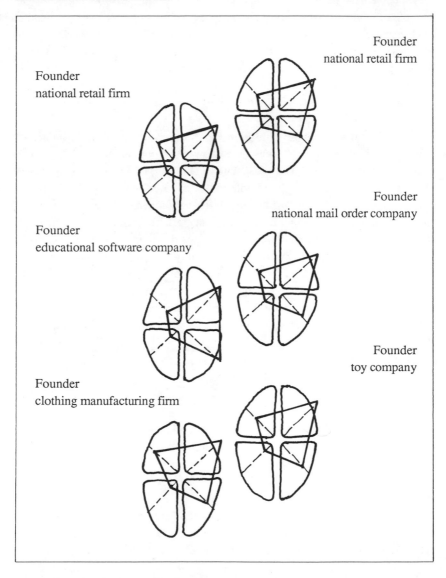

This hypothesis is further supported by the entrepreneur's predictably poor sense of scheduling and his difficulty in accurately predicting how long it will take to accomplish a given task or assignment. When asked for their estimate he will quite sincerely say that it "can be done in, oh, say four months," when, in actuality, it will take much longer, perhaps even years. The combination of their "already completed" vision and their inability to see the total number of steps involved (and the time that will be consumed by each step) makes their estimate miss by a large margin. It's a bit ironic that these thinkers are, on the one hand better than other people at predicting the future and inventing new programs/products which will succeed, while, on the other hand, they are unable to calculate the amount of time necessary for the project's implementation. In a way it's as though they are, mentally speaking, far-sighted and that, like all far sighted people, they have difficulty in seeing things clearly as those things come closer. One such person once observed that when he envisions a new project it is very clear but that as he approaches it, it actually begins to blur and he finds his vision going off into the future again.

Another significant point to make here, is that successful entrepreneurs tend to be very extraverted. We have not mentioned introversion and extraversion in the book thus far because they introduce another layer of complexity which might be confusing for those just developing a familiarity with the model. Here, however, it would be misleading not to insert a brief comment. Introversion and extraversion are psycho-physiological labels which describe the direction of a person's thinking. Introverts are inwardly focused, seeking internal understanding, comfort and mastery. Extraverts are outwardly focused, intent on gaining influence or control over their environment, whether natural, mechanical or human. Significantly, our society has historically valued and rewarded extraversion almost to the point of implying that introversion is abnormal and unhealthy. Important recent research led by Dr. Hans J. Eysenck contradicts this. Conducted during the mid and late 1980's his research suggests that, although certain types of life experiences, particularly ones which are demeaning or stressful, can increase our degree of introversion temporarily, the extent of our natural introversion or extraversion is rooted in our innate baseline anxiety or arousal level, which varies throughout the human population according to a normal distribution function. Accordingly, only 15% of us are naturally highly extraverted, another 15% are naturally very introverted, and the remaining 70% have a balanced need for, or tendency towards, both. Thus, it seems that despite our cultural bias against introversion, both are fully natural.

What's more, in the same way that each of the four core modes has a special type of processing it manages naturally, and a natural and unique contribution to make, introversion and extraversion tend to cause us to focus and use our brains and energy in distinctly different manners, each of which, as with the four core modes, has its own unique and valuable contribution to make to our lives.

Thus, the extremely extraverted Frontal Right has the drive and interest in using his of her new idea or invention to conquer or master his or her environment --a drive necessary for any fledgling business in a competitive market. By contrast, when a Frontal Right person is extremely introverted, he finds it equally natural and energizing to travel within, <u>exploring the patterns</u> in the psyche--as a psychiatrist, artist or poet. And, surely both are equally important to the development and fulfillment of the complete human life: the extravert's vision of a better product, a bigger company, and a better world created and led by him and the introvert's vision of the soul with its evolving patterns, needs and symbols.

So it's worth remembering that although some 70% of us have a balanced need for both introverted and extraverted activities and most standard jobs call for a person with both needs or tendencies, some 30% of us are natural extremists-- attracted to and suited for specialized jobs, which allow for this additional dimension of our psychophysiology.

Having read through the above discussion and looked at the sample profiles provided, you are probably beginning to see that as a result of the way in which the smart-dumb rule guides career choices, people in the same profession tend to have very similar dominance patterns. For this reason, from this point on, we will only be giving you the generalized pattern which we have found in each profession we discuss.

ENGINEERS:

In some areas, such as engineering, it is possible to see the role of dominance most clearly by considering the way in which it affects people's choice of subspecialty. In looking at the profession of **electrical engineering**, for example, it is typical to find people with strong double-left patterns and a Frontal Left lead. These analytic-sequential thinkers prefer precise, detailed work with a physical rather than a conceptual focus, which they can analyze and manipulate.

Interestingly enough, in the field of **chemical engineering** there appears to be not a double-left, but a double-frontal pattern dominating. When Katherine questioned several chemical engineers about the reason for this shift and why the Frontal Right would be important in chemical engineering, their response was: "Within the field it is known and accepted that the best chemical engineers work by generating in their mind a three-dimensional, dynamic model of the molecular structure of the chemicals with which they're working. By rotating such images in their mind's eye and observing what happens, they gain insight into possible problems and probable solutions."

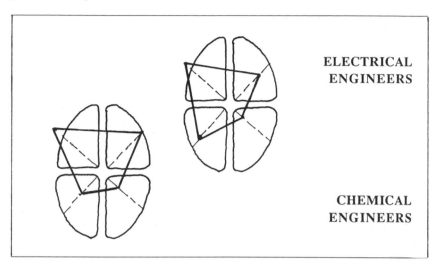

ELECTRICAL
ENGINEERS

CHEMICAL
ENGINEERS

This internal imaging ability is not as necessary for the electrical engineer. Electrical circuitry lends itself to two-dimensional diagrams and does not require the holographic imaging capability of the Frontal Right. Additionally, electrical engineering is highly structured (e.g., on/off switching), whereas that of chemical engineering is more fluid and multidimensional (e.g., molecular chemical bonds). Consequently, the double-left configuration matches the demands of electrical engineering, but does not match those of chemical engineering.

Ironically, the key differences between those individuals who seek work in electrical engineering and those who seek work in chemical engineering go unnoticed, or at least unappreciated, by those in the field and by the colleges and universities attempting to train engineers. According to our interviews, these institutions teach all engineering classes from a Basal Left or double left perspective. It is somewhat parallel to the problem of medical schools training young surgeons without telling them about the need to visualize (create an internal visual model) of their patient. The difference here is simply that engineering students need to learn to visualize the chemicals with which they are working, in order to monitor and predict the effect that certain procedures will have on them. Most successful surgeons and chemical engineers routinely use this process and find it essential to their success. All are self-taught visionaries who simply "stumbled" onto the technique. None of them report having been formally trained to use and depend on the accuracy of their Frontal Right to visualize and solve problems. (See the discussion on "surgeons" under Brain Dominance and the Helping Professions, immediately following this discussion of The Business Community.)

A key question being posed at meetings of the Society For Petroleum Engineers during 1986-87 can readily be understood once you know about brain dominance. The question is: "Why are engineers so narrow-minded and so unimaginative?" The answer is, of course, "When have they ever been trained to be anything else?" Most of the engineers are double left and all have been trained from the Basal Left stabilizing mode. Staying on the path, keeping things in order, doing it the safe way is their strength. They do not use imagination and innovation skills not because they have none, but because these skills reside in a mode (Frontal Right) which is overshadowed by their biological preference and reinforced by their formal training.

Quite the opposite is true for the petroleum geologists who work side-by-side with the engineers in companies like Shell, Arco and Standard Oil. The oil geologist, according to the engineers, is a "dart thrower." "No one," by which they mean no double-left engineer, "can understand how the (Frontal Right, internal image generating) **geologists** know where to look for oil." According to the geologists, they do so by using data to generate a picture of what "must be happening down there." Of course, as soon as you realize that they are Frontal Right thinkers, and you understand how this mode works, what they do seems understandable and practical. By taking a few pieces of hard data, such as sample measures, which they then combine with their understanding of the pressure and other forces impacting the oil, these geologists can produce an internal "movie" of the underground process. By watching this "film" they are able to figure out how and where to drill for oil.

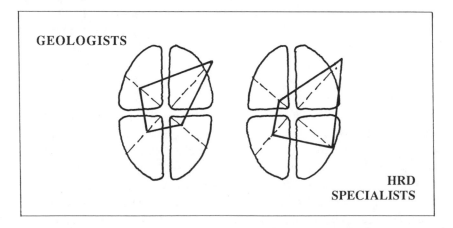

GEOLOGISTS

HRD
SPECIALISTS

HUMAN RESOURCE DEVELOPMENT:

When a person has strong access in the Basal Right mode as well as the Frontal Right, however, he needs a job which is more people-focused than the geologist's. Indeed, when double rights find themselves in a business setting, their usual way of handling the disparity between their loose, open, nonlinear and interpersonal processing, and the generally precise, structured and linear nature of most businesses is to carve out a job for themselves which matches their preferences. Two possible niches are: "human resource development" and the teaching of communication skills within an organization.

JOURNALISTS & LIBRARIANS:

While we're still discussing the business community,there are two other professions that we'd like to cover. They are the **journalist** and the **information manager** or **librarian**. Their patterns tend to look very much alike from the perspective of the four modes. Indeed, upon interviewing several librarians, we discovered that many librarians originally studied to be and/or worked as journalists. What distinguishes them is what distinguishes the entrepreneur from the psychiatrist. The journalist is more extraverted, intent on and interested in the world around him. The librarian is more internal.

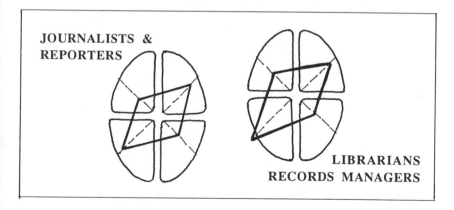

Additionally, their mutually preferred pattern is especially interesting because it proves that any dominance combination is possible and can work. Jung himself felt that a combined preference for the Intuitive and the Sensation functions was not a natural occurrence. Restated as a preference for the Frontal Right and Basal Left modes, the combination still, at best, sounds self-contradictory--a person who seeks to make change while maintaining stability. Our ongoing research indicates, however, that there are a surprisingly large number of people with this particular dominance configuration and that, although it does tend to produce a degree of tension, the worlds of journalism and information management are both benefitting from its existence.

If you think about the combination of skills represented in this pattern, you will begin to understand how it is precisely what's needed to get the job done well. For the journalist, the Frontal Right portion gets satisfaction of seeing the "whole picture" quickly (a good use of the visual brain) and, because a different story is covered daily, enough change and variety to keep it stimulated. The Basal Left brain comes into play to report what's happening in a sequential, step-by-step way. For the Librarian, the Frontal Right is continually being stimulated to look beyond to new and different horizons, to new and different information which might be coming in or which a user needs, while the Basal Left sees that all in-coming information and publications are cataloged, referenced and shelved according to established, sequential systems. Thus, persons with this unlikely profile can and do make distinct and valuable contributions to the world of business.

SUMMARY of DOMINANCE IN THE BUSINESS COMMUNITY:

The following chart shows how several brain dominance patterns distribute themselves throughout the business and professional community:

BRAIN DOMINANCE IN THE BUSINESS COMMUNITY	
DOUBLE LEFTS **with Frontal Left Leads:**	Accountants MBA'S, CPA'S Electrical Engineers
DOUBLE LEFTS:	Lawyers
DOUBLE LEFTS **with Basal Left Leads:**	Bankers, Machine Operators Machine Repair Personnel
BASAL LEFTS:	Ordering & Purchasing Clerks Record Keepers & File Clerks Bookkeepers Personnel workers

DOUBLE BASALS:	Secretaries
BASAL RIGHTS:	Receptionists Communication Specialists
DOUBLE RIGHTS	Organizational Development Specialists
FRONTAL RIGHTS:	Entrepreneurs Geologists Architects
DOUBLE FRONTALS	Inventors Chemists & Chemical Engineers Research Scientists Economists
BASAL LEFT - FRONTAL RIGHTS:	Journalists Librarians

BRAIN DOMINANCE AND THE HELPING PROFESSIONS:

Like corporate America, health care and the helping professions need and attract a wide variety of preference patterns.

THE PHYSICIANS:

A self-selecting process occurs when people choose a career in the field of **medicine**. With the increased post WWII emphasis on diagnosis (analysis), medicine has become even more strongly a Frontal Left profession. Medical education, on the other hand, continues to be a primarily double-left currriculum, emphasizing a combination of analytic and sequential thinking, reminiscent of the training found in engineering and accounting.

Not surprisingly, there are quite a few similarities between physicians, MBA's, accountants and engineers. All of them have strong Frontal Left leads and enjoy work which allows them to analyze and diagnose. Physicians diagnose the underlying cause of an illness; accountants diagnose the underlying cause of a client's financial problems; and engineers diagnose the underlying weakness in a structure. And, all of them recommend startegies to "fix the problem" and "cure the disease."

Once you realize that most physicians have preferential access to the two left modes of thinking, certain legal and public relations problems they are having begin to make sense. From a double-left point of view, a patient's body is a complex, malfunctioning machine which they investigate in the hopes of repairing. They do not necessarily bring to this process any of the Basal Right skills in interpersonal relations. They are not adept at making their patients "feel cared for " nor, given their dominance, do they see any logical reason why they should be. Unfortunately, most of us don't like being treated like a broken machine, and we have difficulty making the doctor's <u>technical</u> skill more important than his <u>lack of personal relations skills</u>.

Although this double-left profile is certainly the most common single profile among physicians, in medicine, as in engineering, there is variation. The range of **specialities** that abounds demands and provides opportunity for this variation.

One of the most distinguished specialities is **surgery**. In the ranks of physicians, surgeons have a reputation for being domineering, demanding and not particularly interested in following the rules. These behavioral quirks are more easily understandable when you realize that as a group, surgeons are not double left (analytic-sequential) but double frontal (analytic-spatial). Whereas the double left may <u>want</u> power and control (due to his Frontal Left), his Basal Left, which is into order and stability, keeps him from creating too much havoc. The surgeon, on the other hand, combines his analytic/power-focused function with the Frontal Right's disrespect for order and sequence. The result is that within health care , and especially among nurses, surgeons are seen as behaving in whatever way they need to in order to get what they want, including throwing a temper tantrum or breaking the rules. As we became aware of this pattern and its behavioral implications, Katherine was reminded of an unforgettable experience when she was thirteen and working as a candy striper "helping out" on the community hospital's nursing ward. She found herself suddenly grabbed by the star OB GYN surgeon who had just had an emergency in delivery and not finding the help he needed, decided to recruit her. At the time Katherine was struck by the fact that although what he wanted her to do might help, it was totally non-standard and possibly illegal, but that those facts didn't faze him in the least.

As fascinating as it is to be able to diagnose and explain these particular behaviors, the question still remains: what attracts these double frontals to surgery in the first place? To answer this question, consider what happens during surgery when the human body must be taken apart and put back together. Unlike a man-made machine, the human body cannot be taken completely apart in order to be worked on. Nor can it be unplugged, drained of all its fuel and lubricants, steam cleaned and then rebuilt. And, finally, although some surgical procedures go quite routinely, the surgeon must be ready at all times to deal with the unexpected. Translated into brain modes these characteristics of surgery means the surgeon must have access to the creative, adaptive mode of thinking in order to handle the trouble-shooting functions and come up with procedural variations as and when needed.

According to many successful surgeons interviewed during workshops at the American Academy of Medical Directors, another reason surgery is so attractive to double frontals is that it demands the use of their internal-image generating skills. As is the case with chemical enginners, excellent surgeons use this imaginative, spatial part of their thinking to construct in their mind's eye a three-dimensional image of the organs and tissues they're operating on. They can then rotate this image and "see" the places they are unable to see (with their normal vision) and by using this image, continue to operate precisely and effectively.

Although this "x-ray vision" is considered indispensable by many successful surgeons we have interviewd, it appears to be exclusively a self-taught skill. None of the surgeons we spoke to could recall ever hearing it mentioned and all were certain it had never been taught in medical school. In fact, until our conversations, they had never even discussed it among themselves out of fear they would be criticized for using a non-rational procedure. The "taboo" about discusing this skill is so strong that even the surgeons training young residents do not explain it to them. When asked by a resident how they had managed a particularly difficult operation in which much was not visible to the naked eye, all of these physicians responded only by saying "Experience, experience."

PSYCHIATRISTS:

Another medical specialty which has both a distinctive and predictable brain dominance is **psychiatry**. Almost everyone appears to know that psychiatrists are the misfits of the world of medicine and, from the perspective of a typical AMA member, the psychiatrist is both a "problem" and an anomaly. On one occasion we actually heard a nonpsychiatrist physician try to reassure himself that "psychiatrists aren't real physicians anyway." This was his way of separating himself from the bizarre behavior and thinking which characterize the strongly

Frontal Right psychiatrist and making sure no one would mistakenly confuse them with the standard double-left physicians.

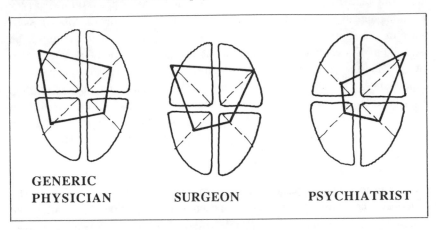

**GENERIC
PHYSICIAN**   **SURGEON**   **PSYCHIATRIST**

Unlike the surgeon whose preference is double frontal, the psychiatrist tends to be almost exclusively Frontal Right. The behaviors they exhibit which express this dominance pattern are their use of metaphor, their sense of humor and their strong penchant for making bizarre comments. Additionally, since psychiatry relies on the spatial brain's ability to perceive patterns and that is a skill found only in the Frontal Right, it is not surprising that psychiatrists test as dominantly Frontal Right thinkers. When psychiatrists work with their clients, they approach their job rather differently than do their analytic colleagues. Although both collect data, much of what the psychiatrist collects is disjointed and not readily measurable. Furthermore, the psychiatrist has to collect the data he works with without being able to isolate it in single systems or components. He must work with the entire gestalt and from that gestalt, using his Frontal Right, create a picture of the significant patterns.

Thus, within the generic category of physician quite different brains find a place to enjoy themselves, "think smart", and contribute.

THE NURSES:

Having briefly explored the field of medicine from the perspective of brain dominance, we can now take a look at brain dominance in the **nursing** profession. Dominance data on two thousand nurses suggests that most nurses are sequential-feeling thinkers (double basal). This profile is not particularly surprising given the fact that for the last several decades nurses have been trained largely as the physician's helpmate--the person who sees that his orders are carried out according to "prescribed" schedule ("turn the patient this often," "give X amount of this medication every four hours," "waken him every few minutes," etc.) and who provides the patient with the nurturing care the physician doesn't have time for. The nurse is both the detail attentive person who sees that the necessary procedures are accomplished and the encourager, the comforter and the morale-builder--the Basal counterpart to the Frontal Left physician.

Within this overall double basal pattern, there are nurses who have a strong preference for one of the modes over the other. Those nurses with a preference for the sequential mode over the feeling mode tend to gravitate, even in their mid-twenties, to **supervisory nursing** positions in which they can monitor and correct schedules and procedures. In contrast, those who have a stronger preference for the feeling mode will elect to remain in **staff nursing** for decades, even when it means being supervised by professionals many years their junior.

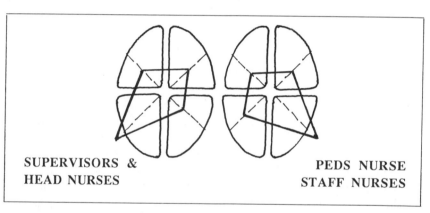

SUPERVISORS &   PEDS NURSE
HEAD NURSES   STAFF NURSES

This split in preference between the sequential mode and the feeling mode explains the conflict which is experienced on many hospital units between nurses advocating "the procedure" and those advocating a more feeling response. A typical scene recounted to Katherine numerous times by nurses themselves provides an excellent example:

"A staff nurse is sitting at the edge of a patient's bed talking with the patient. Her head nurse enters and says: "The manual says staff should not sit on patients' beds. Furthermore, we should finish our work before we go around gabbing." The nurse, aware that the patient is in desperate need of attention and nurturing, is at a loss. After all, you can't proceduralize the time and place for appropriate feeling responses; it's something you simply know based on being sensitive in the moment."

Who's right?   And what to do about it?   Needless to say, a good bit of anger and resentment builds up as these two different types with their two different agendas are forced to work side by side.

Of course, there are anomalies in nursing just as there are in medicine. One is the **intensive care nurse**, who works predominantly with unconscious patients and the machines responsible for keeping them alive. These nurses, who enjoy working in intensive care unit with the machines, are very often double left brain thinkers. For these nurses, an opportunity to practice nursing without having to be nurturing, in the Basal Right feeling sense of the word, is often a welcome relief. Some are even aware that they are more comfortable with the unconscious patients than conscious patients with whom they would have to interact.

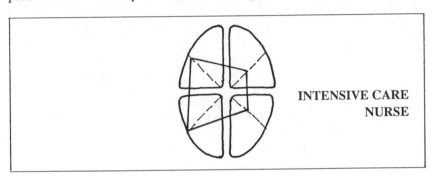

INTENSIVE CARE
NURSE

Despite this overall pattern, in one of our client hospitals we found an ICU managed by a double-right brained, feeling-spatial, thinker. This nurse, following a pattern which could be called "TRIBAL," had hired double-right brained nurses to work in her ICU. Although at first glance this might appear to be an undesirable staffing pattern, conversations with the manager revealed tht the team had worked out ways of "being smart." In their ICU, these nurses used their spatial mode to scan the machines (much like pilots use this mode to monitor their instrument panels). Then, with their feeling/ nurturing modes, these nurses continued to touch and talk to the patients even though they were unconscious. As they explained it to us, "Even unconscious people need to be touched and talked to. It helps their morale and consequently the overall healing process."

We do not know whether or not the overall performance of this unit was better or worse than the norm, nor do we know if they had a higher burn-out rate than on intensive care units staffed predominantly with left-brained nurses. Nonetheless, it is interesting to note the tribal pattern in operation and the supervisor's need to be surrounded by people that matched her own dominance. It is equally fascinating to notice the ways in which those particular nurses redefined the job in order to use their preferences. Whether or not such an adaptation would be satisfying and productive on a long-term basis is difficult to predict.

Another specialty within nursing which seems to attract the atypical nurse is **emergency nursing**. These nurses seem to be somewhat sharper and more decisive than the general staff nurse, concerned with precision as and when need be, but otherwise more fun-loving than the typical intensive care nurse. When we tested and interviewed several hundred of them over a three year period, what emerged was that on the whole, nurses attracted to emergency room work are double frontals. Although the daily routine and one-on-one intimacy of much nursing care might be very uncomfortable for them, in the Emergency Room or Department, they are indeed smart. They enjoy and are adept at problem solving and seek the opportunity to share this activity with the physicians, an opportunity which has not traditionally been available to them in an office, or on the units. Additionally, they are attracted to what they perceive to be in emergency work as continual novelty and change and the challenge to think on their feet in difficult situations where trouble-shooting may be as necessary as practiced knowledge and expertise.

COUNSELORS:

Other right brainers choose careers in counseling to validate their strengths and make them feel "smart." For the double-right brained individual with a very strong lead preference in the feeling mode, this could mean electing to be a **counselor, psychologist** or **therapist** since that career choice provides them with the opportunity to observe patterns of behavior from a perspective grounded heavily in feelings. When such a double right individual also has access to the Basal Left sequential mode, they may prefer to be a social worker rather than a therapist in private practice. This choice balances their need for connection with their ability to work well with forms, schedules and procedures--their skill as a therapist with their skill at keeping accounts ordered and complete.

A double-right with less strength in the Basal Right mode, and a strong lead in the Frontal Right may choose PSYCHIATRY rather than psychology or counseling, because psychiatry is more conceptual, "intellectual" and pattern-focused than straight counseling. This allows them to express more of their Frontal Right pattern skills and removes them somewhat from the strongly visceral Basal Right feeling mode. The difference between the person attracted to being a "therapist" and the person attracted to being a "psychiatrist" is particularly evident in the differing approaches these people bring to their work--the therapist or psychologist being more attracted to "getting personal" and "involved" with their clients, possibly even "giving advice based on personal experiences" or using active techniques such as psychodrama. By contrast, the psychiatrist, being somewhat aloof, is mainly interested in listening.

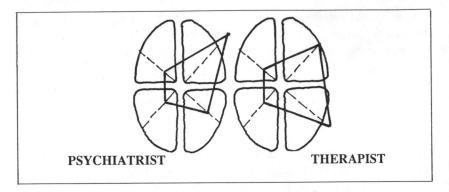

PSYCHIATRIST   **THERAPIST**

TEACHERS:

The most commonly preferred mode amongst the grade school and high school teachers with whom we have worked is the Basal Right, with many teachers actually having either Double Basal or Double Right preference patterns. This is particularly significant inasmuch as the schools and their administrators appear to function largely from the Basal Left. If our sample is accurate, then the time out which teachers take each summer may in fact be necessary for those teachers lacking natural strength in the Basal Left to recover from the year's stress of functioning heavily in the Basal Left. Moreover, this would explain the chronic tension within schools between the teachers on the one hand with their ideas for new and better classes and class structures, and their administrators on the other hand, who are uncomfortable doing anything experimental, preferring instead the tried and true methods.

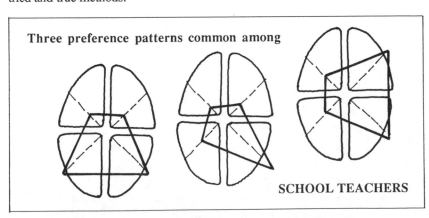

Three preference patterns common among

SCHOOL TEACHERS

SUMMARY OF DOMINANCE IN THE HELPING PROFESSIONS:

In the same way that the business community offers a wide range of opportunities such that someone with almost any pattern can find a niche, so do the helping professions. Some of the more common ones are listed in the chart which follows:

BRAIN DOMINANCE & THE HELPING PROFESSIONS

DOUBLE LEFTS
  with Frontal Left leads: Hospital Board of Directors

DOUBLE LEFTS: Physicians, ICU Nurses

BASAL LEFTS: Personnel Officers,
    Hospital Administrators (old)
    School Administrators

DOUBLE BASALS
  tilted to Basal Left: Head Nurses & Supervisors

DOUBLE BASALS
  tilted to Basal Right: School Teachers
    Staff Nurses

BASAL RIGHTS: Counselors, Pediatricians
    Staff Development Specialists
    Community and Public Relations
    School Teachers

DOUBLE RIGHTS: School Teachers

FRONTAL RIGHTS: Psychiatrists
    Emergency Physicians

DOUBLE FRONTALS: Surgeons
    Hospital Administrators (new)

BASAL LEFT-
  FRONTAL RIGHTS: Community "Organizers"

BRAIN DOMINANCE   AND THE FINE ARTS:

We do not have nearly as much data on artists and those choosing the fine arts as a profession, but some data is available. That data tends to confirm what many people already suspect: the arts attract predominantly right-brained individuals. However, within that general pattern, there are some profiles of particular interest. For example, many **poets** and **composers** have a significant amount of access to the Frontal Left mode. In such cases the Frontal Right remains the dominant lead and the Frontal Left contributes its skills in support of the Frontal Right goals. To get a sense of how this works, consider if you will the works of Robert Frost and Carl Sandburg.

Certainly Sandburg's "The fog creeps in on little cat's feet" is the kind of highly pictorial and metaphoric thought produced by a Frontal Right preferent brain. Equally visual and equally metaphoric is Frost's "Two roads diverged in a yellow wood." And yet, what distinguishes both of these poets from many lesser artists is their ability to be precise in measuring their words, in creating rhythms, in evaluating what to include and what to exclude, all of which are contributions of the Frontal Left analytic mode. Unfortunately, we cannot do an assessment of Frost or Sandburg. However, in assessing almost two dozen poets from a Boston area group, a colleague of ours, Chuck McVinney, discovered that those with similar abilities and styles also had what we are calling Frontal Left support.

This Frontal Left back-up seems to be common to a number of **painters** as well and is evidenced in their interest in and ability to use specific painting techniques with <u>precision</u>. Some years back, Katherine became fascinated with this idea and took it to an **engraver** who is also dean of the Art School at a large university. She suggested to him that there appear to be at least two distinct categories of artists: the first made up of double-right artists who have grand ideas and execute them with vitality, color and flair but with no precision; and the second made up of double frontal artists who have visions they can and do execute with tremendous precision, although perhaps with less vibrancy of color. In the first group she included painters like the landscape and flower painters of the "Okracoke Island artists' colony." Their strong Basal Right lead was further suggested by their search for community and their need to be connected. Another member of this crowd might be Robert Rauschenberg. Although his work shows a distinct lead in the Frontal Right, his preferred modus operandi is often as a member of a group co-creating through a communal effort. In the second (double frontal) group, she placed such artists as Picasso and Rembrandt. To her delight, the dean agreed completely with her assessment, adding that it explained to him where his own ability and precision had come from, and why all artists did not have the patience or ability to work with engraving and lithography.

Educated guesses about how some well known artists might think...

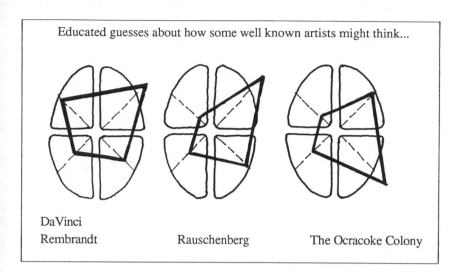

DaVinci
Rembrandt   Rauschenberg   The Ocracoke Colony

Thus, even though we associate "being artistic" with "being right-brianed,"the profiles of artists can be quite diverse.

Another member of the visual arts community is the **illustrator** who captures things in caricature. Not surprisingly, such artists tend to be almost quarter brain Frontal Rights.

While working with a large theatre company in The Pacific Northwest, it became apparent that many if not most **actors** and **actresses** have very strong access to the Basal Right mode. Their favorite way to learn a character is to first observe the nonverbals of a person similar to character and then to mimic their movements. As one acting instructor pointed out, it is much easier to be aware of the gestures and body stance of a character type (say, a military leader) and to embody these before learning the lines. "Once your body is moving in the right way, it is easier to speak the words in a way which naturally express the character."

In a recent television interview, Michael Caine told a revealing story about his first acting assignment, which supports the idea that many excellent actors are strong Basal Rights, even if their directors are not. His role was that of a military leader. Knowing absolutely nothing about acting at the time, and following his instincts, he looked around for someone to pattern on. He fixed on Prince Phillip, noticing most especially how he would hold his hands behind his back as he reviewed the troops. When Caine mimicked this gesture in a rehearsal, the director, who obviously had not noticed Prince Phillip's behavior, commented:

"Who is that? Fire that actor, he keeps his hands behind his back all the time!" Obviously, the nonverbal gestures Caine selected didn't quite match the director's conceptual picture of how a military leader should behave.

The "method school" of acting in which one seeks to get in touch with the feelings and emotions which can be brought to the character (in order to express his motivations) also relies heavily on having Basal Right feeling access. Ironically, with all this apparent skill with the Basal Right, many actors also appear to have exceptionally unhappy lives. Peter Sellers often commented that he did not know who he was. Rich Little, a well-known impressionist, echoes Sellers in his "Who's the real person in here? I don't know." Could it be that the same skill which enables a Basal Right thinker to reach out and "understand deeply" another person, when exercised to excess, as in acting, destroys the individual's own sense of self? This may be the case. Certainly one of the technical terms for the mental ailment reported by Sellers and Little is that of "Poor Boundary Definitions."

Upon reflection, we notice this same kind of ailment has been reported by many housewives, especially those married to exceptionally successful double left or double frontal men. Is the wife who for years has played the role of Mrs. Jones so successfully, anguished today because, after years of using her skill to minimize the boundaries between herself and her family in order to maximize the family's peace and harmony, she has no boundaries left in which to contain herself or no sense of herself at all?

SUMMARY OF BRAIN DOMINANCE IN THE ARTS:

In summary, the majority of visual and performing artists with whom we have worked show a marked preference for one or both right brain modes, using the precision and routine functions in the left to give shape to the visions and emotions they seek to express. Not surprisingly, many such artists actually have very weak access (i.e. an avoidance pattern) in one or both left brain modes.

Given these observations, it is perhaps easier to understand why and how so many performing artists become involved in raising money for good causes such as helping people with special illnesses, helping people in Africa facing starvation and promoting world peace.

BRAIN DOMINANCE IN THE ARTS

DOUBLE FRONTAL:	Composers
	Painters[1]
	Poets
	Woodcarvers
FRONTAL RIGHT:	Sculptors
DOUBLE RIGHT:	Dancers
	Painters
	Poets
DOUBLE RIGHT	Actors
tilted to the Basal Right	Musicians
	Interior Decorators

BRAIN DOMINANCE AND LEADERSHIP:

From the perspective of The Benziger Model, **leadership** is not different than any other profession or job. It attracts a particular type of person, whose pattern of mental preferences enables him or her to execute the full range of tasks embodied in the job of leadership. What is distinctive about Leadership is that more than most jobs, it requires a whole brain thinker who has equal and strong access to all four modes.

As one moves higher and higher in an organization one must think in broader and more conceptual terms much of the time. A great deal of the work involves prioritizing and making complex comparisons and <u>decisions</u>, tasks best done by the Frontal Left. Some of it, the <u>strategic planning</u> aspect, involves the visioning skill of the Frontal Right. Those with more basal access simply would not be

---

[1]Note: remember that painters fall into at least two camps: those who master techniques and whose paintings evidence precision, such as Picasso and Renoir and those whose paintings are more emotive such as Eduard Munch, who did "The Scream," and the communal artists of the art colonies such as Ocracoke Island on the Outer Banks.

able to cope. At the same time, excellent leaders also demonstrate a Basal Left ability to work in the trenches and remain alert to operational concerns, as well as a Basal Right ability to relate well and reinforcingly with other people. In fact, as one moves higher and higher in organizations, it becomes more necessary to work with a wider range of people--the left brained financial people, the Basal Left operational people, the Frontal Right scientists in research and development and the double right brained organizational development people. In other words, for the top executive, all modes are needed and none can be sacrificed.

From the point of view of the whole brained thinker, such a position is ideal. The range of tasks insures not only that he will get to use all four modes, but that he will get to move from mode to mode fairly rapidly. For these reasons, although such whole brain thinkers rarely become experts in a "narrower" field, they do tend to excel at leadership.

Another explanation for why and how the whole brained individual naturally seeks the top of the organizational pyramid can be found in cybernetics, the science of systems. The **First Law of Cybernetics**[2] (sometimes referred to as the Law of Requisite Variety) states: **the unit within the system which has the most behavioral responses available to it controls the system.** An example of how this law applies to human systems is found at the United Nations. Suppose for a moment that you put a Frenchman, a Japanese, a Nigerian and a Russian in the same room with a translator who spoke all four languages. Now suppose you asked the group to develop a proposal for global food distribution. Who do you suppose would control the outcome of the meeting? The **translator**, of course.

Multidominant individuals act naturally as translators. When their dominance only extends to three areas they are most effective at helping others decide how to act. But hindered by their one area of weakness, which is frequently almost an avoidance pattern, these people find there is one group they just can't work with. By contrast, the four-modal individual can, and usually does, get along with everyone. This makes him both a translator and a facilitator. Moreover, like the UN translator, he naturally controls what happens.

One last point which can be made in this area is that leadership profiles shift with the times. Five years ago the typical company president or chief executive officer was whole brained with a tilt to the Frontal Left. Today, more and more of the

---

[2]For additional information on this law and how it impacts human interactions, read The Magic of Rapport: How You Can Gain Personal Power in any Situation. San Francisco: Harbor Publishing, 1981.

nation's top executives are showing a strong Frontal Right tilt. This shift in leadership is normal and predictable given the current economic climate in which mergers, innovation and entrepreneurial behavior are key to success, and in which there is a tremendous amount of change taking place.

BRAIN DOMINANCE IN LEADERSHIP

1975
The Implementer

1986
The Visionary

These patterns were derived from Katherine's own data, combined with the written work of Harold Leavitt, author of <u>Executive Styles</u>, c. 1986.

For the reader interested in history and the philosophy of history, we suggest that this current shift is not unlike those exampled by Irwin Thompson in his book, <u>Archetypes in History</u>, 1971. Thompson's thesis is that there are four types of leaders and that the correct or appropriate type of leader automatically comes to the fore in response to the key needs of his time. His four types are: the hunter, the leader, the shaman and the fool. The hunter might be a military leader like MacArthur or a business leader such as Robert McNamara. The leader is an administrative leader who can handle stable times. The shaman is a spiritual leader like Billy Graham or Jesse Jackson. And the fool is a visionary-intuitive leader like John F. Kennedy or Winston Churchill. What you may notice is that the hunter uses a lot of the Frontal Left, the administrative leader needs a strong appreciation of the Basal Left, the Shaman represents the Basal Right feeling mode and the visionary fool, the Frontal Right.

Although Thompson suggests that these leaders have strengths in only the one or two areas needed at the time, we would like to suggest that, among the best leaders, these "leads" may simply be tilts to otherwise whole brained patterns. Combining Thompson's work with the theoretical and practical knowledge from cybernetics, we can see how the job of leadership in any specific situation holds two requirements:

REQUIREMENTS FOR BEING A SUCCESSFUL LEADER

REQUISITE VARIETY: A degree of Wholeness so that the leader
                     can communicate and work with all groups
                     within the company or community; and

APPROPRIATENESS: A lead which matches the need of the
                     time, so that the specific genius of the
                     leader can be brought to bear on the group's
                     most significant problems or needs.

A final point about leadership is that from a brain dominance perspective, almost all management jobs require whole brain thinkers. Although this need is apparent, our statistics suggest that there simply aren't that many people with four-modal access. The implications of this mismatch between our need for skilled leaders and our available human resources are significant. It may be that we can no longer spend our time seeking the perfect executive, but must commit to a future in which leadership is recognized as a joint function, to be filled by a team of persons who together have a whole brain.

This idea is not as far fetched as it may sound. In a small way, the growing tendency in large corporations to have a Chief Executive Officer (CEO) and the Chief Operating Officer (COO), one focusing on the strategic concerns and one on the operational concerns, is a step in this direction.

A SUMMARY OF HOW IT WORKS:

People are instinctively attracted to work which lets them feel "smart" or, in other words, work that matches their inherent, preferred biological dominance. They can find this congruence in a wide number of areas: medicine, business, the arts, or leadership. But, independent of the area, they will seek the job that has the closest fit. In the event that such a fit is unavailable, they may attempt to tailor a job to match their personal mental requirements.

Ideally, as we grow older, all of us become aware of what Bernard Haldane calls "our dependable strengths." We realize what it is we do well and under what kind of procedural conditions. We notice whether we work best alone or with other people present; whether we work best when we can delegate, when we can collaborate, or when we are directed. In other words, we become increasingly aware of our inner roots, our make-up, our mental dominance.

If, at the same time, we also gain an appreciation of which, if any, of our key choices earlier in our life were made in response to family pressure, limited opportunities or available role models, we can become empowered to create our own reality, one which will enable us to feel "smart" and good about ourselves. Our decisions about what job to do, which assignment to take, which promotion to go after will reflect with greater clarity our self-awareness and our entire life would be naturally and effortlessly brought into alignment with our dominance. In the best of all possible worlds the result would be that we would do less of "those other things" which leave us drained and discouraged and more of the work we enjoy and which energizes us. And, although some may see such a vision as mere fantasy, according to John Naisbitt and Patricia Aberdene in their second book, ReInventing The Corporation, recognizing individuals for the specialized contributions they offer and making the most of those contributions, is a must if we are to continue thriving as a nation and world.

CHAPTER 5
WHEN WORK DOESN'T WORK
(and other issues)

CAREER SHIFTS DUE TO A MISMATCH:

As we explained in the previous chapter, we naturally tend to be attracted to careers which match our dominance. It is important to notice, however, that sometimes this instinctual attraction gets thrown off course. This happens most often when a job or career is misperceived by the individual at the time he is selecting it. As he becomes aware of the problem, the young adult worker will usually attempt to remedy the situation by making a career shift, provided his life situation will accommodate the financial set-backs and insecurities that tend to accompany such a shift.

One example of this would be Katherine's own early choice to be a "long range regional planner." She made this decision by looking at the scope of the work and its function, as well as at some of the leading role models in the field, and concluded that the work was largely Frontal Right in nature. Five years into her career, she realized that in doing public planning, which is where most of the jobs are, a great deal of the work involves processing forms to approve or deny land use changes, variances, conditional uses, and permit appeals (which are definitely not Frontal Right activities). It took her a few more years and a great deal of inner courage to decide that she had made a bad choice and to get out. In fact, it was only once her health had begun to suffer dramatically that she got out of the field.

A second example has been occurring with increasing frequency during the past few years in nursing. It seems that despite the ""smart-dumb" rule, over the years, largely because of sociological factors, many non-basal women have been attracted to careers in nursing. One particular group of these misfits is made up of double left brained women whose analytic capability is equal to or greater than their skill with procedures. These women, who self-admittedly, have been feeling dumb in nursing, are now leaving nursing to go into law school. Once they have their degrees, interestingly enough, many of these same nurses find that in order to "be smart," they don't need to totally throw out their years of experience in nursing. Many of them are being retained by hospitals which desperately need guidance and advice on issue of risk, malpractice and liability in general. For hospital administrators who need legal advice, a lawyer who actually understands what health care is about is a valued advisor. Others from this same group of nurses in transition are finding both satisfaction and success assisting patients who wish to file malpractice suits. In either case, these women are finally free to be "smart" while using their analytic skills to win the day.

A third example occurred with a client of Anne's, a young man who had been trained as a lawyer and was "working his way into a position with the firm" by doing legal research and writing briefs. When he came to see Anne, he was in despair about his job. He hated sitting all day in a small office. He hated researching cases and writing positions. He hated never getting to move around, never talking to anyone, never doing anything creative. By having him complete one of the assessments we use to identify brain dominance,we learned that he was a double right, feeling-spatial thinker whose nature was to relate to people in an imaginative and expressive manner. As you might imagine, this configuration is not at all suitable for law, particularly the kind of law this man was practicing-- working alone and focusing on written details.

When asked how he came to choose law as a career in the first place his response was: "Well, in the first place my parents wanted me to go into it. They told me it would be an exciting and stimulating career. They also told me it was a good way to help people and that it would provide me with the financial security to pursue my other interests like painting, travel and music. And finally, they pointed out that artists rarely make a decent living. So I did what they suggested and went into law. And now I've invested so much time and energy in it that I'm stuck." Fortunately, after gaining a better understanding of his brain dominance and his fundamental unsuitability for standard law, this client was able to make the decision to move into a career he would be suited for and which would provide him with satisfaction. He is now doing just that, working as an artist representative part-time and a trainer part-time, leading seminars around the country on "How to represent yourself in contract negotiations." Both advocating and teaching other artists uses his Basal Right skill. The travel and involvement with visual art both draw on his Frontal Right. While, the workshop content and negotiations put to use some of the things he learned in law.

It is not always easy to change careers and to adjust one's life so as to live more in alignment with one's brain dominance. Nevertheless, most people who have gone to the trouble to change consider it a worthwhile thing to have done. For them, life is too short to spend it feeling chronically "dumb," frustrated and dissatisfied.

Think about it. Do you know someone who selected a particular career only to find that it wasn't what he had pictured? Perhaps this has even happened to you. This tendency to change careers in order to find a deeper level of satisfaction by using our "true self" at work may be becoming more frequent in our society as our natural affluence, longer life expectancy and changing cultural values all allow us more time and permission to use career shifts as a way of finding ourselves. In the last few years this tendency has increased so dramatically that, on the average, a worker will try seven different professions during his lifetime. Some, of course, make do with their initial selection, either because they chose well initially or because they are able to tailor the job to their brains' requirements. For some, the risks of career change will continue to be sufficiently more frightening than the discomfort of not fitting their job. In such cases, the person will probably not change unless or until stress and his deteriorating health force him to do so.

If you or someone you know is feeling uncomfortable at work, before he considers moving, it might well be worth their time to explore what, if any, role his brain dominance is playing in his current reality. In doing so a final word of guidance may prove useful. Some people seeking a shift need to make one, not because their current job requires them to use their non-preferred mode, but because their thinking pattern is broader than the range of tasks which make up their job. For example, a double basal woman working as a bookkeeper would find her job satisfying but not fulfilling. Her natural strength in the Basal Left would enable her to do the job easily and well, but her equally natural strength in the Basal Right would have nothing to do all day. For such a woman shifting to a career comprised of double basal tasks, such as teaching bookkeeping in a high-school, would be both sensible and satisfying.

Although we do not have specific examples of this available to share with you, both of us have served as career counselors, and both of us have seen such multi-dominant individuals, frustrated by their jobs, move to a completely different career, which was appropriate for the part of them they had not been using for years. Although at first they are delighted, within a few years they found themselves moving back towards their first job or career. For such multi-dominant persons it is vitally important that they understand the nature of their mental flexibility and accept that it is not simply a "nice thing" to have because it means they can always pinch hit, but a true physiological reality which demands to be used. For such people, it is not simply variety which is needed but a special type of variety which calls upon the full range of mental skills they have in their personal **mental tool box.**

CAREER SHIFTS DRIVEN BY THE NEED FOR NOVELTY:

There is, however, another kind of career shift which needs to be managed differently, and which doesn't stem from a misperception but rather from the fact that our perception of a given career changes as we really get to know it over time. This shift in the degree of satisfaction provided by a given career is particularly common for anyone who has a lot of Frontal Right in his profile. As you recall, Frontal Rights need a lot of change and get quickly bored with routines. In fact, for Frontal Rights, two or three years in the same job can be an eternity. It is for this reason that they instinctively seek work which has lots of variety on a regular, ongoing basis. Failing to find such a thing, they are very likely to deal with their need for stimulation by changing jobs frequently.

An emergency room physician came to Katherine for help in figuring out his perennial dis-ease, dissatisfaction, and boredom in his chosen profession. As a young man he had considered specializing in surgery but, after looking at emergency medicine, had decided it would be a more challenging and exciting option. Instead, by the end of his first year he had already discovered that it was just a set of very routine procedures, most of which he had long since mastered by heart. He also found that he was having disagreements with other physicians about diagnoses. His personal style of diagnosis was to sense what was wrong with a patient from the doorway. He would observe the patient's energy, body posture, movement, skin tone and color; then, intuitively, he would synthesize this information into a diagnosis. Although he was invariably correct, his unorthodox (translate: nonanalytical) way of approaching things brought him into considerable conflict with the other M.D.s. Moreover, he added, his experience of himself as an outsider and misfit were compounded even more by his Frontal Right sense of humor which was considered bizarre and inappropriate.

As Katherine listened to him, his problem became clear: the boredom and frustration this now middle-aged physician was experiencing with the emergency department was just the natural and normal response of an analytic-spatial thinker who has been around for a time. Initially, the unpredictability of the type and number of patients is experienced as "exciting"--a kind of "troubleshooting," a talent common to double frontals with a spatial lead. Unfortunately, after a short amount of time, when the physician has handled so many knife wounds and so many auto accidents, the kind of procedures he does become predictable and he is likely to think "I know what's coming. I've been here before."

For this strong Frontal Right physician the experience in emergency medicine had become an unexpected and unwanted routine with most of the variables known, predictable and manageable. The career he had seen as full of excitement and variety while in medical school, and actually experienced as exciting and stimulating at the beginning, was now simply a source of chronic boredom, the natural result of his internal mental structure.

Before telling you how he elected to "solve" his career problem, it is worth mentioning a point he brought out during our discussions. It is an established fact that there is an exceptionally high "burn-out" rate among emergency physicians, and his theory was that the spatial-analytic thinkers self-select emergency care in medical school, believing it to be filled with excitement and endless variation (characteristics spatial thinkers thrive on). If this is true, then what is being experienced as burn-out is simply a growing recognition that appearances in the emergency room are deceiving, and that to a large extent, emergency medicine is simply routine care delivered in a schedule-free context. So what can these physicians do for the rest of their lives? If and when medical schools begin to include dominance in the information they provide to those selecting a specialty, some system-wide answers can be generated. Until then, each one will have to deal with his or her "burn-out" experience in a personal way.

Our emergency physician decided to take the medical board examinations for chemical dependency medicine, a brand new specialty in medicine (he took the very first board exam given), and then to specialize in working with teenagers with substance abuse problems. In making this choice, he is carving out a totally new career (in and of itself attractive to any Frontal Right), which resembles that of the psychiatrist. Although we cannot know whether he will be satisfied over the long haul with this choice, we can suggest that working with people's internal problems is vastly more complex than working with cuts and wounds. Thus, perhaps, he will indeed stay interested and satisfied for years.

Lest you think that we have been focusing just a tad too much on health care, and that such problems do not occur elsewhere, let us suggest that there is at least one group of people who have so much Frontal Right that for the good of everyone involved they should automatically plan to change jobs (or projects) often. These people are the entrepreneurs of the world, almost all of whom possess a strong Frontal Right lead. What is particularly interesting and predictable about how these far right thinkers do their work is that once they have a particular concern up and running, say in three to five years, and the trouble-shooting has given way to the routine, these people find themselves suddenly and profoundly bored even, sometimes, to the point of depression. Equally predictable is how they will respond to this eventuality: to regain their interest and vitality they take (or try to take) some of the company's capital to explore and possibly develop a new project they have been toying with.

Of course if the company has been doing well up until this time, it has hired a number of strong Basal Left line people and managers to handle production and see that things are manufactured and shipped on schedule. You can imagine the hue and cry that comes from this group when they hear how the boss intends to spend their hard earned profits. If you have followed any of these situations in the media (e.g., the case of Apple Computers), you are probably aware that the situation typically resolves itself when the founder sells out to a less Frontal Right buyer, sometimes from within his own firm.

We once met such an entrepreneur in California who was, at the time, in the process of selling his sixth company (which, given his profile, was a "smart" thing for him to do). Building a company, especially one which offers an innovative product, enables him to use and validate the adaptive and innovative skills of his change-loving, non-anchored spatial brain. It enables him to identify new products, to use his skill at predicting products that are going to be good money makers and to start up the necessary manufacturing operation. When the new system becomes standardized, with procedures and productivity quotas in place and specialized machinery developed, the need for his style of thinking becomes consistently less until, ultimately, it is replaced by the need for a more rooted, maintenance-focused type of management. If the spatial thinking entrepreneur attempts to stay, he will only find himself bored with the work and begin to inappropriately tinker and meddle around with the procedures.

Strong spatial thinkers need to learn that their ability lies in participating in and leading the adaptive phase of any project. When that phase is over it is time--for their well-being as well as the welfare of the organization or division--for them to move on. Individuals with this preference pattern who are self-aware often exploit this pattern by marketing themselves as troubleshooters and selling their services on a project basis to corporations. In larger corporations, it is also possible for such a thinker to be used internally as a troubleshooter, moving him from area to area as the point man for solving difficult situations. In at least one oil company, the benefit of such troubleshooters is maximized by making their services available to other companies on a fee-for-service basis. Whatever the project, the end product is usually best when everyone involved understands that this dynamic, enthusiastic, Frontal Right thinker will be used only until the project is turned around or up and running, and that at that time, he will, by pre-agreement, hire and train his replacement.

One of the drawbacks of this pattern is that sometimes those who have it, particularly as they age, feel they have not completed very much. Since they so excel at helping things get started--at birthing new ideas, products, and organizations--they may feel sad or frustrated at having missed the realization and completion phases. They will not interpret this sadness in a self critical way or conclude that it means something is wrong with them. Beginnings are the purview of the spatial brain and endings are the purview of the left brain. It is not a character defect that causes Frontal Right thinkers to move from beginning to beginning. It is the way their brains are built.

In summary, there is much to be learned about the interconnectedness of our brain dominance and our career satisfaction. From the examples we have looked at, it seems that a significant amount of the re-selection which goes on in midlife can be traced to an individual's need to be more "smart" than "dumb" at his job. Furthermore, since very few of us select perfectly the first time and we have more freedom to adjust than ever before, more individuals are choosing to change their careers so that their work is in alignment with their overall dominance pattern.

But even with the "big picture" in focus, there continue to be difficult moments and non-rewarding tasks in the total package we call "our job." Some of the most frequently-cited problem areas are: procrastination, time management and decision making. What relationship do the difficulties people have in these areas have with their dominance? And what, if anything, can be done? For fun, we're going to show you some of the answers to these questions.

WHEN WORK SEEMS MOSTLY RIGHT, BUT PROCRASTINATION'S A PROBLEM:

If you are like most people you probably have more work to do each day than you can possibly get done in eight hours. For this reason, you regularly have to decide which tasks to do and which tasks to leave undone. Sometimes the work you decide to leave undone must be completed the next day. Other times you notice "no one much seems to care" whether you do it, in which case, over time, you forget about "it" completely. In either case, much of the energy influencing your decision to put off doing certain tasks often comes from your dominance and your own internal desire to do the things you feel "smart" doing.

A tale of procrastination from medicine:

In the past decade of work we have met more than five hundred physicians who "have trouble" completing the entries they must make in a patient's medical records subsequent to seeing the patient. For 98% of them this "trouble" is that sitting down to record their diagnoses and prescriptions in a meaningful, legible fashion is overwhelmingly boring. Nonetheless, for most of these physicians, the knowledge that this information is <u>key</u> (a Frontal Left flag word) to properly treating the patient and to protecting themselves in the event of medical or legal problems is sufficient to motivate them to complete the records. It is interesting to note that many have enough residual frustration at having to spend time on this "important but dull, time consuming" task that they have taken to using a dictaphone and letting someone else transcribe and complete the records.

Let's look at this problem through the lens of brain dominance. The task of recording information accurately is a sequential and detailed procedure. The response of the 490 physicians is that of an analytic thinker who appreciates the value and importance of records but does not have a strong enough sequential thinking pattern to want to do the work himself. For many it is a frustrating experience. Analytic skill is basic to being a good diagnostician and physician. But being analytically preferent, when finished with one patient and one analytic task, such a physician wants to go on to another diagnosis, another analytic task. In other words, he wants to progress from one "smart" experience to another "smart" experience. To write out a detailed, sequential report of what he found, thought, and recommended would engage the Basal Left more than Frontal Left and by comparison would not be nearly as mentally rewarding to the physician.

In the case of many physicians, the medical records build up throughout the day. Only at the end, when there are no more patients to see and no more opportunities to feel "smart", do these physicians turn to the task they find so unpleasant. It is also true that during the time they are theoretically completing this task, these physicians are open to interruptions and distractions--by a phone call requesting a consultation or by another doctor walking by. This difficulty concentration or <u>lack of concentration</u> is the typical and predictable result when anyone does a task which does not match his or her dominance.

At first glance, the solution would appear to be a workable one, in that "only the physician himself is inconvenienced" by his needing to stay late. It is, however, worth noting that the solution could have an unfortunate effect on the physician's home life, and not simply because his lateness upsets any mealtime routine which other family members might have. What happens when we put off until the end of the day those tasks which we would rather not do at all because we simply don't enjoy them is much more insidious. When we come home immediately after completing a task which matches our dominance, we are positive and "up," ready to talk with our spouse or play with our children. By contrast, when we come home immediately after completing an hour or more of unsatisfying work, work that is outside our area of dominance, we feel quite differently. We may feel slightly angry and imposed on. Our energy will be low and we will certainly not be oriented toward healthy relating. It is likely, therefore, that this hour of tedium at the end of the physician's work day may also cause difficulty in his home life.

What these physicians are facing, the procrastination they are trying to manage, is simply the normal, natural experience we all have when we work at a job we love, but with a nonnegotiable part we hate. In talking with a wide range of people who find themselves in such positions we find is that the most satisfactory way of dealing with this "Putting off being dumb" is to sandwich these tasks between tasks which are guaranteed "highs" (tasks which match our most preferred mode). It takes a bit of conscious planning but it can be accomplished. The result is that we tend to feel strong and solid and generally positive about ourselves when we begin the task, because we are basking in the afterglow of doing a "smart" task; and even if the non-preferred tasks makes us feel "dumb" or bored or down, we are able to regain our general sense of well-being by the immediate "shot in the arm" provided by another high which follows the undesired task. Using such a strategy of **personal energy management** suggests that we would be well-advised to end the day on a high so that we don't need to "take time out" before we are ready and available to be with those we love.

Let us return for a moment to the ten physicians (the 2%) for whom completing medical records is more than just tedious. For these people, the rational explanations (re: the importance of these documents) just go in one ear and out the other. Months can go by without them completing a single record. In fact, it is usually only when they are faced with the prospect of being denied privileges that these physicians get motivated enough to sit down and focus intently on their records.

The difference between the first group, the 98% for whom it is simply tedious, and the 2% who find it nearly impossible is that the 2% were all strong spatial, adaptive thinkers, with less strength than their colleagues in the analytic mode. None of the physicians in this survey were sufficiently preferent in the sequential mode to actually enjoy the task of record keeping. Yet those with a strong lead preference for the analytic mode could will themselves to complete the task, because they perceive its importance. For the ten spatially dominant physicians who lack the analytic ability to review the situation and appreciate the value of the records, the situation is entirely different. Their very nature, the structure of their spatial brain, leads them to resist the record keeping (a repetitive task) so much that most of them found it almost impossible to conceive of completing it.

Precisely how these physicians might learn to manage their "problem" is not clear. In cases where resistance is this strong, the sandwich technique can be used most successfully on a once a month rather than a daily basis. It may also help to simply accept that the basic problem with the task is that it is too repetitive for a Frontal Right thinker. As one physician pointed out, although each person is unique, when you have a specialty practice you will often see the same condition and prescribe the same prescription over and over again. Accepting this, one physician we know created a number of standard paragraphs which he numbered, so that all he had to do to complete his medical records was to note a series of numbers on the person's chart. His secretary, whose satisfaction from Basal Left activities is predictably higher than his own, takes the records and types in the paragraphs which he later initials. Although we were delighted with this solution, and indeed have known other Frontal Right physicians who have developed and use similar systems, we are sad to say that we were told by a more left brained physician that form-alized medical records are expressly forbidden and that this approach is actually illegal. For this reason, we would like to emphasize that we do not suggest the approach. Of course we are also aware that few Frontal Right thinkers are likely to be stopped by such "minor matters" as legality.

Tales about procrastination from Katherine's office:

Much of the time we procrastinate, we are doing so around tasks that, like the physician's medical records, should be done on a daily basis. With this type of procrastination the unpleasant, undone task hovers around us like a gnat or mosquito, putting us in a slightly unpleasant or defensive humor. In other cases, we procrastinate tasks which only need to be done once, but can, by an adept procrastinator, be left completely undone or go unnoticed for quite a long time. Although this latter type of procrastination seems more pleasant in that we manage to be totally oblivious to it after we've dropped it from our conscious awareness, it is often much more hazardous to our long-term welfare. Such was the case when Katherine started her business.

Not having a particularly strong Frontal Left and only a minimal Basal Left, one of the things that never occurred to her was the importance of having a standard formal contract she could use with all her clients to guarantee that she got paid <u>what</u> was expected <u>when</u> it was expected and to protect her in the event of last-minute cancellations. And, although a few friends had strongly recommended she institute such a procedure, it was easy for her to ignore them and avoid the task. Then, before she knew it, her business had grown and she was too busy thinking about new program designs and media backup to worry about such things as contracts. She hired an office manager who was wonderful and who took care of all the Basal Left functions. She kept all the records straight, processed all the forms with only an occasional query and handled all the client questions and billing. She was a dream come true because, with her strong preference for sequential thinking, she would do <u>almost </u>everything that Katherine did not want to do. Katherine's business doubled in short order thanks to the detail-sensitive procedures and organized foundation built by her office manager.

Unfortunately, they only had three-quarters of a brain between them; neither was a strong analytic thinker. Because Katherine is such a weak Basal Left thinker, she would regularly set fee schedules and then, just as regularly, ignore them so her office manager was perpetually confused by all of Katherine's "special agreements." Additionally, although Katherine finally did develop a Letter of Agreement which the office manager could use with all clients, there were ongoing clients for whom no such Letter of Agreement existed and with whom Katherine had only a verbal contract.

The problems caused by Katherine's weakness and attendant procrastination will appear quite predictable to those of you who are double left brained thinkers, but to Katherine they were an unexpected source of emotional pain and financial loss. What happened was that two of her ongoing clients, organizations which had originally approached her with pronouncements that "written contracts are unnecessary and we never use them," and with whom she subsequently had no contracts, began to shift the conditions of their verbal agreements pushing for significantly more service for the same fees.

Obviously, this entire situation was unnecessary. Had Katherine sent them a contract or even a one-way letter of understanding prior to delivering the services, there would have been fewer unpleasant experiences and loss of money. Unfortunately, as simple as it sounds to create and use a contract, it is not so simple for someone with Katherine's brain dominance. Thus we can begin to see how important it is for us to notice where the weaknesses in our dominance pattern are causing us to ignore, overlook or procrastinate on important tasks, for those weaknesses can sabotage our successes. We may never enjoy the type of natural energizing concentration while doing tasks which involve our nonpreferred modes. Yet, if and when we learn to accept and plan for our weaknesses, we may find that we are freer to actually do and enjoy the things we love simply because we don't have to spend time worrying, trying to cover the bases and back-filling because we didn't do something we would have taken care of had we a different set of mental preferences.

Procrastination: Turning away from or putting off a task, often one ill-suited to our natural self, at times accompanied by a turning towards what interests us.

Concentration: The natural absorption in a task or content which accompanies doing things which match our natural self and preferences.

Lesson: Everyone can concentrate easily and naturally. When Concentration isn't easy and effortless, or when we find ourselves hoping for interruptions, the chances are quite high that what we're doing doesn't fit our thinking style.

PROBLEMS WITH TIME:

One of the most interesting places to see the effect of dominance in our lives is by observing how we manage time. We once knew a woman manager who had a terrible time getting any work done. After we talked with her at some length the cause of her problem became apparent: as a strong feeling type with not very much access to either left mode, she found much of her work frustrating. At best, scheduling and monitoring tasks were simply unsatisfying. On the other hand, she was adept at listening to and empathizing with people, and she was also sensitive to their feelings. When an employee came into her office, it was an opportunity to be "smart" and use her feeling-based skills to be supportive. Furthermore, once she got them talking, she certainly did not wish to hurt their feelings by cutting them off; so she managed to spend much of her time "socializing" instead of working.

In the medical community a similar problem arises for many pediatricians. This specialty attracts physicians with a strong feeling access who enjoy working with the more "touching" clients like kids and moms. Since the need to touch is most often sublimated into the more socially and professionally acceptable "chatting," the pediatrician is more likely than any other physician to dally with the patients regardless of how tight his schedule is. Chatting with the patient or parent, establishing a personal connection and making sure they feel heard are very much a part of his practice. Also, of particular concern and importance to him is making sure not to rush the patient "in" and "out" as if seeing them was "just business." Although this behavior makes him popular with his patients, it often drives his Basal Left office manager into a frenzy. It also manages to reduce the number of patients he can see in a day and hence his billings. This in turn, quite naturally, doesn't please his more left brained colleagues who, being more "efficient," generate more money and often feel that they are "carrying him" as a sort of good will gesture.

That both the female manager and the pediatrician have unusual difficulty staying on schedule and "getting work done" is a source of frustration and confusion to them and those with whom they work. Yet, in actuality, the problem is not in managing time but in scheduling a work day which will be satisfying to the person with a strong preference for the Basal Right feeling brain.

In the case of the female manager, one possibility could be sharing a leadership position with another, more left brained manager. The more we come to understand about leadership, the more we see it as a complex task requiring a whole brain package of skills. As this perception spreads and is accepted, we predict that shared leadership will eventually become an everyday way of structuring organizations. Our Basal Right manager is not adept at managing schedules and needs someone to perform that function. At the same time, there are numerous left brain managers who are not at all adept at assisting people who with an emotional trauma (as a result of illness, alcoholism or death) or who are in conflict with another employee. For such left brained managers, having a "partner manager" who is adept in the area of interpersonal counseling could be invaluable.

In the case of the pediatrician, much of the pressure comes from trying to force this Basal Right thinker to move through a schedule which does not allow time for what he feels are necessary conversations. Simply scheduling fewer patients for him would appear to be a poor solution from a cost-effective perspective (which is ultimately how most business decisions are made), but it is not actually that clear- cut a decision. Recent studies demonstrate that physicians who smile and bond with their patients are sued significantly less often than physicians who do not. By extension, a group practice which has one physician, the pediatrician, who literally "puts on a smiling face" and builds good will with the community (note, he is usually also the physician who participates in community affairs) could well prove the cheapest and best liability insurance a group can have.

What else happens in the area of time management? The people who tend to work by a schedule are the Basal Lefts. Unfortunately, what can happen to them is that they get so "scheduled up" that they have little or no time for impromptu activities or meetings. Another problem Basal Lefts have is that because they generally need to review material in detail, they tend to need more time and information in meetings than their more Frontal Left bosses want only a brief summary of the most significant facts and recommendations before making a decision.

A third problem for strong Basal Lefts in managing time is that although they may attend a time management class or two, they are repeatedly frustrated. Most time management classes teach a technique called the 80/20 rule which states that 80% of the tasks you perform produce only 20% of your results; while conversely the other 20% of your work accounts for a full 80% of your results . Given this formula, the would-be master of time management is simply advised to sort out which tasks fall into the 20% category and which fall into the 80% category. Unfortunately, this theoretically simple task is not so simple for a Basal Left, who does not know how to compare apples and oranges. But more about that when we discuss decision making.

By contrast, the Frontal Left is a natural master of time. This person is able to sort readily through tasks, paperwork and information to determine what is worth doing and what should be immediately jettisoned into the wastebasket or "circular file." Similarly, when listening to a report or presentation, the Frontal Left is adept at listening only for key information, analyzing it quickly and taking immediate, decisive action. Like superman, he or she pushes through work towards the goal of success faster than a speeding bullet.

For the Frontal Right, time management is almost a moot question. For one thing, these people tend to not wear watches or observe clocks. For another, when they are truly interested in a problem, it absorbs their attention for prolonged periods of time during which they block out anything or anyone else trying to get their attention. In such instances they may miss scheduled appointments, meals and even sleep. When interested, they don't need to try to fit everything into an eight- hour day because they never work only eight hours. By contrast, when they are bored they almost never show up at the office, and so again may well miss scheduled appointments and meetings.

**DOMINANCE
AND DECISION MAKING:**

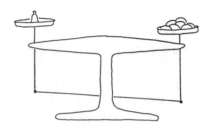

Decision making is another area in which our work pattern or style is strongly affected by our dominance. In decision making, the general rule that applies is: **"You make decisions from your preference unless your environment forces you to do otherwise."** In other words, someone who has a strong feeling (Basal Right) lead makes a decision based on her feelings unless the boss has specifically told her to approach an issue another way. It is interesting to note that although she may comply with this request, she may not necessarily feel "right" or <u>comfortable</u> doing so. In such cases, she is likely to seek out other feeling types with whom she can discuss the problem and from whom she can elicit support.

This same seeking of others' opinions is used by feeling types in order to solve or sort out and solve a complex problem. For them, one of the best ways of deciding what to do is to find out what most people want to do. To accomplish this, those who have a strong preference for the Basal Right feeling mode are likely to amble around, chatting with lots of different people to learn their opinions. Although these people will listen to logical arguments, they are more likely to be impacted by the person who quietly tells them about a <u>"gut feeling"</u> they have. Although Basal Rights are known for collaborating, it is more frequently the case that they will let the majority decision stand, provided the agreed upon solution does harm to no one. Thus, for feeling types, the time required to make a decision is the time required to talk to everyone about it, to collect their feelings, and to identify a decision with which everyone feels comfortable. Controversial decisions which seem to be a major source of disagreement are decisions the Basal Rights frequently refuse to make at all. In some management books, managers with strong Basal Right access are referred to as "country club" managers because they prefer to stay away from difficult issues so that they can keep things to running smoothly.

As you can imagine, a strong Basal Left procedural thinker approaches decision making very differently. People with this preference want clear and detailed guidelines for all decisions within their area of responsibility. If none exist, they are likely to try to obtain some before proceeding. They'll ask others: "Where has this been done before? How did those people make their decision? What did they decide?" Thus, for procedural thinkers, the time it takes to make a decision is the time it takes to review all the details of the decision, matching them against an approved set of guidelines. Since they can do this by themselves, they may very well spend their decision making time alone.

Strong Frontal Right adaptive thinkers are equally predictable in their decision making behavior. In areas of their strength, such as selecting a new approach to solving a difficult or complex problem, they tend to make quick "intuitive" decisions which are often correct, but which they can't easily support with facts. When forced to slow down and consider facts, they often become confused and lose touch with their own internal sense of what's happening. Once this has happened, they are generally easily talked into backing away from their original position. Such experiences have been reported by many successful entrepreneurs, who freely admit to having made major errors because they allowed themselves to be talked out of an intuitive decision by their left brained colleagues or staff.

In areas of their weakness, such as scheduling, performance evaluations or contract negotiations, the strong Frontal Right thinkers are equally predictable. They avoid such decisions or make them in such an off-handed, overly optimistic manner (which is frequently in error) that the decisions cannot be implemented. Comments like, "sure, we'll have it done in a month" or "I know we're just getting started, but we'll be in a position to pay you top dollar within three months" are often simply wishful fantasies.

Strong Frontal Left analytic people also have a preferred style of decision making. They prefer to make their decisions about consequential things and not waste their time on things that will not matter in the long run. They are famous for reminding people of the 80/20 rule, which says that eighty per cent of the result is obtained from twenty per cent of the tasks comprising the job. Moreover, they themselves often use this rule to justify dropping those tasks which promise only a small payback. This allows them to take on additional high yield tasks. They call this prioritizing. Also, when looking at a given problem, one which they feel is worth their time, they prefer to have only the key facts. As such, they prefer half-page summaries and charts rather than long reports. After studying the key facts they will analyze the impact of each of the options and then select the best as a solution. Frontal Lefts are the founders of the cost-benefit school of decision making.

WORK RHYTHMS, HOURS AND SPEED:

Although they are less tied to dominance than some of the other patterns we have discussed, the hours, rhythm and speed at which we work also reflect our dominance.

Where **hours** are concerned, double basal (Basal Left and Basal Right) people work regular hours unless their help is specifically needed. Basal Left thinkers prefer to work regular hours and if they think a job may require them to stay late, they may not take it. Alternatively, if they're in a job in which events are making the hours and working conditions erratic, they may join a union which will fight to get the workers their desired 9 to 5.

Basal Right thinkers tend to work long hours because they like to help and can be counted on to stay to "help out." A frequent reason they stay late is to help a Frontal Left who putting in the extra time to achieve more power or influence.

Frontal Right thinkers work in fits and starts and tend to stay late and long. When they get hooked on an idea which is of personal interest to them, they will often work non-stop through the night, totally oblivious to time. When they are "stuck" and can't figure something out, they are just as likely to go for a long walk or to play tennis for hours, much as the chemist John Critch relates doing when stuck in his work on the DNA-RNA double helix.

Frontal Left people work long and hard to get someplace or to gain control for they are aware of and buy into the concept of the organizational ladder. These are the people who believe that if you want to be on the fast track you need to demonstrate it by making the commitment to work long and hard hours.

Where rhythms are concerned, the Basal Left thinkers tend to be the slowest and the most methodical. Basal Right may work equally as slowly, but, in their case, it's because they need to stop for frequent chatting breaks with their boss, their colleagues, or perhaps a client. The Basal Right's pace also depends more on their mood; if they are sad they may work rather slowly; when they are happy they will pick up the pace. Regardless of their mood, they rarely work for a prolonged, uninterrupted period of time alone.

By contrast, Frontal Rights tend to work very quickly. At times, their energy seems to spiral into a frenzy of activity. This spiralling is what tends to separate the Frontal Right from his Frontal Left colleague, who also tends to work quickly but with a sense of control.

COMMONLY ASKED QUESTIONS ABOUT WORK:

You say that Basal Lefts are usually picked as supervisors and operational managers. Why is that?

The reason Basal Lefts are well suited to being operational managers is that they like to attend to routines, details and the necessary procedures in order to keep things running smoothly. Someone with more access to the feeling mode might be distracted by how people are feeling about their work. Someone with more access to the spatial, experimental mode would most likely delay productivity by intermittently designing and implementing improvements in the schedule or procedures. A Frontal Left, analytic type might consider simple operational management beneath his level of skill and try to rapidly move upwards.

What happens when a right brained thinker is promoted into management?

The usual result is that they do not do the mandated job as well as their left brained counterparts. Since they don't perform as well, they become discouraged when they are passed over for promotion or given poor performance reviews. When Frontal Right research scientists are promoted by their companies into tasks requiring a significant amount of double left thinking, significant problems occur. This situation is particularly common in companies like Shell, DuPont and Standard Oil which have all promoted scientists into managerial positions because the non-scientist left brainers they had used previously had difficulty gaining the respect and cooperation of the scientists in their Research and Development Labs. Unfortunately their solution is not much of an improvement. When a scientist is promoted to such a management position, the demands of his new position--the monthly reports, budgets and other control functions of management--cause him to feel "dumb" and subsequently drained.

Such mismatched or dominance-crossed promotions may go far to explain the Peter Principle, which has gained so much attention in the past decade.

I'm a triple mode translator. Does that explain why I've changed careers so often?

It is common for tri-modal individuals to have a number of different careers during their lifetime. They initially choose a career which matches the strongest of their preferences. However, since this does not represent all of who they are, after a time, they become bored with it and seek to move into another of their strengths. Unfortunately, when they reach this point, they commonly conclude that their first choice was just a **mistake** and often reject it altogether. In the case of a tri-modal thinker, the first choice is often not wrong so much as too focused. As such, the best second choice will be one which will hold onto the opportunity to use the preference they were using in their first job, while adding opportunities to use their other areas of preference. When a tri-modal person is ready to use all three of her preferred modes she may be attracted to management positions where diversity is a daily if not an hourly necessity.

Is it better to have a boss who has the same preferences you have, or one whose preferences are different from your own?

How well you get along with a particular boss is the result of the interplay between at least six variables: your dominance, level of self-esteem, and degree of maturity, and your boss' dominance, level of self-esteem and degree of maturity.

If you and your boss have a similar dominance pattern, the two of you will probably get along quite well since you both see the world in the same way. In fact, you are likely to really appreciate your boss as a person and enjoy relating to him. You will also tend to give him the benefit of the doubt in difficult situations. Nonetheless, if your boss is hiring only people who think like he does there will problems. Because to some extent all jobs are whole brained, there will be a part of the job that nobody wants to do since it is outside everyone's dominance. If the boss gives you the work, you feel dumped on. If he does it himself, he is likely to feel resentment and eventually burn out. Thus, the problem with such tribal configurations is that they are not sufficiently flexible to handle well all parts of the job, they do not have the necessary Requisite Variety.

When you and your boss have <u>overlapping</u> patterns, that is a part of you matches your boss and part of you doesn't (e.g., he's a double left and you're a double basal) you will relate well in the area you have in common--the Basal Left procedural mode. The two of you should have no trouble handling schedules, routines and standard procedures. However, when part of that system breaks down, your boss is likely to become more crisp, decisive, and critical (his analytic Frontal Left), while you become more concerned with the interpersonal ramifications (your Basal Right). What makes this situation difficult is that your boss will not understand you at all when you take this feeling-based approach and it will be disconcerting for you to be so "out of rapport" when you are usually so in agreement. If you want to talk to your boss at this time, you will need to <u>communicate in his language</u>--the language of the Frontal Left. This means you will need to be precise in your choice of words, present key points and argue logically. It will do you no good at all to present things from a Basal Right point of view. Having an overlap with your boss gives you a basis for collaboration but it also leads you to believe you are more completely understood than you in fact are. To do well in this situation you must recognize the differences as well as the similarities between you and your boss.

When you and your boss have <u>totally different</u> patterns you will either be a resounding success or a complete failure at working together, depending largely on how mature each of you is and whether or not you succeed in bonding sufficiently well to effectively collaborate. In our work with team building we have found that the best product comes out of Whole Brain teams. We deliberately put together people with differing dominance patterns in order to create a single "whole brain" team which can function in place of a single leader/decision maker. According to Naisbitt and Aburdene (authors of <u>Megatrends</u> and <u>Reinventing the Corporation</u>), an organizational structure in which the leadership position is held by more than one person is emerging in the top corporations around the country and is one of the trends of the future. What makes this difficult to accomplish is that all of the individuals involved need to be sufficiently mature and have sufficient self-esteem to make the collaboration work. If either person is overly invested in his way of thinking and has not accepted that he can benefit from help, the disparity in dominance is likely to cause problems.

In one situation we were asked to assist by our client, the vice president in charge of one division who had been unable to get her budget approved since the arrival of a new chief executive officer (CEO) three years earlier. Although our client understood that the recent years had been a time of severe cost cutting, she was also certain that her division was suffering more than it needed to. A rapid analysis of the situation showed that the vice president, a strong Frontal Right, was a success because she had a strong instinctual sense for what the clients wanted and which new products would sell. Unfortunately, the new CEO appeared to be a strong Frontal Left. Despite her track record, when she went into to request a budget for the coming fiscal year, he expected her to justify her requests in a logical manner which, for her, was almost impossible. Sending her in to negotiate with this new CEO and his new fiscal management team was as inappropriate as sending someone with one year of high school Russian to negotiate a treaty with the Soviets.

When we pointed this out to her, she came up with her own solution almost immediately. The next time she had to present a budget, she would take a strong Frontal Left with her to argue for her position. With this strategy in mind, she looked to her staff for the best Frontal Left and to us for a bit of strategic coaching on how to co-present her budget. In the end, the results were well worth the time she spent to sort out the problem, for according to our client, they got every penny they asked for--all because she took Margaret, a strong Frontal Left, to the budget meetings in which she would repeatedly turn and ask: "Now, Margaret, what exactly was our thinking on this?"

IN CONCLUSION:

Almost every aspect of our work life is affected by our internal, physiologically-established, mental preferences. Regardless of who we are, there are things we will not do well and situations in which we will not get along well with others. This is even true for the whole brained person, for although they can do almost any kind of job and understand any type of person, focusing for prolonged periods of time in one area or talking at length to a person whose dominance is highly skewed will tire them. Thus, their strength is also their weakness, as is the case with us all.

How can we live a complete life with these inborn limitations? There are many ways. The first step is to learn who we are and to gain a real appreciation for how our dominance has been guiding and influencing us. Then, we can begin to put the Two Rules of Thumb for insuring effectiveness and success to work. We can (1) choose tasks which enable us to use our preferences; and (2) ask for assistance with tasks requiring our non-dominant modes. The following pictorial summary will assist you in integrating the content of the last two chapters on work, before you go on to Part III which explores the relationship between your dominance and the your personal life.

The Basal Left Brain's Thoughts about Work

Basal Lefts feel smart and capable when asked to meet deadlines, stick to the established procedures or proofread.

Basal Lefts also tend to feel dumb or frustrated when asked to negotiate, argue for their budget (or whatever they want), nurture, be supportive, innovative or imaginative.

Therefore, Basal Lefts tend to select careers in which attention to detail and procedure is the key to success.

The Basal Right Brain's Thoughts about Work

Basal Rights feel good and energized building and maintaining harmony and connection, being sensitive, attending to and helping others.

Basal Rights also tend to feel dumb or frustrated when asked to negotiate, argue for their budget, enforce deadlines or schedules, strategically cut costs, do a cost-benefit analysis using measurable criteria.

Therefore, Basal Rights tend to select careers in which caring and touching are the keys to success.

The Frontal Right Brain's Thoughts about Work

Frontal Rights feel excited and turned on when exploring, playing with new ideas, using metaphors or being creative.

Frontal Rights also tend to feel dumb or frustrated when asked to prove an idea is correct using logic, read all the forms or follow the procedures precisely, analyze a budget or be nurturing.

Therefore, Frontal Rights tend to select careers in which imagination and enthusiasm for change are the keys to success.

The Frontal Left Brain's Thoughts about Work

Frontal Lefts feel energized and smart when using logic to analyze and solve problems or make complex decisions.

Frontal Lefts also tend to feel dumb or frustrated when asked be supportive or nurturing or come up with a totally new solution.

Therefore, Frontal Lefts tend to select careers in which logic and analysis are the keys to success.

PART III.

USING WHOLE BRAIN THINKING TO IMPROVE THE QUALITY OF YOUR PERSONAL LIFE

Rule #1: To develop or nurture your self-esteem,
as well as insure your immediate effectiveness and success,
select activities which match your dominance.

Rule #2: To assure your survival, as well as guarantee your
long term effectiveness and success, manage activities and people
not matching your dominance by enlisting assistance from
complementary brains.

CHAPTER 6
YOU'VE GOT TO BE KIDDING

If you've come to the conclusion that dominance affects practically all of what you say, do, think or value, you're well on your way to understanding dominance. Dominance isn't the total picture, of course, but it's so close to our core identity that it might be described as part of our genetic roots. Consequently, we can anticipate seeing its involvement in virtually every area of our lives. And although the specific rules which apply to each area of life differ slightly, they are all variations on the same general theme: the Two Rules of Thumb for insuring success and effectiveness, which in this chapter we will be applying to your personal life: your friendships, your marriages and your children.

FRIENDSHIPS:

Most of us select friends who **mirror**, at least partly, our mental preferences. Furthermore, when we meet a person who mirrors us completely, that is, whose dominance pattern matches ours perfectly, we are likely to feel so comfortable with this person that we will make him or her into our "best friend." This then is the basic rule of dominance and friendships: we choose our friends because they are like us. We also call this the **Mirror Rule**.

At first glance, it might seem very narrow-minded of us to actively choose to be surrounded by people who see the world as we do. However, choosing friends who effortlessly mirror our thinking and values serves a valuable function: they foster our sense of mental and emotional well-being.

"A faithful friend is the medicine of life."
Ecclesiasticus

Think for a moment of someone you would consider a "best friend." Notice how you and your friend are interested in similar things and have formed similar opinions. Notice that your conversations are noteworthy for the amount of agreement there is between you and the sense of satisfaction you feel following the interaction. Notice how you feel heard and validated. In conversations between best friends this harmony and agreement exists, not because they are trying to make each other feel loved and accepted, but because of their similarity in dominance.   This congruence of mental preference is also reflected in their nonverbal signals and the pace and rhythms of their speech.

Having the same dominance allows our best friend to follow our thinking easily and effortlessly which, in turn, gives us the impression that what we think is "good, " "clear," "right" and of value. Even better, the process is completely natural; we don't have to ask if they are in agreement, since their expressed interest and their nonverbals tell us they are. By contrast, someone whose dominance differs from our own will not be able to follow our thinking easily and effortlessly.   Despite efforts on their part to express interest (e.g., by asking questions or nodding in agreement), their nonverbal signals will reveal confusion and boredom. Even though they may say, "Yes, I understand," their eyes will be a bit glazed or out of focus and their brow will be wrinkled as they try to understand what we mean or why we value something.

Another thing that happens when we converse with someone who is our mental mirror is that as we begin to express an idea they may begin to smile or nod, even before we have finished, because they can already see where we are headed. Contrast the pleasure you feel at this experience with the discomfort you feel when trying to explain something important to someone who does not understand you; you will begin to see the important psychological benefit of mirroring.

"A friend is, as it were, a second self."
Cicero

A third, benefit of talking with such a friend comes, not when we are talking, but when we are listening to them talk. As we listen to them expressing their thoughts, dreams and concerns, we notice that what they say "makes sense to us" and that we ourselves "thought that just the other day."

Thus, a best friend is not just a passive, responsive mirror (as might be provided by an adept active listener); he is an active initiating mirror. He does not simply parrot back to us what we think and feel, he actually agrees with it. We feel connected or "as one" with him and the gulf between ourselves and others disappears. We belong.

Understanding that this kind of connection comes from an underlying congruence in dominance may provide some insight into why so many of the communication classes offered to adults fail to produce lasting results. The difficulty with trying to make connections and trying to reach out to others is that real and full acceptance comes only once we identify with the other person.

To summarize: "In friendship, likes attract" and are valuable to each other because being with someone who thinks the way we do enables us to feel connected, accepted, strengthened, affirmed--to develop positive self-esteem.

QUESTIONS AND ANSWERS ABOUT FRIENDSHIPS:

What type of thinkers find it easiest to find friends?

It is easiest for the half brains to find friends because the half brain patterns (double left, double right, double frontal, and double basal) appear most frequently in our society. Furthermore, because these patterns are so numerous, there are many "tribes" or groups which these people join and which they can access should they want to find like-minded friends.

For example, double lefts, who arc often engineers or accountants, frequently belong to business organizations and to clubs that focus on such hobbies as fishing, stamp and coin collecting, model building and model-train operation.

Double basals, often teachers, clerical workers and nurses, tend to enjoy church groups and structured organizations that help others. Double frontals, such as chemical enginers, surgeons, architects and research scientists, tend to enjoy mountaineering, hang gliding and flying (many actually have their pilot's licenses). Double rights, including some entrepreneurs and organizational development specialists, can often be found involved with community theatre since they enjoy acting, or in art classes or attending exhibits.

If someone has these patterns and they are not finding friends, they are probably not looking in the right places. In such cases, reviewing the careers that people with their brain dominance tend to select may help them to generate ideas for where and how to meet new friends.

Why don't I have a best friend? Could this have something to do with my dominance?

If a person has a strong preference for only one mode (quarter brained), he or she may have difficulty finding a best friend since there are simply not as many people around who think the way they do. Such quarter brain people find many people with whom to talk, since the total number of people who have a preference for that mode is substantial, but most of these people will be half brainers who also have a preference for another mode. Over time, the half brainer will try to shift the discussion--its pace or its topic--into his or her other preferred mode. Unconsciously, the quarter brainer has a strong interest in keeping it focused in his or her one preferred area. It is not uncommon for this resistance to be experienced as constraint by the half brainers. So after a time, the half brainer is likely to abandon the quarter brainer in search of a broader match.

Of significance here, however, is the fact that the quarter brain individual eventually can find another quarter brain with the same preference or expertise. And when this person is found, he or she is a friend for life.

How about multidominant people? Do they find it easier or harder to find a best friend?

Interestingly enough, people who are **multidominant**--with a preference for three or four modes--also have difficulty finding a best friend. In their case it is, however, because they tend to leave others. Since there are so few multidominant people and since it is even less likely that they have ever known anyone with their specific pattern, such a person may never have had a best friend or even truly understand what the term means.

In order to manage their need for a mirror, multidominant people tend to instinctively build "**Composite Mirrors**," using one friend to mirror one of their modes, and another to mirror another mode. Because none of their friends is <u>completely</u> comfortable for them, they move back and forth between these partial mirrors in order to create a full sense of self-acceptance. The results of this composite mirroring can be quite troublesome. For example, the multidominant person will find giving a party difficult because his friends won't necessarily like each other. In fact, they may actively put each other down, as they compete for his or her approval. The multidominant person may also experience internal conflict about his relationship to each of the mirrors. When they first get together, his experience may be one of delight but, after a few hours, he may be bored and want to get away. This shift from interest to disinterest is normal and natural for the multidominant as his brain tries to balance the attention and time spent in each mode. Unfortunately, this pulling away may feel like rejection to those people making up the multidominant's composite mirror, and so the multidominant will need to use great tact and finesse in handling his friends.

Multidominant individuals tend to make up their mirrors from a series of half brainers because the half brainer's mental flexibility is more in sync with their own. Occasionally they use a quarter brainer to pick up the mode not represented by their half brain friends. However, this will be a difficult relationship since the narrowness of the quarter brain's focus will rapidly become oppressive to the multidominant.

Finally, one of the problems multidominants have making friends is the time it takes to build friendships. As one strong triple-brainer put it, "Even when you find the pieces, it's really difficult to build the friendships because friendships take time and, if you're a multidominant, you need three times as much time because your mirror is made up of three people. Considered that way, it's almost impossible."

What about <u>trust</u>? How does that fit into brain dominance?

We are much more likely to trust people who have the same dominance as we do because they naturally support the things we value and naturally understand our fears and weaknesses. Generally, they affirm rather than discount us when we show them a part of ourselves, which encourages us to feel safe.

Contrast this to the risk we feel sharing ourselves with someone who has differing mental preferences. In the latter case, the chances are great that we will experience a put down and/or a criticism--if only in the person's nonverbal signals--making it considerably more <u>difficult for us to risk</u> opening up to or sharing ourselves with that person.

Moreover, since it is easiest to build trust with our "mirrors," we tend, over the years, to create more opportunities to share with them than with others, thereby. cementing the bond of trust that exists between us. At the same time, our discomfort with people who are different may cause us to actually avoid many trust-building opportunities with them, thereby reinforcing our initial discomfort. In turn, we may generalize our mistrust of a specific person to include all people with that brain preference. Thus, over time, a strong Basal Right or Frontal Right may come to automatically mistrust all Frontal Lefts. This kind of **aversion** for a certain quadrant often comes out of experiences in which we feel we have been rejected by a representative of that group. In addition, if the quadrant is one we have little strength in, our experience of unfamiliarity and strangeness may be so strong as to preclude any possibility of trust.

MARRIAGE:

It's probably no surprise to anyone that the principles which govern how we select our life partner vary dramatically from those we use to select our "best friend," although most of us would be hard pressed to understand why.   Far from being a "perfect mirror" for us, thinking as we think, acting as we act and choosing as we choose, our spouse is often as different from us as the day is from the night.

This, of course, is something we all know and accept. Our common folk wisdom that "opposites attract" is reenforced by such lyrics as: "You say tomato, and I say tomah-to. You say potato and I say potah-to. Let's call the whole thing off." It's all very clear. We know we choose to marry "unlikely" partners, and as the song suggests, we know that our un-alikeness can and does cause real problems. Yet most people don't call the marriage off, most people do plunge ahead-- desperately attempting to assure themselves that things will be ok, and that they do have some common ground with their spouse. After all, the newlywed observes, "We use the same tooth paste. We like the same coffee." And eventually, at a loss for words which would clarify their behavior, most people attempt to explain their selection of a spouse, by simply acknowledging that "people marry for irrational reasons."

Only quite recently with the insights provided by brain dominance have we come to understand that our choice of a spouse is perhaps one of the most rational choices we make. The simple explanation, from a brain dominance perspective, is that we marry in order **to have the best chance to survive** as well as to grow. Paradoxically, this means we marry someone who is very different from us. Someone who can handle those problems in life which frighten, baffle or are otherwise uncomfortable for us.

This then is the **rule of marriage: we seek a mate who will complement and complete us** in order to guarantee our survival. You might say, **we marry to get a whole brain.** Importantly, this is more than a mere a surface "attraction of opposites." It is a deeply seated drive linked directly to our core survival instincts. As such, it is also an excellent example of the Second Rule of Thumb which states: to insure your survival, as well as guarantee your long term effectiveness and success, manage activities which do not match your dominance by enlisting assistance from complementary brains.

You might say that our partnering behavior is simply another example of the **first law of cybernetics**, discussed in chapter 4. You may recall that this law, fundamental to all systems, states that "The unit within the system with the most behavioral responses available to it controls the system." Accordingly, when we marry someone whose brain dominance differs from ours, we increase our own ability to respond through our spouse appropriately and thereby successfully.

In many marriages one or both of the partners seem both aware and appreciative of the wholeness their spouse brings, even if the differences occasionally grate on them. There are the classic stories: the woman who can't even balance her checkbook marrying an accountant who can manage money for her; and the crazy inventor who marries the practical, down-to-earth woman, who sees that groceries get bought and bills paid. In all of these cases, the individual's **ability to survive** is enhanced by the variety of skills present in the couple.

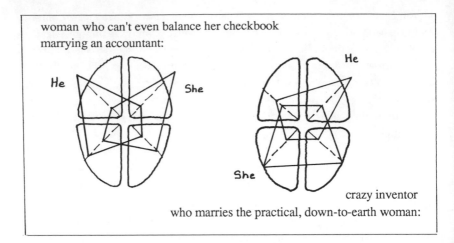

woman who can't even balance her checkbook
marrying an accountant:

He   She

He

She

crazy inventor
who marries the practical, down-to-earth woman:

Moreover, beyond our need to survive, we all share another need first identified by Abraham Maslow: the **need to learn and grow.** By marrying a person whose brain thinks very differently from our own, we create a learning opportunity for ourselves. We can learn from the brain we married how to think in ways we may never have even imagined. If Carl Jung was correct that the task of life is really to develop all four functions within ourself, then marriage provides us with the opportunity to not only survive, but to succeed at life: to learn and grow, on a daily basis as well as over our lifetime. Thus, in the very best marriages, each person offers himself as **the loving tutor** to his spouse.

The Problems:

Unfortunately, many marriages do not turn out as positive "learning experiences." Although some of the challenges and road-blocks encountered in marriage occur independently of dominance, at least three distinct problems can be traced to dominance. These are: **conflict, atrophy** and **miscommunication.**

Conflict occurs when, instead of appreciating our partner's being strong where we are not strong, we get <u>irritated at our partner's differences</u>. The two arenas in which conflict arises most frequently are behavior (how we do what we do) and **choice making** (where we go and what we do). A strong Frontal Left married to a strong Basal Right might complain: "She always wants to go to parties and be with people. I want to be left alone, to stay home and read." While the strong Basal Left married to a strong Frontal Right bemoans: "He never follows through with things and is always chasing after some wild idea. Why can't he be more stable and dependable?" Such apparently irresolvable complaints are the natural result of instinctual complementary coupling.

"She always wants to go to parties and
be with people. I want to be left alone,
to stay home and read."

"A theatre party?
Yes, Sharon, we'd love to come.
Tomorrow night at seven?"

Conflict occurs around decisions about what you're going to do

A second problem that occurs in many relationships is **atrophy.** Here, instead of encouraging our partner to tutor us, and learning from our partner how to become stronger and more competent ourselves, we back off from using their preferred mode. This can occur for two reasons: laziness on our part, or possessiveness on the part of our partner. In the first instance, we make our spouse totally responsible for doing those things we don't like to do. In the second, our spouse assumes all responsibility, refusing to allow or accept our help. In either case, the prolonged nonuse of our nonpreferred mode can mean that what little strength we had in it originally begins to weaken or atrophy.

Consider Stuart, a newly divorced forty-five-year-old double left business man, who is unable to socialize and make friends on his own, because for the past twenty years his Basal Right nurturing wife handled "everything." After all, it was she who was so comfortable with people and such a good hostess, why shouldn't she have managed their friendships? Imagine Mary, a fifty year-old widow who, after twenty-five years of giving her Frontal Left husband all the responsibility for managing their money, does not know the first thing about using a checking account. Clearly, both of these people are paying a high price for having surrendered their original competency. For even if such surrender felt "good" and "safe" in the beginning, in the end it is isolating, paralyzing and tragic.

The third problem with marrying a complement is that <u>expressing ourselves so that we are understood by our spouse</u> is likely to be difficult. In fact, many couples report **"We simply don't communicate."** Actually this is a natural, although perhaps unwelcome result of marrying to survive. Because the two of you have such different lead functions, you will also tend to use different words to convey your thoughts and feelings. A good example of this is a conversation Katherine overheard one morning in a hotel coffee shop. The topic being discussed was a short term loan for which the husband had applied:

He: "The penalty clause is **excessive.**"
She: "It sounds **unfair** too."

He: (After a brief pause during which he seemed to
       be trying to make sense out of what she said)
       "Well, it <u>is</u> **excessive.**"

Did this couple realize they were saying the same thing? We think not. In fact, we think this is a good example of "does not compute." She understood only that he did not like the clause. At the same time, he was baffled by the notion that fairness had anything to do with a loan agreement.

Unfortunately, however, this type of conversation is typical of complementary brains trying to communicate. Each person feels confused by what their spouse is saying, as well as misunderstood by their spouse.   Yet despite the fact that neither one is actually "getting it," they typically continue to try--to put out signals which say "Go on, I'm listening," because they do value their spouse and do not want to lose them--even if they can't understand them.

Alternatively, they may decide that trying to make sense of what their spouse says is simply too much work. When a person makes this decision, he or she stops listening when their spouse begins to speak. This shutting down or avoiding in communication may be intentional or unintentional. Either way, it is caused by the discomfort inherent in trying to communicate outside of one's preference.

Let's reiterate the basics. Guided largely by instinct, we tend to marry someone whose mental preferences compensate for our weaknesses, thereby enhancing our chances for survival. Our selection, however wise in the grand evolutionary scheme of things, presents real life problems: probable conflict, the possibility that we will lose what little strength we have in our weaker modes and the promise of ongoing communication difficulties. Nonetheless, few people vary from the rule when selecting a life partner, especially a first partner.

QUESTIONS AND ANSWERS ABOUT MARRIAGE:

Your theory linking the 'attraction of opposites' to an instinctual need to survive is fascinating. Could you be more specific. Are you actually suggesting that our dominance could affect our decision to marry one lover rather than another?

That's correct. Although we may date people whose dominance patterns are similar to our own, when we get serious, when we actually decide to "tie a knot," we seek out a person whose strengths will compensate for our weaknesses.

This is well illustrated by the tale of Kit and Bruce. Kit was a triple dominant with a weakness in the Basal Left who found herself dating and deeply in love with Bruce, a double left lawyer with a strong avoidance in the feeling mode. At first the relationship seemed to work; she felt grounded and secure with his stable Basal Left and he felt eased and comforted by her Basal Right access. In addition, since they both had access to the analytic mode they could spend hours being friends and discussing subjects of mutual interest. One day Bruce was gone; no fight, no explanations, just gone.

Some years later, when Bruce did marry, it was according to the complementarity rule. Bruce had an avoidance in the Basal Right, and he instinctively chose a woman whose strength and expertise in that mode could counterbalance his extreme deficiency.

An additional possibility is that Bruce sensed on some level that Kit was more "whole brained" than he was. In fact, a secondary pattern we've observed is that people tend to select a spouse whose **range of access** matches their own. In other words, people with one lead tend to marry people with one lead, people with strong access to two modes tend to marry people who also access two modes and so forth.

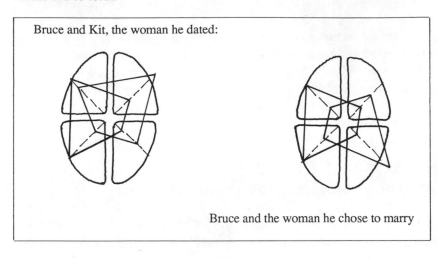

Bruce and Kit, the woman he dated:

Bruce and the woman he chose to marry

Another wonderful example of how **we instinctively sort out our friends and lovers** is the story of two double left engineers, Jane and Fred. This marvelous tale began some fifteen years ago when Jane and Fred, both in their early twenties, met at work. They had a lot in common, including their dominance patterns. Naturally, they began to spend more time together: talking, eating lunch, going to movies. This "Bobbsey twin" phenomenon continued, as Jane recalls, for five years, during which time they grew closer and closer, although they never discussed marriage.

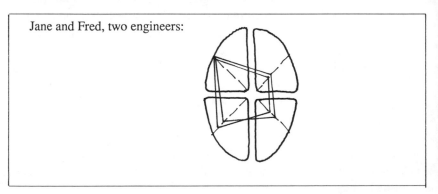

Jane and Fred, two engineers:

Then, things began to happen. Fred met Mary and decided to get married. And, although Jane was quite amenable to Fred's marriage, they stopped spending so much time together as she had nothing whatsoever in common with Mary. Within a few months, Jane met and married someone herself.

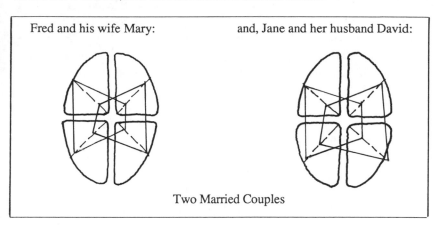

Fred and his wife Mary: and, Jane and her husband David:

Two Married Couples

From this point on, as Jane tells the story, the two couples have been routinely double dating. Only when they get in a car, instead of following the traditional "men in the front, women in the back" pattern, Fred and Jane always sit together in the front seat so they can talk about a new computer design, while Mary and Dave always sit together in the back talking about their gardens and the children. "What's more," Jane says, "When we all go to a party, Dave and Mary find each other in minutes, and talk for hours. But then of course that's exactly what Fred and I do....You know Fred and I will always be friends, but I wouldn't have been comfortable married to him. I need Dave, and I love him.

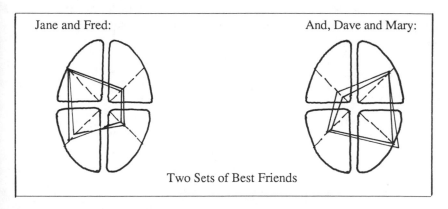

Jane and Fred: And, Dave and Mary:

Two Sets of Best Friends

Some people would be jealous of their spouse talking with someone else all the time. What, if any, connection does jealousy have with dominance?

If we marry someone who complements us, we will probably <u>need</u> to be with or talk with someone else fairly regularly who is like us and who naturally affirms us. Sometimes this need stimulates jealousy. In Jane's tale, one of the things she shared with us was that some of her female friends had come to her expressing their concern that Mary might be "taking Dave away." Her response to her friends showed both strength and understanding. She told them, "Actually, I'm glad they have each other. They're good for each other and they have so much in common--they even worry about the same things."

As Jane told her tale, it occurred to us how wonderfully she put things. Perhaps we should all take care to see that our spouses have a best friend. Not only would it be an excellent strategy for managing their worry (which would preclude our having to listen to them talk for hours about things we don't fully understand or value), it would also enable our spouses to feel good about themselves. This in turn would help to make our time with them more enjoyable and rewarding.

You've shown how our dominance affects our selection of a spouse, but what happens <u>once we're married</u>? How does dominance affect the way in which we relate or get along?

Let's begin by looking at how complementary couples who are "happily married" manage. In one such couple, the husband is a double frontal orthopedic surgeon, with a <u>strong Frontal Right lead</u> and an avoidance pattern in the Basal Left, while the wife, a grade school teacher, is a double basal with a <u>strong Basal Left lead</u>. In other words, they complement each other almost perfectly--he is strong where she is weak and she is strong where he is weak. Given their preferences, she naturally manages most of the routine tasks, including the bill paying, while he provides the element of novelty and adventure.

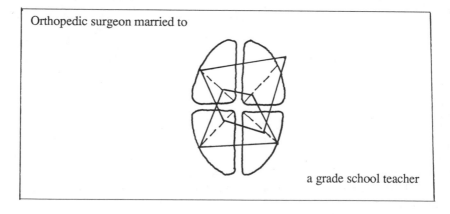

Orthopedic surgeon married to

a grade school teacher

What is interesting is that early in their marriage, while he was in medical school, her strength in the Basal Left was a god-send to them both. Being so weak in the Basal Left mode, he had great difficulty with much of the medical school curriculum which required a tremendous amount of memorization of facts and details. His wife, with a mind made to manage detail, helped him not only by drilling him repeatedly before all tests, but also by making sure he stayed on task to complete the more left brain assignments which he would have otherwise walked away from. He recalls, "Without her, I never would have gotten through."

Another example of **how the happily marrieds do it** is offered by Jeff and Margaret. Jeff is a double frontal surgeon. His wife is a double basal. Happily married for twenty-five years, they began to manage their complementary patterns early on by establishing "territories." His territory, "being a surgeon," enabled him to use both of his frontal lobes regularly, and thereby to feel smart and good about himself. Additionally, it brought in enough money to support them both and the children they eventually had. At the same time, Margaret's work around the home enabled her to feel smart, performing lots of basal tasks while contributing to the family.

For Jeff and Margaret the territories of "work" and "home" made perfect sense during their first two decades of married life. As they began their third decade together, and as their children left home, however, Margaret found less and less to keep her busy. There were fewer groceries to buy, less laundry to do, no kids to chauffeur around or take care of.

How Margaret solved her problem is a wonderful story. She went to a secretarial school for training in typing and general business procedures, and then took over as her husband's office manager, thereby enabling the couple to continue functioning as a team. An interesting point is that Margaret doesn't see herself invading of her husband's territory because she doesn't consider herself a "part of the work world." She is just "helping out," seeing that her husband's office runs smoothly, in the same way she made sure everything at home went smoothly. In other words, the shift in setting doesn't affect the basic structure of their relationship.

What about this idea of establishing territories? Is that a useful way to try to manage the differences inherent in a complementary marriage?

Territories can be useful. However, they need to be created to match the specific dominance patterns of persons involved. It is worth mentioning that the general territories which Jeff and Margaret found so useful, **work** and **home**, worked for them because of their particular dominance patterns. For another couple, say a double left husband with a double right wife, the same division could be disastrous. The husband would be satisfied with work (possibly a career in engineering or accounting), but the wife would constantly be experiencing <u>mixed feelings</u> about her role at home. When asked to be nurturing to her husband or children she would feel smart, and yet when asked to perform the routine tasks of shopping, meal preparation, laundry, etc. she would feel tremendously drained and fatigued, or even "dumb."

You've given some examples of what how complementary coupling can work--but I know a lot of couples who can't seem to make it work. Would you give some more specific examples of marital problems which can be directly linked to dominance?

Of course, not all complementary couples run smoothly. Terri and Mark, for example, found that living together meant simply one problem after another. Terri, a double right brained office worker with the Chamber of Commerce, and Mark, a double left brained mechanic with an avoidance pattern in the feeling mode, came to our attention when they came to Anne for marital counseling.

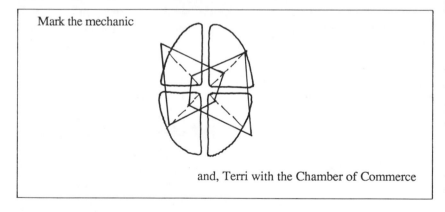

Mark the mechanic

and, Terri with the Chamber of Commerce

Terri's inability to comprehend why her husband got so hostile and angry when she met or chatted with her friends and acquaintances. It seems that whenever and wherever they would go out together, Terri would invariably meet lots of people she knew. Of course, this was quite understandable, given her job with the Chamber and her Basal Right attraction for connecting with people and making friends. However, "one thing would lead to another" and Terri would end up getting engrossed in a lengthy conversation or, alternatively, would invite whomever she had run into to join them at their table. In either case, Mark would become furious--refusing to talk with anyone and demanding that they leave immediately. Later, once they were headed for home, he would say, "I don't know why you have anything to do with those people. You don't really mean anything to them. And they don't really care about you at all." At which point, if Terri tried to explain her point of view (her interest and delight in people), Mark would retreat into a gloomy silence which would last for days.

Ironically, due to his extreme avoidance of the Basal Right feeling mode, Mark couldn't tolerate in Terri the precise thing he had married her for: her warmth and friendliness. Having no usable Basal Right function himself, no natural attraction to people or skill in relating to them, social situations left him feeling uncomfortable and inept, and needing his wife's support. When he saw her "giving attention to others," his discomfort would grow into feelings of rejection, invalidation and jealousy. Since Terri's Basal Right nurturing skills were not being directed at Mark to help him through his discomfort, Mark's inability to process his feelings ultimately exploded in rage and a vehement devaluing of Terri's other relationships.

Mark's form of retaliatory punishment of his wife--his anger and prolonged pouting--were especially difficult for Terri, since as a strong Basal Right she was particularly sensitive to any disharmony with her husband. In fact, as she realized, she found herself in a no-win situation. She hated being cut off from her husband during his periods of silence and withdrawal following each "incident," but on the other hand, the choice he was giving her, to isolate herself from all others, to disconnect from her friends and acquaintances with whom she shared a range of experiences, was no more tolerable or acceptable for her. Thus, eventually, as you might have anticipated, Terri and Mark were divorced.

Unfortunately, the problems which tore apart Terri and Mark are typical of the problems which many couples face, particularly when one or both members of the couple haven't developed sufficient emotional maturity to handle and appreciate their partner's differences. In cases where a general psychological immaturity coincides with an avoidance pattern, many couples do not make it. It would, however, be a mistake to say the problems were all caused by brain dominance. Ultimately, our maturity carries more weight than our dominance in determining our ability to succeed as part of a "happily married couple."

Discussing maturity raises the issue of psychology. Is it brain dominance or psychology that makes us try to control our spouses?

Brain dominance is something we are born with. Its primacy comes from the fact that it is biochemically based and predates our psychological profile, which develops after our birth in response to how we are treated by the world. Both are powerful factors which interact with and influence each other. In the case of **control**, we have observed that there are certain dominance patterns which, when placed in relationship to specific other patterns, are predictable.

The following story provides a useful example: In a women's support group which we observed, there was a woman who, given her buoyant personality, her expressive gestures, her totally nonlogical manner and her chosen career in social work, obviously had a strong Basal Right lead. During the session she explained how whenever she got excited and enthusiastic about something, her husband would come up to her and, taking hold of her wrists, move her arms down to her sides where he would hold them while instructing her to "calm down." Her husband, it turned out, was a banker with a strong double left profile and an avoidance pattern in the Basal Right. Given our natural tendency to marry someone who is strong where we are weak, it's just possible this man had married his wife for precisely the strengths he was trying to suppress or still in her.

Why? The answer is unclear and complex. Possibly because to him feelings and expressiveness were not only foreign and unfamiliar; they were, due to his avoidance pattern in the Basal Right, a source of real fear. Yet, it is likely that dominance alone does not cause one person to try to control another in this way. Although possibly dominance, unguided by supportive and informed assistance, leads to avoidance, and that avoidance in time leads to the need to control what we have avoided. In other words, our <u>dominance tends to feed our psychology</u>.

You've mentioned <u>avoidance</u> as a common problem in most marriages. What do you mean by avoidance and how does it work?

Avoidance is intentionally or unintentionally "turning off" or "spacing out" on your partner because he or she is presenting material you aren't interested in or have difficulty understanding due to the difference in your dominances. Here are some examples of what we mean.

A striking example from a workshop Katherine gave for several corporate lawyers and accountants, most of whom showed a distinct weakness in the Basal Right feeling mode. She asked them to write an article that would speak to a strong Basal Right reader. After ten minutes, the group had written: "Pregnant woman killed in car accident this morning." Katherine pointed out to them that although this was a subject any Basal Right would find interesting since it was of "human interest," it was not written in the <u>language</u> Basal Rights would understand or use. Nor was the brevity of their article typical of the Basal Right speech pattern. To help, Katherine suggested each imagine returning home at the end of a day to be greeted by his wife, who immediately begins to tell him about a terrible accident she has seen. She then asked: "What would your wives say?" All six men began talking at once. For a moment Katherine thought she had found the key to helping them learn to speak and use a mode other than their natural lead. But then, they all stopped. The reason they stopped was that, although they all knew the first sentence that would come out of their wives' mouths, none of them knew the second. Over the years, since they found their wives' "chatter" uncomfortable, they had learned to "tune her out," while paying just enough attention to give her the impression that they were actually listening. Their approach was, as they explained, much more effective than trying to stop their wives from talking.

Another example of avoidance happened to Katherine one night as she and an accountant she had been dating were driving home from a long weekend. It was late and he was driving while Katherine relaxed. Suddenly, he began talking about the stock market, a subject of great interest to him since he had a Frontal Left lead. Since she actually did care about him (if not the stock market), Katherine tried to pay attention. Nonetheless, after only a few minutes, she noticed she had not heard much, if anything, that he had said. Instead, her awareness had shifted to noticing his face, his smile, the curve of his dimples--all his nonverbals. In other words, without Katherine doing anything consciously to make it happen, her brain had shifted its attention away from what it could not easily understand (the left brain information about stocks) to what it understood best (his Basal Right's nonverbals).

Avoidance is a way of staying smart and screening out those things that make you feel dumb, incompetent and irritated. Since we are all likely to feel this way when asked to process in our weakest mode, some avoidance is probably an inevitable part of any relationship. Too much, however, can lead to distance between the partners and set the stage for divorce or a "purely functional marriage."

Why would it be helpful for a couple to know each other's dominance pattern? It certainly is not going to make the differences go away.

A friend of Katherine's who specializes in marriage counseling routinely uses brain dominance as a therapeutic tool. One of her clients explained the value as follows: "It's not that the differences go away. It's just that we see them and ourselves differently. It <u>helps us to be less irritated</u> and to not take things so seriously. We used to get irritated by each other's quirks. Now we just recognize them for the natural behaviors they are. In fact, we even laugh about them-- together. We also don't feel the need to try to change each other anymore."

Knowing their brain dominance has freed this couple to laugh more and control less. We think that's a considerable improvement. Author and psychologist Sheldon Kopp, in his second book End of Innocence, said that he grew up the day he accepted not only that his mother didn't love him, but as well that, 'It wasn't personal,' in that his mother would have had difficulty loving any child. In a similar vein, you might say that understanding each other's dominance helps couples to grow up--to learn to not take 'personally' the apparent slights and misunderstandings which result from their differences--the differences which are in fact the basis for their mutual attraction.

In another situation, learning about brain dominance saved a marriage. In what we call "The Case of the Misdiagnosed Father Complex," a client of Katherine's avoided a trip to the divorce court by learning that her problem with her husband was physiological (caused by dominance) rather than psychological. The story goes as follows:

Mary was a woman who had already been married and divorced numerous times by the time she came to one of Katherine's workshops. According to the psychiatrist she'd been seeing for the last fifteen years, her problem in making her relationships work was that she had a "father complex." According to the psychiatrist, this complex was evident in the fact that each time she married she chose a man who behaved just like her father. From his perspective, in order for her life to improve, Mary would need to work through this complex. Mary never fully accepted the psychiatrist's diagnosis. Yet, since she kept marrying and divorcing the same kind of man, she had begun to assume, "He must be right."

When Mary attended Katherine's workshop, she realized two points of fact. First, she and her father had complementary thinking styles. And, second, it was completely natural for her to marry men whose brains complemented her own. That these men coincidentally thought just like her father may have been confusing, but it did not mean her choice of husbands was "wrong." Following the workshop Mary arranged to have her current husband's profile done to confirm her analysis. She also stopped seeing her psychiatrist, deciding instead to spend the money on fun activities she and her husband could enjoy together. At last report, Mary and her husband are happily entering another year of marriage.

Of course it is certainly possible that Mary had some real issues with her father. Most of us have areas of pain and sensitivity where our parents are concerned.

But did that make her choice of husband "wrong?" For once Mary was able to understand the reason for her selection of these men and to make sense of the difficulties she was having with them, she could separate her childhood issues with her father from her adult relationship with her husband. This in turn freed her to enjoy him for what he is and what he brings to her present life.

You continue to emphasize the phrase: Marrying to get a Whole Brain. Do all couples who marry to get a whole brain actually get one? Don't some couples end up with only three fourths of a brain?

There are many couples in which the husband and wife have a combined strength in only three of the four modes. Since we tend to instinctively seek someone whom we perceive to be strong in our area of greatest weakness, it sometimes happens that the person we choose is not a perfect complement. Someone who is strong where we are weakest, but who also shares a strength with us. In such cases the couple will have more shared interests as well as a common language or mode to which they can retreat in conflict situations. The disadvantage of such a situation is simply that not having a whole brain, they don't have all their bases covered.

Sam and Jennifer's marriage is an example. Sam is an advertising executive with a diagonal preference pattern for the Basal Left and Frontal Right. Jennifer, a typical entrepreneur, has a double frontal pattern tilted to the far right, and an avoidance pattern in the Basal Left.

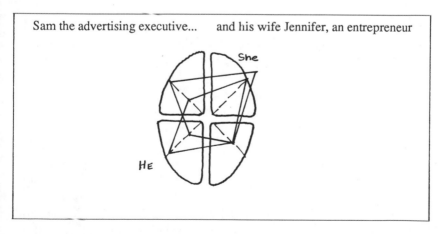

Sam the advertising executive... and his wife Jennifer, an entrepreneur

As a couple they have strength in the Frontal Right adaptive mode as well as both of the left's modes, but only moderate access to the Basal Right feeling mode.

Although they enjoy each other and are prone to sharing flights of fancy, their mutual deficit in the bridging/nurturing mode has caused some predictable problems, particularly now that they have children. Children, as we all know, need nurturing, something neither Sam nor Jennifer do naturally. Thus although they both love their children, their way of caring for them is to teach them to take care of themselves and each other.

Another problem which Sam and Jennifer have faced is the result of her avoidance in the Basal Left stabilizing mode, coinciding with their mutual strength in the adaptive Frontal Right. Over time, to compensate for Jennifer's weakness with routine and details, Sam has increased his use of his own Basal Left, at the expense of his Frontal Right. Although they both have primary strengths in the Frontal Right, Jennifer's is so much greater than Sam's that he has "backed off" so as not to suffer in comparison. Subsequently, Sam is spending much more time in Basal Left activities than is healthy or appropriate for him, given his original preference pattern. Were his "backing off" behavior to continue over several years, Sam could be a good candidate for a midlife crisis.

Fortunately, Sam is taking steps to reown his Frontal Right preference and to once again see himself as a creative person. He is also being supported by Jennifer, who is making a conscious effort to not go into competition with him around Frontal Right tasks. Jennifer is exploring her own problems with the Basal Left and beginning to build some competency in that mode. Again, personal maturity and responsibility are important elements in the "happily married" scenario.

Barbara and Michael are another couple who have a combined strength in only three modes. Barbara, a therapist, is a strong double right with an avoidance in the Basal Left. Michael, a journalist, has the same diagonal preference for the Basal Left and Frontal Right. Barbara's and Michael's shared access to the Frontal Right enables them to share a good bit of amusement as well as an enthusiasm for adventure. Their mutual weakness in the Frontal Left analytic mode, however, means they have ongoing, predictable problems with making decisions and managing money. Additionally, Barbara and Michael tend to have sudden conflicts when Michael unexpectedly shifts from his spontaneous Frontal Right way of doing things, which Barbara also enjoys, to his more careful Basal Left approach which is planned and organized. Since Barbara has so little Basal Left she doesn't understand why her husband suddenly wants to be places on time, or put the house in order, or be told to whom she has written checks and for how much. As strongly right brained as she is, Barbara is most comfortable with her husband when he is in his Frontal Right. When he does "go left," she is often very upset, even though his Basal Left strength, which offers her a sense of safety and stability, is part of why she chose to marry him.

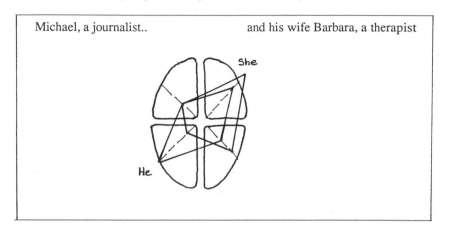

Michael, a journalist..   and his wife Barbara, a therapist

She

He

One final point about these overlapping marriages. In many of the ones we have encountered, although not all, two things are true: at least one member of the couple has a <u>very</u> strong lead in the Frontal Right, and they all have a mutual preference for the Frontal Right. This atypical pattern of spousal selection by Frontal Rights has also been noted by Dr. Frank Farley at the University of Wisconsin. Farley's twenty years of research on people he labels "Big T's" (thrill seeking individuals) suggests that most highly creative people seek the high level of stimulation derived from "thrills." As an aside he notes that, whereas most people tend to marry people substantially different from themselves, Big-T's tend to marry each other. One explanation for this might be the low level of social tolerance for many Frontal Right behaviors, such as day dreaming, laughing inappropriately, leaving things in stacks and generally not following the organized procedures which underlie so much of our educational and professional activities. Possibly Frontal Rights seek some validation by marrying each other.

If most of us marry to get a whole brain, do whole brained people need to get married at all?

The pattern that emerges around marriage and multidominant individuals (triple and quadruple brains) is that, if and when they marry, they tend to do so later than their friends and contemporaries. As one of them put it, "I knew all along that I wanted to get married but the men I met simply didn't believe me." This tends to suggest that their whole brainedness makes them less likely to be viewed as available partners by prospective mates. As one married whole brained woman told us, "It's certainly true I got married late in life. What's also true is that I have a very hard time convincing my husband that I need him. He doesn't see it and neither do the children. My boys have told me again and again "Mom, you don't need anyone." You know, it's the oddest feeling to be told that by your sons and husband. I can't explain to them how and why I do need them in a way they understand and accept."

When asked why they marry, whole brained people usually say that it is for the connection--that no one can really thrive alone and isolated. Furthermore, just because they don't **need** to be married as a biological imperative, doesn't mean they don't **want** to. Their main problem seems to be in convincing potential mates that it is okay to marry someone who doesn't need you in order to survive (particularly since the mates are probably not whole brained and the survival rule DOES apply for them). And it may be that on some level they sense they are relating from a one-down position, i.e., their spouse offers four modes while they only offer two. We assume it takes a fairly secure person to handle such a situation.

Do people with similar dominance patterns ever marry?

Yes, people with similar dominance patterns do marry--most often when it is a second marriage for one or both partners, or a "late in life" marriage. When two people with similar preferences marry, they are likely to enjoy each other very much and to have a tremendous, initial friendship. However, over time, the incompleteness of their combined access, the fact that they are not whole brained as a unit, will begin to produce problems which neither of them can handle. How well they cope with those problems largely depends on whether or not they anticipated the problems going into the marriage and made provisions for handling them. A conscious decision to "violate" the rule is preferable to an unconscious one, as you will see from the following anecdotes.

The first couple came to our attention when they attended a special Brain Dominance Workshop for Families sponsored by their church. They had virtually identical double right preference patterns, with which they had lived as a couple for some eighteen years. Our questions revealed that the husband's first impression of his wife (nineteen years earlier) had been that she had a dominance quite different than his own. As he tells it, "I still recall the night we met. I was only eighteen and my buddy John and I had gone to the drug store to get an ice cream soda. She was working behind the counter and fifteen minutes later I told John 'I'm going to marry that girl.' You see, what I remember is that when she was making our sodas she was so neat and clean and orderly. She had this way of making sodas 'just so' and everything was tidy. I figured she was the one for me. You know, I also still remember how surprised I was when we started dating and we turned out to be like two peas in a pod. Neither of us ever paid any attention to time, which meant that we were both usually late. We both laughed a lot. We both enjoyed simply wandering along the country roads. I think if the term best friend has a meaning, we were best friends."

As we talked to the couple it became clear that they were, in fact, a two-person mutual admiration society and authentic best friends. The children, however, were shocked at their father's description. For although they agreed that he was nearly off the scale in his own tilt to the right, they saw their mother as a strong Basal Left thinker. In their eyes, she was the detail-oriented planner, organizer and administrator of the family.

We then turned our attention to the mother. How could it be, we asked, that your husband sees you as a carefree, fun-loving, spontaneous person and your children see you as factual, cautious and planned? She was silent for a moment, as if lost in thought, and when she finally spoke she said something we have never forgotten: "That explains it. Twelve years ago I had a massive hemorrhage of the left cerebral hemisphere for apparently no reason at all. What I recall about that time is that I simply didn't want to do any more left brained thinking. Of course, I didn't have a label for it then and I couldn't explain it well, but in a way, my hemorrhage was a way of saying 'Stop making me do this.' After all, now that I'm damaged, they can't make me do it because I'm not able to."

Raising children, making house payments, doing laundry for four, planning and preparing meals all require the use of the left brain's skill in prioritizing and in handling routine tasks. The husband, not a skilled left brain thinker himself, had selected his wife for those particular abilities and never stopped to consider that his initial assessment might not have been accurate. The wife, who did have some learned competencies in the left, (such as soda making which she had learned from her grandfather who owned the drugstore) decided order was preferable to chaos and set about using her nonpreferred modes to run the household and do what needed to be done. For eight years her adaptive behavior continued except, of course, when she was alone with her husband. During those times she would revert to her preferences and be the happy, fun-loving , double right he described. Unfortunately, most of her time was spent in her weak areas and, if she is correct, the result was a stroke. Since she was unable to verbalize her dilemma, she made a nonverbal statement and damaged her left cerebral lobe so that everyone would know it was her weakness, not her strength.

Such a story is an excellent example of what can occur when one or both members of a couple misperceive the other's dominance. What is wonderful about this case is that both people were able to hang on to the love they felt for each other. More often, love is eroded by the problems depression, and anger which which occur when a person performs for long periods of time in one of their nonpreferred areas.

A second example of how like-brains manage in a marriage concerns Norm and Jean who also have virtually identical double right profiles. In explaining their situation, Norm pointed out that this is a second marriage and that their children, all from their previous marriages, live on their own. In other words, many of the Basal Left pressures of raising children and running a complex family structure (that caused so much trouble for the preceding couple) aren't things which Norm and Jean have to manage.

And yet, they still have a problem. They have to be careful not to **compete** over "who's best at working with people" and "who's the best photographer" and "who's the most creative." Norm recalls that in his first marriage (to a very left brained woman), he enjoyed the position of being "the artist in the family." In this second marriage he has to share the glory and figure out how to not compete.

In John and Sarah's relationship, another marriage of like-minds, the couple learned about brain dominance prior to making their decision to marry and determined that they would have to **cope with the areas neither partner wanted**. To protect their love and guarantee that no one would get stuck with these "problem" jobs or feel resentful because their spouse wasn't taking care of it for them, John and Sara made a list of the left-brained tasks that neither of them really had the competency to handle. They then reviewed their list to separate the tasks into three categories: ones they could do together, ones they could alternate handling and ones they would need to hire someone else to do. To date, their strategy appears to be working for them and they have a happy marriage.

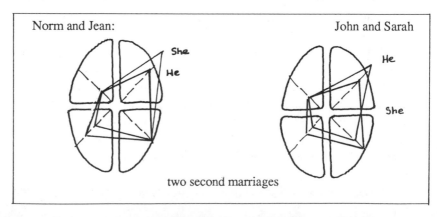

Norm and Jean: John and Sarah

two second marriages

If more couples were aware of their dominance going into their marriages, they might develop **conscious strategies** for handling the problems and avoid unnecessary conflict and disappointment. This thought has occurred to many people with whom we work. In fact, it seems to have such appeal that one person is working on a dating service which would provide dominance counseling, while another, a psychiatrist, is designing a pre-marital counseling service which will assist couples to deal effectively with each other's dominance and manage their shared pattern of strengths and weaknesses.

You've told several tales about right brainers who have married each other rather than "live with a lefty." Do left brainers ever marry each other?

We actually know of far fewer cases in which both partners are double left but there are some. Again, these marriages tend to be second marriages in which one or both members of the couple have had bad experiences in an earlier, more traditional complementary relationship. Most report that their decision to marry their current spouse was in part rooted in a desire to avoid a repeat performance of their first marriage.

One such marriage is between Fred, a double left executive with a Frontal Left lead and Martha, a double left bookkeeper with a Basal Left lead. The couple describes themselves as "content." And yet, according to Fred, although they "get along well", their marriage "lacks something." When questioned further, he'll speculate that the "something" which it lacks is the fun, enthusiasm and sense of adventure--which are, of course, typically provided by the right brain.

Another left brain couple observed that although they enjoy being together very much, their mutual lack of people skills is causing problems with their social life. It seems that more than once, after putting months into building a relationship with another couple, they suddenly find the other couple not calling them or returning their calls, and they have no idea why. Furthermore, lacking the Basal Right ability to recognize hurt feelings early and reestablish harmony, they do nothing. That someone else might know what to do, or have done something already, is a mystery to them.

IN SUMMARY:

Differences in dominance lead us to the altar and provide us with opportunities to learn and grow. They also lead us to inevitable conflicts about how things are going to be done. If the conflict gets bad enough, or if we are not mature enough or skilled enough to handle them, our differences may eventually lead us to the divorce court. Alternatively, likeness in dominance may lead us to be "friendly spouses." But it can, just as naturally, lead us into anger and resentment if one partner is forced to do for both what neither one can really do for himself.

In the final analysis, therefore, there are no right or wrong choices in marrying. What one chooses spouse-wise is a matter of personal preference. Whether one does it by instinct or for comfort, in the end it is really a matter of deciding which lessons in life you want to take on, and choosing accordingly.

FAMILY LIFE WITH CHILDREN:

We have seen in the preceding section how people who marry to get a whole brain learn to cope with and, in some cases, fully accept their spouse's very different thinking pattern. Although it is common for each partner to feel somewhat disappointed that their spouse doesn't fully understand them, each also knows on some level that this difference is something he needs--that it is a strength undeveloped within themselves, without which they would be less prepared to meet the full gamut of life's challenges. We also noted the differences between our selection of a spouse who has a mental preference in our area of greatest weakness and our selection of a best friend whose mental preferences are almost identical to our own, and who therefore can and does effortlessly affirm our self-esteem.

When children enter or join the family, these two patterns of relating come together. While the parents continue in their relationship with each other to seek complementarity, all family members, including the parents, in the context of the total family, seek the affirmation and companionship which comes from being fully accepted and comfortable.

Thus, we are generally likely to feel:

- most comfortable in a family in which there are others with our mental preferences;

- most comfortable with and closest to the family member or members whose lead preference is the same as ours; and

- less comfortable if and when something happens to shift the balance.

As you can imagine, there are many concerns and issues involved in understanding children and parenting well which relate, at least in part, to brain dominance. Because there are so many, we are addressing them in the Questions and Answers. Some are addressed in the Questions and Answers section immediate following this discussion. Others, of equal importance, are addressed in the Questions and Answers section in Chapter 7: Your Whole Brain Over Your Lifetime. In this latter section, there are specific guidelines for assessing and validating a child's dominance.

QUESTIONS AND ANSWERS:

Does Brain Dominance run in families?

This question is perhaps better restated as: If two left brained people marry, do they have left brained children? And, if two basal people marry, do they have basal children? And so on.

First off, this is a difficult question to answer because the drive which causes most people to marry to get a whole brain precludes our having the type of data we would need in order to answer it. There simply aren't that many instances in which two right brain people marry, or two left brained people, or two basals or two frontals. And, when this does occur, it is most common in second marriages which frequently do not include children.

Given these constraints, it is possible to say that indeed if and when two people of like dominance marry, there is a greater possibility that they will have children of similar dominance. A greater possibility is, however, not the same as as absolute rule.

At least two cases have come to our attention over the years which suggest this. In the first, two double lefts married and had four children, three of whom were double left and one of whom was a double right. In the second, two double right parents had three children, two of whom were double rights and one of whom was a Basal Left.

What happens when one child has a distinctly difference dominance from the other family members?

One cartoonist calls this **"The Enigma"** effect. And, naturally, how it is experienced depends on whether you are a part of the majority or the one who is seen as different, the enigma, the weird kid, the misfit. Those who think alike clearly set the tone for "how things get done around here." This tends to mean that they see the "problem kid" as a misfit who isn't trying and isn't cooperating. It is typical in such instances for the parents to develop a strong sense of "Where did this child come from?" and sometimes they may even joke about the difference by suggesting that the hospital must have switched babies on them. Another frequent comment involves one parent suggesting that the child is "a throw-back to some long deceased relative on their spouse's side of the family."

By way of contrast, the individual who has the distinctly different pattern tends to feel invalidated by the family. Because no one in the family structure values the same things and thinks in the same way, he may have difficulty building his self-esteem. To the extent that he feels pressured by the family to adapt to their way of thinking, he may also feel resentful and angry.

In our society as a whole the most frequent person to find a misfit is the Frontal Right--in many classrooms and offices such a person is regarded as odd, weird, strange and or a goof-off. In the personal setting of the family, however, there are no rules. Someone with any pattern, especially if it is heavily focused in one and only one area, can be an outcast. It all depends on what the specific profiles of the other family members are. Here are two examples.

In the first, which we refer to as **The Case of Miserable Martha,** Martha, a quarter-brained Basal Right, found herself in a family of two Double Frontals (her father and her eldest brother) and two Double Lefts (her mother and her older brother).

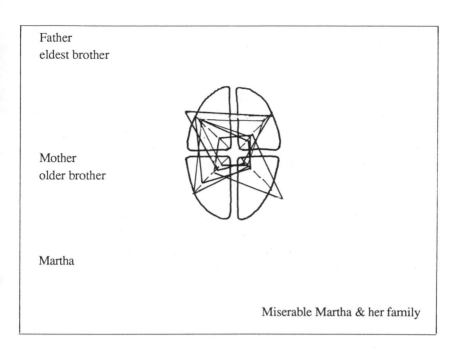

Father
eldest brother

Mother
older brother

Martha

Miserable Martha & her family

The father was a career diplomat so, by the time Martha was fifteen, she had already lived in eight different countries. This constant moving around and lack of "roots", combined with the repeated "loss" of friends, seemed not to affect anyone else in the family, but for Martha it was a terrible experience. Each time the family would be "uprooted", Martha would find herself seriously depressed and in heavy grief. Unable to find any emotional support or comfort from her family, who saw her behavior as "childish" and "self-indulgent", Martha increasingly isolated herself in her room where she would cry for hours.

As if this weren't enough, the father, who was a high-achieving Frontal, constantly put pressure on Martha to "be a success like your brothers" (one of whom eventually got his Ph.D. in physics, the other who became an engineer). To make his point, he would bring her articles about successful female executives, bankers and lawyers, stressing that this is what he "expected" of her and that it was the only level of performance he would consider adequate. Since this was totally impossible for Martha, given her dominance pattern, every attempt she made to excel in the academic areas which would lead to such careers resulted in failure. This led the family to conclude that she was "stupid" and "lazy" and they let her know it (along with the fact that she was "an embarrassment" to them). Finally, when she was fifteen, the family solved its problem with Martha by shipping her off to a boarding school. And during the three years she was away at school, no one from her family wrote or visited her, nor was she ever invited home for holidays.

Ironically, Martha had one very special talent, which, though obvious, was never acknowledged or appreciated by her family. Of all the family members, Martha had the greatest aptitude for learning to speak the different foreign languages quickly and easily (which is consistent with her strong Basal Right profile). Unfortunately, she did not do as well in the classroom study of the language, where more emphasis is put on writing, spelling and grammar (Basal Left), and so it did not change her family's opinion of her academic incompetence.

Now an adult, Martha has spent years in therapy trying to undo the damage to her self-esteem caused by her upbringing. And although learning about brain dominance has helped her understand that she was just "the wrong person in the wrong family" and also helped her appreciate the person she is, it unfortunately cannot take away the pain of those years of rejection and invalidation.

The second case which illustrates the enigma phenomenon is that of **Norman,** a strong Basal Left thinker brought up in a family of "crazy right brainers."

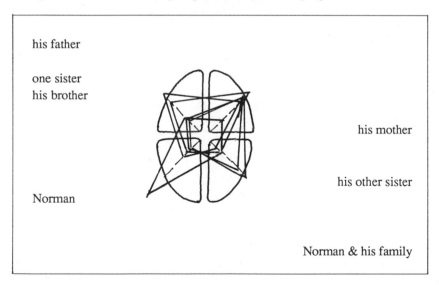

his father

one sister
his brother

his mother

his other sister

Norman

Norman & his family

Where Norman would seek to establish rules and schedules so that he would know when to be where and what to do, the rest of his family--his inventor father, his interior decorator/entrepreneur mother, and his two artistic and musical siblings--persisted in more spontaneous behavior. If they were all home and happened to eat at six, great. If not, "well, no matter." If someone felt like going out to get pizza, those who were there and wanted to go would go, and those who were not would fend for themselves. If dirty laundry was turned in somewhere near the weekend it might be clean by Monday morning, and then again, there's nothing wrong with retrieving a dirty shirt from the hamper. To make matters worse, while all of this was going on, Norman's double right family, so very interpersonal and gregarious and interested in helping, would try to help Norman by suggesting that he "have some fun," "take an art class" or "laugh once in awhile."

As the years passed and Norman's differences persisted (in spite of repeated attempts by the family to "rescue him from himself"), Norman's parents began to feel that although they had been successful parents with their other two children, they had most decidedly failed with Norman. Not long after this, shortly after his eighteenth birthday, Norman announced that he had decided to enlist, and his parents' growing sense of powerlessness to "help Norman" was turned into total despair. After all, to the double right-brained parent, voluntarily joining the army can only mean "our son wants to kill people." Which, by the way, is not at all how a double left-brained parent perceives the same reality. For them, joining up means: a cost effective way to pay for one's college education, an opportunity to travel and see the world before settling down, and last but not least, a way to sow one's wild oats away from home.

Fortunately, what happened with Norman is that his father, learning about the Whole Brain Thinking model only days before his son was to leave for Boot Camp, rushed to find his son and wife and to have everyone's profile done. Once this was accomplished, Norman's very right brain family was actually able to see, accept and be happy that what Norman was choosing, after eighteen years of shaky self-esteem and feeling "big dumb-small smart," was a step which would allow him to use and be recognized for his sequential-routine thinking skills. They could finally see that Norman was choosing to be "big smart, small dumb."

Can the sense of isolation and feeling like a misfit, which comes from being an enigma to one's family, occur to other family members?

Most definitely. The key point here is: look at the context. Anytime anyone is in a situation in which his or her mental preferences differ strongly from those of the rest of the group, he or she will begin to experience a sense of "not belonging", "not being loved" and "not being adept."

An excellent example of this is **The Case of the Misfit Mother**. The family's profiles revealed Jeanette, the mother, to have a strong preference for the Basal Left mode. While her husband Frank and both their children were Frontals--one of which had with an actual avoidance pattern in the Basal Left (the daughter).

How those patterns played out is as follows: The disparity between Frank and Jeanette's patterns (Frontal v.s. Basal) was not a problem when the couple was first married. They had their differences, but then so did every couple they knew. When the children began to grow up (approximately ages seven to ten, the precise age during which the frontal lobes mature according to Luria and Piaget), Jeanette found herself becoming increasingly a misfit in her own family.

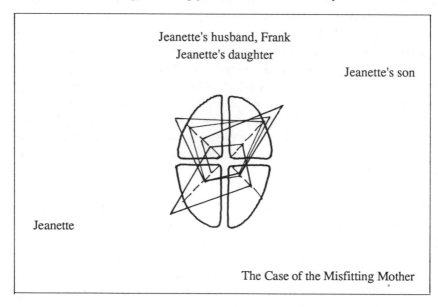

Jeanette's husband, Frank
Jeanette's daughter

Jeanette's son

Jeanette

The Case of the Misfitting Mother

Although Jeanette was attentive and dedicated as a wife and mother, the children, who were coming into their own with respect to their frontal dominance patterns, began to prefer and seek out their father's company.   Unfortunately, at the same time, they also began to actively resent and reject their mother's strong Basal Left. This dislike for the "way mother acts" led the daughter to develop a set of "gotcha games" the kids could "play on mother". For example, since they knew it was important to her that they be on time, they went out of their way to make sure the family was always late. And because she wanted them to have dinner together at a regular, fixed time, they purposefully arranged their extracurricular activities to conflict with the dinner hour. In addition, whenever they were having a discussion with their father and the mother came into the room, they would stop talking until she left.

Although it seems incredible that the father did not notice and put a stop to this behavior, it appears that since his own relationship with the kids was so good, it "never occurred" to him that it might bother his wife. And since he himself thought "her rules were silly" and that "she couldn't really understand the things they discussed anyway," it may have made perfect sense to him that the three of them acted as they did.

From interviewing Jeanette (the mother), it became clear that she had known for years that she was an "outcast" in her own family and that her children "didn't like her", but that she had never been able to understand why. When asked how she coped with the emotional pain of being rejected, she responded in a very Basal Left way: "I just did the things I knew I was supposed to do as a wife and a mother and I kept the family together. And, after all, that's what's really important, isn't it?"

Not everyone can respond with such stoicism to being ostracized by their family. In another case we know of, the strongly Basal Right mother became severely depressed and suicidal by being cast in the **role of the misfit** (her husband and both children were Double Lefts). For her, the fact that her children preferred their father's company was proof of her "failure as a mother" (which to a Basal Right feeling type is a terrible thing indeed), and it was only after she learned about brain dominance and her family's specific profiles that she was able to stop blaming herself and move out of her near suicidal depression.

Here again, Sheldon Kopp's insight (that he finally grew up the day he understood that although it was true that his mother didn't love him; it was also true that it wasn't personal) is very helpful. It is our feeling that Kopp's wisdom is something from which we can all benefit. Learning to accept that the behavior of another may well not be personal is an important life lesson and the key point we are trying to make here is that such acceptance is often easier when you also know "the reason." Martha, Norman and Jeanette all learned that in their lives and in their families, their feelings of being different, an outcast and a failure, were caused largely by the fact that their mental dominance patterns really were different and that that was ok. Learning this single fact helped each reevaluate the experience and accept that the rejection they felt was not personal. As such, it freed them to accept themselves.

What about the situation in which no one feels particularly isolated, yet one parent clearly feels uncomfortable with one of the children?

You can be uncomfortable around one of your children for one of two reasons. First, it may be that the child's dominance is so different from your own that indeed you do feel that the kid is an enigma. If you are a double basal, with strong procedural and foundation building skills as well as a ability to connect with feelings, and you have a strongly Frontal Right daughter, she is likely to think so differently that you do not know what to do with her, how to spend time with her or how to enjoy being together. Your sense of dis-ease and perhaps even nervousness with this child may be quite similar to the way you feel in the presence of adults with the same preference. It's just that with an adult you can say that "one can't like everyone," but you feel guilty when you don't enjoy your own child.

But there is also another explanation, which at first may seem odd. It is possible to feel uncomfortable with a child because he is just like you. In this instance, the discomfort stems from your not having accepted a part of yourself. The tale of David and his son Martin is an appropriate illustration here. David, the father, was born a double frontal, capable of both analytic and synthetic thinking. Over the years David chose to abandon his Frontal Right lead, while maintaining his natural strength for analytic thinking, because experience had showed David that no one appreciated a roving prankster. Thus David was made uneasy by his double frontal son whose Frontal Right behaviors and skills were a constant reminder of the part of himself which David had rejected.

Either way, whether because the child's mental preference is completely different from our own, or because it is too much like a part of us, the discomfort we feel tends to focus on an aspect of ourself which we have not fully accepted, resolved and fully integrated.

In some families there is a child who naturally seems to mediate problems that occur between the parents. There has been some thought that birth order may be involved here. Is there any evidence that brain dominance might explain a part of this as well?

Yes. Imagine a situation in which double left man and a double right woman have a double frontal daughter. In such an instance it is probable that the father will relate best to his daughter's analytic thinking skills, using his time with her to debate the pros and cons of something which has happened or to discuss a critical analysis of a book they have both read, none of which he would do with his wife. At the same time, the wife and mother relates to the daughter's Frontal Right focus on freedom and variety, her use of metaphoric thinking and her playful sense of humor. Over time as the daughter's bond to each parent develops, she will also tend to become aware that although she enjoys talking with each parent and can generally see where each is coming from, they themselves do not enjoy the same types of conversations and often misunderstand badly what the other is thinking or feeling. Subsequently, she may act as a natural bridge between her parents, attempting to clarify for each what it is that the other is thinking and why.

What if any relationship exists between birth order and dominance?

As far as we can tell, birth order has no role whatsoever in the creation of the child's original dominance pattern. Dominance is a biochemical reality which must, on some level, have genetic roots. However, it is possible and even likely that birth order plays a role in reinforcing or discouraging particular patterns after birth. For example an analytically-preferent female child if the eldest or only child, and particularly if born into a family in which the father is a successful analytical thinker, may well be reinforced for her preference. This reinforcement will occur in full opposition to society's more conservative image of the acceptable girl as a feeling Basal Right. In contrast, the analytic female child who is born later in the birth order may well be discouraged from holding onto her birth preference, and encouraged to see her natural thinking and behavior pattterns as unfeminine.

Similarly, although all male children with strong natural preferences for the feeling mode are discouraged by the systematic programming in society which tells them to "fight back," "keep a stiff Frontal lip," and "remember that big boys don't cry," it is likely that the youngest male in the birth order, particularly if surrounded by many female role models (siblings and adults), if born with a Basal Right lead would be able to hold onto his natural feeling strength at least through early adulthood.

What about twins and brain dominance. Would <u>identical twins</u> tend to have the same dominance?

At birth this would seem to be true. What happens over their lifetime is a different matter. In some of the cases we have studied, one of the twins makes a conscious decision to develop other mental strengths in order to develop a sense of themselves as a separate person. In one of the cases in which this occurred, what also happened several years later, was that the twin who had elected to shift or adapt her identity went through a traumatic mid-life crisis in order to re-embrace her natural dominance.

Why is it that certain children are "problem children" at school while others are not?

The problem child at school is most often a strong double frontal with analytic and internal-image focussed skills. This tends to be true for two reasons. First, most schools are set up to teach in a Basal Left mode. Kids learn things in sequence and are expected to do everything according to a rigid schedule, staying focused on one subject for a full period even if they already understand the content, and switching focus at the ringing of the bell even if they are still interested and in the middle of a problem. Obviously this approach, replete with simplistic Basal Left tests with true and false and multiple choice questions (when used exclusively), is dysfunctional for all but the strongly Basal Left child.

The second cause for the "problem child" is the human context. Thinking back to what has been said about brain dominance and careers, it should not be a surprise to anyone to learn that the majority of elementary and secondary school instructors are double basals, adept at working with procedures and routines as well as at nurturing. Thus, the child with a frontal preference tends to naturally be a misfit in most school. The only difference is that the stronger the child's Frontal Right, the greater the probability that he or she will act out "problem behaviors."

What about the favorite relative. It seems that some children select and gravitate towards a particular relative or friend of the family?

This can happen any time a child finds an adult whose dominance is so similar to their own that if the adult were younger or the child older, they would fast become best friends. It can also happen when a child is either unable to validate their preferred mode of thinking, or alternatively, only able to validate one of their preferred modes within the context of their family. In such cases, if and when the child finds an adult role model, preferably their own sex, they will seek out opportunities to be with that person in order to experience the natural ok-ness which comes from being with a person who mirrors us.

SUMMARY:

Families are perhaps the smallest and most intense experience we have of communal living. Most of what happens in other groups can be derived from those patterns which we played out in our family unit. Thus, when we seek affirmation and validation by identifying and bonding with family members who think the way we do, we foreshadow our behavior at work or in a club or church group, as we seek out friends to affirm our essential way of being. And when we seek to be able to use our dominance in the family, to do things on time and on schedule if we are Basal Lefts or spontaneously if we are Frontal Rights, or with another person if we are Basal Rights, or rapidly and precisely if we are Frontal Lefts, we are simply foreshadowing how we will go about doing our work, actively seeking opportunities to do tasks which make us feel "big smart, small dumb."

The crucial difference between families and the work world is that "blood is thicker than water. " Within the family structure we may be enabled to take chances: to grow and to learn in an environment which basically wishes us well. It is important to remember that the lessons we learn at home are in part accidental, for they depend to some extent on what our birth pattern is and how well it meshes or does not mesh with others in the family. When we go out into the world of work we may or may not meet with similar reinforcements and challenges. What's more, the context may or may not be the same.

If there is one rule to be derived from observing brain dominance in families, it is that context is all important. In order to determine what someone might be experiencing we need to look at what their dominance is, what the dominance patterns of those around them are, and finally what activities they are being asked to do.

CHAPTER 7
YOUR WHOLE BRAIN OVER YOUR LIFETIME

Everyone is born with a set of preferential patterns around which they must develop their lives. And, whether we are discussing handedness or brainedness, the rule is: **first, know thyself and to thy own self be true; then seek to grow and become more.**

For some people, following the rule comes naturally. Those who are fortunate enough to have the opportunity to value, use and develop their native preferences from an early age develop a coherent and positive sense of who they are, as well as a set of competencies which correlate with their preferences. For these people, life appears to flow smoothly. From an early age, their self-esteem and sense of life-direction are strong. And, by the age of twenty or twenty-five they are doing what comes naturally, in a socially-approved position in the home or on the job. Sometime later, typically around the age of forty-five, they begin to experience a sense of needing to grow, which they will act on by taking a class in something "different" or by doing something outside their range of expertise. When asked about these new and unprecedented actions, these people generally explain that it isn't that they are dissatisfied with themselves or their lives, it's only that they are curious about these other "new" areas. We describe what these people are experiencing as **mid-life spread.**

For other people, however, life doesn't flow so smoothly. Not everyone is born into a family or community in which "who they are" is understood, welcomed and accepted. Many young children, as well as adults, find themselves under a tremendous amount of pressure to "fit in" by turning away from their natural preferences and embracing a set of more socially acceptable competencies. Feeling-preferent boys are told to toughen up. Analytically adept girls are told that "argument" isn't "feminine." And internal image-generating children of both sexes are punished as fanciful daydreamers. Somewhat later, the feeling preferent man is discouraged from entering a "female" profession, the analytic woman is told she is an "aggressive bitch," and the internal image-generating adult is told they need to settle down, be practical and make long-term commitments. Additionally, in most organizations everyone, regardless of their dominance, is told to follow the same behavioral "rules"--use the forms, follow the procedures, attend meetings on time, keep to the agenda. In other words, behave as a "good Basal Left." For the Basal Lefts in the organization. such dicta are comfortable reaffirmations of their preferred way of being. For everyone else, they are simply one more set of rules to conform to and a rejection of who they really are.

Faced with such nonnurturing environments, there is a strong temptation for the misfit is to adapt, to protect him or herself like a chameleon does, by matching the coloring and pattern of the environment. Most especially, to the misfitting child, the judgement and rejection of others is felt as a threat to his still-developing self-esteem, which centers largely on his sense of belonging. Given this situation, the child has basically two choices. The first is to adapt in order to fit in, the second is to resist and remain an outsider or misfit. Later as adults we often have an additional, more empowering option, to change our environment. However, children are limited typically to the first two options.

If the child chooses the first option or path, that is, if he chooses to adapt in order to fit in, he will over time, often decades, learn two things. First, he will learn that **when one adapts in order to fit in, one's sense of self-esteem is weakened rather than strengthened.** Secondly, he will learn that although he can develop a competency in an area outside his native strength, **using these nonpreferred competencies over extended periods of time will bring fatigue or boredom, but not joy.** And if the child persists in living with this adapted sense of self for decades, using his nonpreferred modes almost exclusively, at mid-life he will almost certainly experience what is known among life-career counselors as a **"mid-life crisis."** In such cases, this crisis should be seen, not as a tragedy, but as a great opportunity. For it is this crisis which enables the individual to remember who he was/is, and to decide to embrace and reown his original self. And it is only through such an internal reevaluation that the adult who has abandoned his "self" as a child can fully heal.

Of course, many opt not to heal. Many middle-aged individuals facing such an internal crisis resist hearing what their bodies and minds are trying to tell them. For these people, the fear of having wasted years of their life is compounded by their confusion at how to develop skills in the area they abandoned. When you add to this their already weak and eroded sense of self-esteem (from years of adaption), the situation becomes intolerably frightening. For these people, the goal becomes, above all else, to keep things on an even keel, even if it means consuming large amounts of alcohol or mind-sedating drugs. And thus, for them the crisis is replaced by either illness or by a persistent depression.

If, on the other hand, the "misfit" child elects to follow the road less travelled, to hold fast to his own sense of self regardless of the feedback from his environment, a completely different set of learnings awaits him. First of all, he will learn that he must always be prepared to defend himself, for indeed, being a self-declared misfit, he will always be under attack. Given this need, he may develop either an active and aggressive defense pattern or a passive defense strategy. If he develops an openly hostile pattern, he will probably be known as an angry young man. If he develops a passive strategy, often that of avoidance, he will most likely be known as a difficult young man who keeps to himself a lot, and is perhaps a drop-out or a run-away. Either way, his defensive behaviors will begin to cause trouble. In the first instance, he may get into trouble with the law or with the organization for which he works. In the second, he will find himself repeatedly isolated, without the support of friends and colleagues. For such a person, the preeminent need becomes finding a place in which one can be true to oneself **without being rejected**--so that there is no longer a need for the defensive behaviors.

Examples of this type of adjustment are multiple. The strong Frontal Right or double frontal, who is perceived as an angry and difficult employee, leaves the organization for which he works at age twenty-nine and within two years is renowned as an innovative and successful entrepreneur in the computer field. The analytic woman, who was considered an angry and difficult nurse, but who decides at age forty-five to leave nursing and attend law school--finds herself five years later as a happy, well liked and respected lawyer.

Either way, whether we are accepted for who we are at birth so that we grow and prosper in our early years, reaching out in mid-life to grow further, or whether we are rejected as a child for who we are and spend years attempting to deal with what it means to be a misfit, there is reason to believe that all of us are lead eventually towards the same goal: a goal Carl Jung called "the development of all four functions," Abraham Maslow labelled "self actualization" and still others today call "Whole Brainedness."

Another way to understand how our brainedness shifts and develops over our lifetime is to compare it to what the American Plains Indians said about their Medicine Wheel. According to Hyemeyohsts Storm in his book <u>Seven Arrows</u>, they believed each person is a living medicine wheel and born at a specific location on the wheel. In one's lifetime, they observed, one must walk around this great wheel, passing through each of its four cardinal directions, and knowing even as one goes that one will always be most comfortable seeing the world from the perspective of the position of their birth. And only as one returns to that place of birth, does one, for the first time, truly recognize oneself.

NORTH
WISDOM
BUFFALO

WEST
INTROSPECTION
BEAR

EAST
ILLUMINATION
EAGLE

SOUTH
INNOCENCE & TRUST
MOUSE

THE FOUR GREAT DIRECTIONS OF THE MEDICINE WHEEL

QUESTIONS AND ANSWERS:

I'm still unclear about why anyone would deny their basic identity or dominance. Is this adaption conscious, and why would anyone choose to adapt?

There are at least five distinct reasons--some more conscious than others--which appear to lead people to turn away from their birth dominance. Many but not all of these begin to affect us in childhood. The five reasons are:

REASONS PEOPLE TURN AWAY FROM THEIR NATURAL PREFERENCE

- the need to feel accepted, to belong, and to fit in;
- the need to avoid punishment for being different;
- the need to establish a separate identity;
- the absence in one's immediate environment of the "stage props" required by their natural preference;
- the need to insure that something that needs to get done gets done in a marriage or partnership where neither person has the required preference.

Let's take a moment to look at each of these forces.

First, there is the need to feel accepted. You might think that this need to belong is the same as the need to avoid punishment for being different. But in truth, they are distinct. For a young child, one who is still dependent on the actions of the adults in the family for survival, being different can be uncomfortable. Furthermore, as a child begins to mature, the drive to look to his or her sex role model for behavioral cues is strong. Although there is evidence that all children are vulnerable to such a need during their first dozen years, we can predict that the child whose natural dominance is in the feeling mode, the one who is most sensitive to the disharmony created when they are "different", experiences the most intense pressure to adapt in order to fit in.

An example of this type of adaption which comes to mind is our office manager's daughter. When we first met Sunny, she was a bright energetic eight year old. From watching her and listening to her tales of discovery as well as her mother's tales of woe, it was easy to see that Sunny was a double right thinker with a strong Frontal Right lead. Although Sunny's mother was aware of her daughter's preferences and like any loving parent tried to help Sunny feel good about herself, validating Sunny's Frontal Right behaviors was not an easy task for Joan (a strong Basal Left). Thus by the time Sunny turned ten, she was already showing marked signs of adapting. At first, this adaption was subtle and directed towards harmonizing her own identity with that of her Basal Left mother. In order to do this, Sunny began to parrot many of the rules and dicta which she had heard her mother state. If questioned about how or why she knew something to be true, she would simply say that it was so. Later, by the age of twelve, Sunny's sensitive Basal Right again began causing problems as she felt herself so intensely different from the girls at school. At this point, however, we might argue that the pressure to adapt was coming more from a need to avoid the punishments which were being directed at her for being different.

Indeed, the second motivating force pushing young children and teenagers to adapt towards the norm is the desire to avoid being called names and being made fun of by their peers. Katherine distinctly recalls being made fun of for her natural enthusiasm for learning which included: always knowing the answers, always asking questions which took the information further and always getting good grades (all rather typical behaviors for Frontal Lefts and double frontals). So strongly did she feel this disapproval that in sixth grade she purposefully flunked art in order to prove she was "like her classmates."

Other types of punishment and invalidation come from the adults in the mitfit's environment. These include: being given extra homework or assigned extra study hall time for daydreaming or doodling (both natural patterns of thinking for a Frontal Right) and being grounded for not keeping one's room neat and orderly or not doing routine tasks in good Basal Left form. Ironically, in this era of renewed interest in creativity, one of the single most disturbing "punishment" still being meted out comes from the art teachers who, in the interest of Basal Left "correctness", label a drawing in which the roses are colored green or brown as "wrong" or "no good".

In considering the above information on childhood and adolescent adaption, it is worth noting that because of the current structure of our society and it's role models three natural dominance patterns are rejected or attacked more frequently than others. This is important because it suggests that children with these natural patterns may require more help and understanding than their peers in building a positive sense of self-esteem. The young Basal Right, feeling-preferent male is more likely to be made fun of by his peers and seen as a child to be "developed" by his parents and teachers than a naturally left brained boy. Over and over this child is likely to be told that he needs to learn to fight back and act like a man, and that he should remember that big boys don't cry, as he hears himself being labelled a "sissy" and a "cry-baby" by his classmates. Similarly, the young Frontal Left female is likely to be receiving messages that her excellence in math is fine, but that she should be learning to baby-sit, to cook, to sew, to be a girl scout, all the while hearing herself labelled a "tomboy" or "unfeminine" by her peers. And finally, Frontal Right children regardless of sex are generally seen as a behavior problem because, although they are quite bright, they get bored quickly and tend to disrupt class, even if only passively by doodling. It is also true that young Frontal Rights are often punished for not being particularly social, and for preferring to go out exploring on their own. The name which these children most often hear is "weirdo."

But trying to fit in, whether to receive love or to stop punishment, is not the only reason people adapt. A third reason that people adapt is one which many of us never experience: namely, to establish a separate and distinct identity. From our research, this type of adaption occurs most often in the case of identical twins. What seems to happen is this. Identical twins naturally have the same dominance. During their formative years, this sameness may be seen as a problem simply because others cannot tell the twins apart. However, during these same years the natural bonding between the twins appears to hold them together. For some sets of twins, however, reaching adulthood brings the challenge to establish a separate identity.   To meet this challenge, one or both twins may begin to dress differently, live separately, and/or establish a distinct set of skills.

As one twin put it: "We were both good at music, but I had to have my own identity, so I stopped playing the piano and began to study accounting. It was as far away from music and my sister as I could get." Initially, this decision to assert different strengths was seen as helpful and throughout her twenties and thirties, Sandy felt strengthened by this choice. Then suddenly in her forties a peculiar thing happened. Although her twin continued to live comfortably and happily, Sandy began to feel uneasy. Her work with a therapist informed her that what she was going through was known as a mid-life crisis. The upshot of the crisis was predictable: Sandy realized that she had to reembrace music. Even though the earlier adaption had been consciously chosen for an important and valid reason, and had indeed helped Sandy establish self pride and achieve an identity of her own, in order to be ultimately happy, healthy and fulfilled, Sandy had to return to find her original <u>self</u>.

A fourth and somewhat different reason underlying many adaptive patterns is an absence in the person's environment of the "stage props" needed to fully develop their preferred mode. The traditional office, for example, is abundantly stocked with Basal Left sequential forms and files, but devoid of any Frontal Right stimulation. Another limited environment is that of the mother at home with two young children, the chores and the television--in which there are plenty of basal opportunities to feel and organize, but no Frontal Left opportunities at all. Finally, there is the dilemma of the misfit child who must live and try to actualize themselves in an environment designed and controlled by its parents. If there are no paints, you can't paint. If there are no musical instruments, you can't learn to play one. If there are no machines or tools, you can't learn to work with them.

Katherine's life is an example of this. Katherine appears to have been born with a strong double frontal preference. But in the home in which she was raised(with two very right-brained parents), there were very few machines. If one ever broke, it was discarded or put in the cellar. What tools there were (a hammer, a saw and a screwdriver) were scattered and uncared for--frequently abandoned somewhere outside and left to rust. In fact, Katherine recalls that as a child, she thought all tools developed rust on them simply from aging. Given this type of environment, there was not a great deal of opportunity for Katherine to use and develop the strengths native to the Frontal Left analytic mode. Although in school she continually excelled at math and enjoyed the year she was allowed to take debate, and although as a child she would occasionally try to repair some machine on her own, the absence of machines and machine-minded people in her home environment (combined with the fact that when Katherine was in school, "shop" was for boys only) kept her from pursuing the area in depth. Hence today, although she understands and can use analytic thinking, Katherine has never fully grasped it in the way someone who has had the opportunity to work with tools and machines from an early age will, mainly because it is the act of actually working with tools and machines that provides a real understanding of the principles of cause and effect, mechanical advantage and leverage.

Finally, the fifth key force pressuring individuals to adapt is being in a partnership, personal or business, in which tasks which need to be done require the use of a mode which neither partners prefers. In this case the partner who has a penchant of "being responsible" due to having been the eldest child in his or her family of origin will adapt in order to see that the task (paying bills, for example) is done. Or, alternately, the partner with the strongest Basal Right will adapt and do it, motivated by a need to keep the peace. Of course a one time focue outside one's area of strength is not the type of adaption which causes problems. The problems arise when someone accomodates over months or years, doing daily tasks that neither they nor their partner want to do.

From all you have said it would seem that almost everyone adapts. Is this true?

No, not really. In the first place, many of us are born with patterns for which we are naturally rewarded (for example, the double left male or the double basal female), For these people, life welcomes them as they are and rewards them for doing what comes naturally. Not surprisingly, it is this same group which tends to have the strongest and most positive sense of self-esteem from an early age, and which seems the most baffled by the fact that so many other people are not as "at home" with themselves. Katherine distinctly remembers how she and her "misfit" friends didn't quite know what to make of a double left male they knew. His self-esteem was so strong compared to their own that they saw him as "having an inflated sense of himself," instead of simply a healthy sense of self-esteem. One memorable tale about Roy was his response to being turned down by the class beauty for a date. Roy told them: "No big deal. She's the one who's losing out." As insecure and misfitting teenagers, his school mates were appalled. Yet through the years, Roy has maintained his self-esteem and lived a full and successful life as an author and member of the GAO (Government Accountancy Office), where he is responsible for checking to see: if the money which has been budgeted is being spent in accord with the purposes for which it was budgeted; as well as what efforts have been made by involved organizations to bring their operations into alignment with new laws, whether governing integration or the manufacture of fuel-efficient cars. An excellent match for his double left talents, Roy's job naturally reinforces his sense of himself as capable, contributing and smart.

In addition to those who don't adapt because they are successful doing what comes naturally, there are many children who, subjected to the kind of pressures we've discussed (rejection, name calling, punishment), choose to resist rather than adapt. No one is certain about why this happens or what causes some children to adapt and others to resist. Certainly a case could be made that it is the kind of parental role modeling and support they receive. Additionally, some of our work suggests that Basal Rights who have a strong internal need to keep the peace and eldest children for reasons we don't quite understand as yet, both tend to be mroe adaptive than others. All we really know is that, according to Dr. Henry Berman, a pediatrician familiar with the model, some people consistently adapt and others, just as consistently, resist. According to Berman, if a person is going to adapt to fit in, it is generally evident by age seven. Furthermore, such persons are likely to continue to adapt more readily as and when needed throughout their lives. Similarly, those who resist adapting are easily identified by seven and equally prone to continue resisting adaption throughout their lives.

More importantly, because the heavy adapters define themselves by matching those around them, establishing a strong sense of self may be a life long problem.

Indeed, their continual wearing of masks and playing of roles often causes them to feel enraged that they have never really been accepted for themselves. By contrast, the non-adapters or resisters, who continually meet with disapproval and rejection as they hold on to their identity, may develop a strong, if not fully positive sense of self.

Thus far when you've talked about adaption, you've cast it in a negative light. And yet, being flexible and able to adapt is seen as a positive trait by many people. Isn't some adaption positive?

Yes, in some cases, adaption is positive. However, the examples we have discussed to date are all of people who consciously or unconsciously chose to give up their birth preference for one they felt was more acceptable. We call this type of adaption "**replacement adaption**" or "**falsification of type**". There is, as your question points out, another type of adaption in which the person realizes that his natural preference will not be accepted or successful in a given situation and subsequently chooses to develop an additional mode which he then uses situationally. This second type of adaption is called "**additive adaption.**"

The following anecdotal examples will clarify the difference between these two types of adaption. As you read them, pay special attention to the way in which each occurs as well as to the long term impact on the person.

This first story is yet another example of replacement. Leslie was born with a strong Frontal Left. As a young child, being raised in her grandparents' home, she recalls sitting at the dinner table arguing over word meanings with her grandfather, a double right brained entrepreneur. As Leslie describes it, the two of them would begin to discuss a word and inevitably get into a disagreement over the fine points of the meaning. To prove her point, Leslie would finally get up from the dinner table and fetch a dictionary (with which she would prove that she was correct about the word's meaning). Her grandfather would then yell at her that she was "just like her father" (a double left lawyer). This "terrible insult" always reduced Leslie to tears and she would run from the room crying. After a few minutes, her grandfather would come into her room and apologize for making her cry. Unfortunately, at this point he would <u>always</u> add: "But you need to learn, honey, that no one will ever love you if you don't stop arguing." With this kind of repeated negative reinforcement, it is not surprising that Leslie turned away from her analytic skills in favor of the more feminine, nurturing and harmonizing skills of the Basal Right. It was not until Leslie was thirty-two and exposed to the brain dominance model that she began to understand what had actually happened to her as a child, and why as an adult, although exceptionally competent in interpersonal and nonverbal skills, she never derived any deep joy from being a therapist or teacher. It also became clear to her why, regardless of what she accomplished in these areas, her sense of self-esteem remained low.

Michael was born with a strong preference for the right brain, especially the Frontal Right. As a young male, whenever he would ask his father, a physician, for permission to take the family car or to stay out late, his father would ask him to explain to him why he should allow his son to do these things. Through trial and error, Michael learned that when he answered his father using sound logic, his father's preferred mode, his father gave permission. In fact, one of his clearest recollections from his teen years is of the night when he finally developed an argument which was completely acceptable to his father. On that night, his father responded by saying: "You have given me an answer that demonstrates you know how to think. Now that I know this, you don't need to ask again. You may take the car and stay as late as you decide you want to." What Michael learned from these evening encounters with his father was not that he needed to totally give up his Frontal Right preference, but simply that in particular situations he could be more successful by switching to his analytic mode. Thus, as Michael matured and entered the job market, he held on to his sense of himself as an intuitive, image-directed thinker, but added to it his ability to respond analytically where appropriate. By age thirty he was a bank vice president earning an excellent income. The fact that the bank was more conservative than he was did not cause him particular problems. Nor did he have trouble handling the analytical, Frontal Left loan decisions he was called upon to make. Since his own sense of himself was so firmly intact, he was able to use the competencies he had developed without conflict. And, when the time was right, he was able to leave the bank and set up a business of his own without feeling like a failure.

Thus, for Leslie, adaption led to a weakened sense of self, a lowering of self-esteem, and a lack of real satisfaction in her work, despite her success. For Michael, additive adaption enabled him to be more successful than he might otherwise have been without costing him his strong sense of self or confusing his sense about what he needed to be happy.

You've talked a good deal about people adapting as kids in order to belong. What happens when someone, say a forty-five year old adult, realizes they abandoned their original dominance as a kid, and now wants to reown the mode they deserted?

The Rule of Thumb with reowning is: it is a good deal easier to re-own a mode than to develop access to a mode you have never used. Generally, all one needs do to reown a mode is follow the instructions for developing access given in the next chapter. There is, however, another consideration. When we as adults approach reowning our area of childhood preference, we do so "in context." This means we do so as a spouse, or as a parent, or as an employee. Thus, although we may be excited about making a change, we may well run into some serious resistance from our family, friends or colleagues. If we have been acting like a "good Basal Left," doing all the family chores and bills, we can expect that our spouse has a vested interest in having us continue these behaviors. After all, it is highly probable that what originally attracted our spouse to us was the belief-- based on our behaviors-- that we were a strong Basal Left thinker who would attend to all the details of their lives. In such cases, special attention will need to be given to helping the other person to accept our new identity.

Another example comes from one of Anne's clients. This woman, Geri, was born with a strong access to both frontal areas. Her adaptive pattern was one we have not actually discussed as yet. It occurs when a person has two strong leads from birth and adapts by abandoning one lead in favor of a more acceptable mode, while keeping their other in tact. In Geri's case, in order to be accepted as a female, she gave up her Frontal Right and added a competency in the Basal Right, feeling mode. Her resulting Frontal Left/Basal Right pattern worked well in that she used her Frontal Left at work and her Basal Right at home. When she finally realized that her feelings of emptiness and her lack of self-confidence came from the fact that she had rejected an important part of herself early in life, she opted to reown her Frontal Right. As a single parent, Geri did not meet with resistance from a spouse. However, her teenage daughter became openly antagonistic to Geri's attempts at change, and went out of her way to criticize her mother for not trying to be the Basal Right nurturer the daughter wanted her to be. To the daughter, it was of no importance that trying to be Basal Right was making her mother miserable. It was the way mothers were supposed to be and that was that. We can only hope that as Geri's daughter matures her concept of what it means to be a mother will become more flexible. As far as we can tell, mothers come in all shapes, sizes and dominance patterns.

Could you please give some additional examples of people who have turned away from their dominant functions early in life?

One of our clients was a very right brained woman whose family owned a drug store. As the store was seen as a "family enterprise," everyone in the family helped out from an early age. Our client's job was to work at the soda fountain where she learned from her grandfather the specific procedures for making sodas, floats, shakes, etc. One of the things which was emphasized frequently was the importance of keeping the counter clean by wiping it with a towel after every customer had finished and gone. Working at the soda fountain was fun for our client because it meant sharing time with her family and helping out, which her strong feeling function delighted in doing. Although she wasn't naturally interested in keeping everything neat and clean, if this was what would bring praise from her grandfather's lips, a clean counter could be managed.

When she was about eighteen, a young man came in with a friend and ordered a soda. He was beginning to think about settling down, and was struck particularly by our client's attention to detail and her tidiness. According to him, when he left the soda fountain twenty minutes later he told his friend he was "going to marry that girl". Which is exactly what he did. Years passed and the couple was very happy. They particularly delighted in each other--which is understandable given they were both double rights. Unfortunately, as they began to build a family, they were required to do an increasing amount of Basal Left, routine tasks. And, given that his original perception of his wife was as "neat and orderly and liking to keep things clean", the husband simply left all these things for her to do.

When we met them, they had been married for twenty years and had two teen-age children. When we interviewed the couple and had them complete an assessment to identify their mental preferences, we learned that they saw themselves and each other as very right brained. From the children, however, a very different perspective emerged. Both children saw their mother as very Basal Left, since she had almost single-handedly run the entire household and been the one responsible for stability and routines. What also came out was that our client did this knowing full well it was not her thing. In fact, when exposed to the model and to her results, our client said simply: It is all very clear now. Five years ago I had a hemorrhage in the left hemisphere of my cerebral brain. At the time there seemed to be no cause for it. Now that I can see how I have spent years working in my nonpreferred area in order to keep everyone else happy, it makes sense. I had been trying to find a way of explaining to everyone that all the organizing and scheduling and routine cleaning and shopping I did were simply not satisfying, but I couldn't find a way to explain it. I guess I "decided" to have a hemorrhage in order to make them see that I was not a Basal Left thinker.

In a way, although our client had certainly suffered tremendously by the time she came to us, this story is one of triumph. She did, after all, reown her original self and together with her family, found ways of getting the routine tasks accomplished without depending on her competencies.

How do we know if we have adapted? That is, if we were born with some other preference than the one we "identify with" now?

That's an excellent question. The simplest answer is: discover as much as you can about yourself as a young child. Some ways to do this are:

HOW TO GET IN TOUCH WITH YOUR ORIGINAL DOMINANCE

• <u>Remember</u> your earliest years. How did you like to spend your time? What activities did you enjoy the most and what about them specifically did you find so enjoyable? How did you fill your leisure time when what did you was totally up to you? Did you prefer to be alone or with others? Who, in particular, did you seem to enjoy the most and what do you think their dominance pattern was? In developing a data base about your self, you might wish to include memories of kindergarten through fifth or sixth grade--what classes or projects you enjoyed and which you disliked and why.

• <u>Ask family members</u> what they recall about you as a child;

• <u>Remember</u> specifically which <u>classes you enjoyed</u> and did well in: were you good at mathematics (Frontal Left) or geometry (Frontal Right) or spelling (Basal Left) or art (Frontal Right) or in intermediate or high school foreign languages and music, perhaps even playing an instrument (Basal Right), or sports (double frontal)?

• <u>Remember</u> how you did and felt when you had to take <u>tests in school.</u> Did you prefer and do well on the true and false tests (Basal Left), the multiple choice tests (Frontal Left) or the essay tests (Left and Right Frontal)?

• <u>Look</u> at the areas which you currently consider to be your areas of dominance, identifying for each activities and tasks in which you rely heavily on that area. Then consider, while doing those things are you energized and happy, feeling comfortable and satisfied? If so, the chances are greater that these are natural strengths. If instead you feel slowed and 'blah' either during or after completing the tasks involving a particular area, the chances are greater that this area is not a natural dominance, but rather an area of learned competency.

When you have gathered as much information about yourself as a child as you can, stop and review everything you have learned about yourself, while keeping in mind the following question: which mental strength or weakness does this suggest? Usually, by the time you have completed the above self-analysis, you will have a pretty good sense of who you were when you were young.

You are using the terms dominance and competency to mean different things. What exactly is the difference?

We use the term <u>dominance</u> to identify a <u>mental strength or lead function</u>. When we refer to a person's <u>natural dominance</u> we mean more precisely those areas for which they appear to have had a <u>preference from birth</u>. By contrast, when we refer to a person's <u>competency</u> we mean <u>skills which are developed through usage</u>. It is possible for a person to develop competencies in a nonpreferred area as well as in an area of natural strength. Sometimes, when people have used a nonpreferred area for a very long time and built up a lot of strength in that mode, they will begin to confuse their **competency** in that mode for **preference or dominance**. This is particularly true if they have gotten a lot of validation for using that competency.

Why is it that a competency doesn't simply become another area of dominance?

This is an excellent question, but also one which is not particularly easy to answer given our current level of knowledge about brain chemistry and development.

Before answering it, let us take a moment to show you why we have concluded that a competency is not the same as a natural dominance. What we have found in our work with hundreds of clients is that when a person uses a competency which they have developed in an area of natural preference, that is when they do what really comes naturally for them, they are energized and tend to experience pressure to do more of the same type of work as eu-stress ("good or beneficial stress" as defined by Hans Selye). This is dramatically contrasted by what happens when someone engages a competency, no matter how expert, in an area for which they did not have an initial preference. In this latter case, the person will tend to be fatigued by the work more easily and experience pressure to do more of the same as distress.

Now, why would this be? One possible explanation is offered by the story of the monkey's finger. In the tale, the monkey was given a task of pushing the same button again and again with one of it's fingers. As the task was repeated over and over again, the researchers observed a "strengthening" of the neural pathways involved in the moving of the one finger. In this medical school tale, the research clearly suggests that when a person thinks a thought they build a neural pathway. When they think the same thought again they strengthen that neural pathway. And, when they engage in the same task repeatedly, an observable, structural change occurs in the brain along the pathways used to perform the task.

From our perspective, this research is indicative of what happens when anyone develops a competency, whether or not it is in an area of preference. What then is preference or dominance? Our own thinking about this is that it is a neurochemical match. Imagine if you will that your brain is actually four discrete machines. Now imagine that each machine runs on a slightly different fuel. (This should not be so hard to do. After all, we are all familiar with the fact that different machines use different fuels, as in leaded and unleaded gasoline in cars. We also know that although a machine may be able to run on a fuel other than its preferred fuel, in order for it to be maximally effective, it must have the fuel it was designed to use). So what we have in your brain is four machines, each needing a different fuel and perhaps a different lubricant, which are most likely to be found among the neurotransmitters and the neuropeptides. It is a logical next step to consider that each person is probably born with a unique combination of these fuels and lubricants, and that if they happen to have more of the "fuels" which are required by the Basal Right, then they will have a natural preference for that mode of thinking. If, on the other hand, they happen to have a deficiency in the fuels required by the Frontal right , then even though they may build strong pathways in that area of their brain through repeated usage, that mode will never function with the same ease and fluidity of their natural preferences.

They are simply two completely different things--competency being tied to frequency of usage and preference being tied to having the optimal neurochemistry. Obviously a person is happiest when their development has enabled them to have competencies in areas which are designed to run smoothly and effortlessly for them biochemically.

You mention that those who adapt away from their birth dominance at an early age go through a mid-life crisis. How does this relate to the crisis identified by Gail Sheehy in _Passages_?

In our opinion, it is the same crisis simply described from a different perspective.

Not everyone experiences a _mid-life crisis_. What would you say about these people?

They probably had no internally driven need to find themselves, as is the case for someone whose natural dominance was welcomed and developed. As we have already noted, these people are more likely to encounter what they describe as a mid-life spread. This "spread" is motivated by a desire to grow and expand but lacks the urgency of a mid-life crisis.

You mention Sheehy's Passages. What about her Pathfinders? Is there any particular brain dominance pattern which correlates with being a "pathfinder?"

We haven't done any real work in this area, although the question is an interesting one. Our guess is that pathfinders might be relabeled the creative geniuses of life and, as such, probably all have the same distinctive brain dominance: a strong lead in the innovative, change-making Frontal Right, supported by at least a moderate competency in the Frontal Left .

You talk about the importance of developing one's nondominant functions. Could you give some examples of people who have managed to integrate their nondominant functions?

We have a physician friend who selected hematology as his specialty in medical school. Once out of medical school, he went to work as a researcher at a large hospital connected with a well known medical school. For about five years, he taught and did his research quite happily, developing as he did so an excellent reputation. Then one day he learned his mother had cancer, and for several agonizing months, he watched her become increasingly ill. When she finally died, our friend was devastated. Here he was, an expert working in cancer research, trying to find cures for the dreaded disease, and yet for all his expertise, he had been powerless to actually help her in any meaningful way during her final months and weeks. Perhaps not surprisingly, the existential and spiritual pain he felt at this time motivated him to redirect his career. (If you will, he took a few steps around the medicine wheel). He began practicing actively as an oncologist and working with cancer patients and their families. Because of his strong motivation, and possibly some innate Basal Right access, he managed to develop a real competency in the caring and nurturing skills demanded by his second career and within a few years he had developed a reputation as one of the finest oncologists in the Los Angeles Area. Even more importantly, he felt better about himself.

When we met him, he was just entering a third phase of his career, leading a group of professionals, at the hospital with which he was affiliated, to develop new solutions for some of the pressing organizational and delivery problems facing health care. The new task was much more frontal, requiring skill in both logical and adaptive thinking. What we found most interesting was that as the months passed and he became more and more engrossed in this new direction he was able to observe: "My old energy is back. I am excited and alive." What he was noticing is the natural and normal result of "being smart" and doing a task which matches your natural preference or dominance.

Upon reflection, he realized that during the decade he had been working full time with oncology patients, developing and exercising his feeling function as much as possible, he had never felt the surge of energy and the natural high which comes from doing what you are physiologically built to do. Again it is the difference between a preference and a competency. What is important is that he elected of his own free will to grow and develop in order to be a more complete person. When, months later, he phoned to tell us how he was doing, we were both deeply moved when he told us that after considering an offer to go into full-time management, he had decided against it. He would work in management, but he wanted to maintain his oncology practice too. It doesn't hurt to exercise a weak arm. Perhaps that is the only way it can be ready and available if and when we should need it.

In the example you just cited, the man's motivation to develop his feeling function came from the trauma surrounding his mother's death. Do traumatic events generally play a key role in a person's decision to develop a nondominant function?

Not always. As we have already discussed, many people who have grown up with sufficient validation and opportunities in their areas of natural strength move naturally in mid-life to explore their nonpreferred modes. Where trauma seems to play a key role is when the traumatic event highlights the area of weakness and when it occurs early in a person's life. In the above example, the physician was in his early thirties when his mother died of cancer and the specific nature of the trauma was such that had he already developed his feeling function, he would have been able to respond more meaningfully and more satisfactorily to his mother's needs. Her death simply made him graphically aware of an area of personal weakness.

Another traumatic event which often prompts the development of a nonpreferred function is divorce. Typically, when a couple divorces, each person becomes painfully aware of the things which the other person handled and which they themselves either never or no longer know how to manage. It is not uncommon, following a separation for a man unskilled in making friends and getting along with people to read widely in that area and even take evening classes in communications, or for a recently divorced woman, inept at the mechanical work her husband had always handled, to take a class in automotive repair or electrical wiring. Each of these acts helps the recently divorced person gain a sense of balance and wholeness, a sense that even alone they can manage. Each also reflects an opening or expanding into a heretofore undeveloped or weak mental mode.

Will chronic or prolonged stress have the same impact?

No. Chronic stress tends to sap a person's energy. Even though they may believe that they could benefit from endeavors which would develop their non-preferred mental modes, persons subject to prolonged stress tend to require rest and should limit their activities to those which are naturally energizing (hence, in their preferred modes).

Perhaps we should add that one probable cause for chronic stress is being forced to act from one's areas of weakness for a prolonged time. In such cases, what tends to evolve is what we call a **repressed brain dominance pattern**. By trying to hold their own while actually using their weak modes, these people develop a pattern which appears balanced, but involves no real excellence or achievement.

What happens if a person ignores their nondominant function?

According to Carl Jung, ignoring what he calls "the shadow function" can be dangerous. A person who has an undeveloped feeling function will tend to make enemies, or at best not make friends, and will tend to repress rather than process their hurt and rage over life events such as rejection by a lover or the death of a loved one. A person with an undeveloped routine function will consistently get into trouble over details and suffer because a bill was not paid or a clause in the contract was not noted. Such a person will also tend to have difficulty keeping track of the papers which seem to accumulate in contemporary life: tax forms, bank statements, appliance warranties. The person with an undeveloped analytic function will tend to have tremendous difficulty and develop extreme stress when required to make difficult decisions. And the person with an undeveloped innovating function will tend to take fewer and fewer risks as they age, staying closer and closer to home and the routines they established early in life.

Although these "problems" may not appear so dreadful, Jung's observation was that the longer a function was ignored, the more troublesome it became. Two examples will serve to illustrate how right he was.

The first is of a man who had an almost total avoidance of the feeling function. As a youth the effects of this weakness were barely noticeable, visible only in the fact that he had few friends and that those he had were limited to his social circle and had simply been a part of his life for years. Then, as a young man he was sent to Viet Nam as a captain. There, each day he would decide who to send out where. And each night he would sit and write the pro forma letters to the parents of the men who had been killed in action. When he came home, he would talk with no one about what had happened and how he felt. He simply went to work day after day and long into the nights at his uncle's legal firm, accruing accolades by the dozen for his excellence in the profession. Throughout this time he did not date. Then his father died and he was left to live alone in the house he had been raised in. And still he spoke to no one. Ten years later, now an even wealthier and more successful lawyer, he began dating a woman he had met several times at the home of childhood friends. But things did not go smoothly. She suggested they try going together to see a therapist she knew. He went twice and reported it was the single most frightening thing he had done in his life. As sometimes happens, even with the help of a therapist, they were not able to resolve their differences. Five years later he was still single and not dating. When discussing his life with Katherine, a friend of many years, he commented: "My feelings are like pandora's box and I do not want to open it. I cannot cope with it. I prefer to live as I am." Such a story is heart-rending. It bespeaks of a terrible waste of human life and energy. Yet it is actually quite typical of those who cannot face developing their shadow function.

Another example is less tragic but equally illustrative of the impact ignoring a weakness can have over time. This is the story of a triple dominant individual whose area of weakness was her Basal Left. The weakness began to show up early in her life as a tendency to spell poorly (even though she had a large vocabulary) and a tendency to make addition and subtraction errors (even though she liked math and understood calculus). In graduate school the principle effect of her weakness seems to have been her insistence in doing a major paper and taking an extra three credit course instead of doing a thesis. The difference between the thesis and the major paper was that the thesis had to be typed correctly according to a form, with all references noted in footnotes and with a bibliography, but that the major paper required much less procedural "correctness". During her early career, her lack of tolerance for procedure began to rear its head as she grew resentful of all the bureaucratic procedures she was supposed to follow. Then for a few years things seemed to improve. She was awarded a personal secretary whose natural lead in the Basal Left enabled her to attend to the details of report writing (spelling correctly and catching typos) and accounting (adding correctly) which came so hard for her. Soon, however, her entrepreneurial tendencies took hold. She opened a business of her own and because she was operating on a shoe-string, the ultimate responsibility for attending to the details returned to her. The tales of woe were amusing, if costly. In the first few years her lack of attention to detail and lack of tolerance for forms meant that she did not see that all clients were sent contracts to sign, which on occasion resulted in a client canceling at the last minute. It also meant that when a client or colleague said: "Oh we don't need a contract, a hand shake is enough", she went along with their suggestion, which ultimately lead to two major disagreements as to what exactly she was supposed to do for each and for how much money. Later when she moved her office to a larger location, this same weaknesses cost her again when she failed to realize that although she had gotten bids from four moving companies and a second bid from the lowest in order to confirm its accuracy, the bids were in no way binding, and she was, therefore, legally bound to pay the movers the full moving bill (which amounted to three-hundred per cent of their estimate). It would be easy for Sharon to accuse others and life of being unfair, but in truth, the beginning of the problem lies in her own dominance. If and when she can use her routine function when it is called for, she will find many of the complications in her live disappear.

There seem to be many intermediate and high school drop-outs today. What effect does our public school system have on a child's dominance?

In order to understand the impact the schools have on our children, it is first necessary to understand the structure of the schools. Of course, we cannot comment on all schools. We believe, however, that the mode which is given the most attention and opportunity to develop is the Basal Left mode. This actually should not be too surprising, inasmuch as the schools and their curricula, like the majority of American businesses, were developed during the industrial era. Society needed and wanted people capable of working with routine functions: whether on assembly lines or in offices. With the advent and popularization of the computer, however, a good bit of what used to be done by human hands can now be done by machines. It is quite possible, therefore, that just as the form of American business is shifting to become more whole brained, so too will the public schools. For those who question the link between these changes and our changing society, we strongly suggest the reader look at Naisbitt and Aburdene's second book, Re-Inventing the Corporation.

Another reason why so many of our schools are structured for the Basal Left mode is that the majority of people who work in the schools, teachers and administrators alike, are basal thinkers. And, frankly, it is not easy for basal thinkers to teach and model frontal thinking skills.

What's more, frontal people are not likely to begin taking jobs as public school teachers--not until and unless the schools are restructured. Why not? Well, it is actually pretty simple--once you understand the smart-dumb rule which governs a person's selection of a career. Most people with a strong Frontal Left like to make difficult decisions using logical arguments and critical analysis. Most people with strong Frontal Rights like a lot of variety and the opportunity to be innovative and problem solve creatively, as well as to take risks. None of these skills is involved in the standard teaching format. Instead, most teaching involves using interpersonal Basal Right skills to present Basal Left, sequenced information.

Given their predominantly basal structure, what then is the impact of the public schools on our youth? Generally speaking, basal children, particularly those with a strong Basal Left lead, find the schools enjoyable (or at least satisfying). For the non-Basal Left child, however, the story is dramatically different, as Katherine's work with a senate committee on developing an educational system for the street kids discovered. For the child with a strong Frontal Left, the schools are basically an experience in boredom. These kids feel the their teachers are slow and perhaps even dumb by comparison with themselves. Nonetheless, being adept at analytic thinking, these same kids stay in school, because they see society as a machine, and they have figured out that the key to gaining leverage in it is a high school diploma and one or two college degrees. For the strong Frontal Right or Double Right, however, our schools, as they are, are a source of invalidation and lowered self-esteem. These kids may be learning-disabled with respect to language and reading. Moreover, they lack the analytic skill to appreciate the value which a high school diploma might have. Hence, they drop-out. Interviews with drop-outs in Washington and Wisconsin have indicated that most drop-outs are adept at fine arts, frequently being excellent dancers, musicians, and/or actors (all strongly right brained pursuits).

Given family and peer pressure, not all Frontal Right or double right kids drop-out, although a revealing conversation with a Chicago area psychiatrist suggests they might have been better off doing so. In considering the kids he had on his adolescent psych unit at a large urban hospital, he commented: "You know, more than 85% of the kids we see here are double right brainers who are confused and irritated by the facts and figures they've been asked to memorize in school, yet who excel in dancing and acting."

Although these observations are disheartening, there are many people, mostly Right-brainers, who are more sensitive to these problems and are already seeking to reform the school system. How successful they will be unless and until American business and our national government decide that their future survival and success depend on the transformation of our schools is another question.

It seems from all you've said that it is very important for parents to reinforce and validate their child's dominance. How can I know what my child's natural preferences are?

A child's natural dominance is generally visible from about the age of two. Hopefully, the following suggestions will help the interested reader to identify their child's dominance.

IDENTIFYING A CHILD'S DOMINANCE

The child probably has a strong Basal Left lead if she or he:
> seems to need more routine
> prefers to eat at the same time daily
> prefers to have the same food for the same meal
> prefers to be told what to do and how to do it
> likes train sets which go around on a track
> likes to read books about the real world
> prefers true/false tests
> wants his/her room kept "just so"

The child probably has a strong Basal Right lead if she or he:
> likes to change clothes often and play dress up
> is chatty
> knows everyone in the neighborhood
> is known by everyone in the neighborhood as friendly
> touches and likes to be touched
> enjoys and often wears bright colors
> likes to read biographies, romances and animal stories
> likes and remembers to take care of pets
> giggles or is silly often
> likes to help or to share experiences
> likes to be in the same room with others rather than alone
> isn't particularly good at tests

The child probably has a strong Frontal Right lead if she or he:
> wanders off or explores
> daydreams
> draws a lot, often expansively covering entire page
> is good at visual or spatial games: pick-up pairs
> prefers a lot of stimulation
> prefers to run, jump & climb, while making loud noises
> may not read as a young child if other stimulation is available
> if or when stimulation is limited may read voraciously
>> especially about new and different things
> is good at geometry
> prefers essay tests in which there is no one right answer
> seems to have a shorter attention span
> may know answers in school without knowing how or why
> may often be "ahead of the teacher"

The child probably has a strong Frontal Left lead if she or he:
> gravitates towards tools and machines
> tries to take apart small machines such as portable tape players
> is articulate, but not "chatty"
> likes to construct things using tools
> is good at math
> seems to prefer multiple choice or essay tests
> likes to argue
> sets "goals" for himself

If you have difficulty identifying one lead function, try backing into the answer by figuring out what your child is not. Then, once you have identified your child's probable lead preferences take time to test what you have determined. In other words, increase the amount of activity available to your child in his or her preferred mode(s) and decrease the amount in his or her nonpreferred modes. If when you do this, your child seems to be happier, more content or more comfortable, you are most likely correct about his or her dominance.

It is important to note that you cannot check to find a child's preference if you are not already offering them a full range of opportunities. In many homes there are areas in which few or no "stage props" exist. If this is true of your home, first find a way to fill out the range of options. Then check to see what your child naturally chooses and rechooses. One way to accomplish this which some families with have found helpful is to seek out an adult who has a natural strength in the area which is not represented strongly in the home environment and ask that person to come over with some stage props and spend time with the child. Sometimes this filling out of the options occurs naturally when the child notices that they really enjoy hanging out around or helping a particular neighbor. In fact, before trying to adjust your own situation, you might check to see if your child has a pattern of going over to a particular adult's home regularly. If so, ask both you child and the adult what seems to go on when they are together.

Then once you are clear about your child's natural dominance pattern, you can help your child develop a coherent sense of self-esteem by finding ways to validate that dominance. If the dominance is one which does not match the socially approved role models and/or is not affirmed in the school which he or she attends, this will be all the more critical.

What are some specific suggestions for reinforcing and validating a child's dominance?

The chart on the next two pages will help you identify specific ways in which you can reinforce and validate each of your children. As you read, look for three things. First, notice what you are already doing that's right. Next, look for new ideas--things you can do to validate each child. Finally, notice what if anything you are doing with the intention of "helping" one of your children, which although helpful, empowering and appropriate for children with one dominance pattern, may actually be damaging to your child, given his or her dominance.

WAYS TO VALIDATE YOUR CHILD'S
NATURAL MENTAL PREFERENCES

If you have a Basal Left child:
- create 3 or 4 step procedures for doing as many things as possible, then be sure to go over each procedure slowly and a step-by-step manner with your child.
- compliment your child for his or her ability to do things on time.
- compliment your child for his or her ability to do things according to the procedures he/she was given.
- if you want something done differently, make a point of telling your child, "You and I will be changing procedures, let's learn or load the new procedure," and be tolerant of any emotional discomfort he or she feels around the changes you introduce.
- ask your child to teach a house guest the procedure for something (i.e., washing dishes or feeding the cat).
- tell your child that everyone has things they do to contribute to the family, and ask him which of the tasks he has learned would most enjoy doing regularly as his contribution. Then reward him for doing it with a thank you.

If you have a Basal Right child:
- spend time with your child, just "playing".
- ask you child to guess what someone is feeling. Then have them tell you why the think that might be true and what about the person's stance suggested it.
- ask your child to come with you to do a favor for someone or to take a gift to someone.
- suggest your child make or find a gift or card to give as well--a drawing a pine cone or a magic pebble or seed are all excellent gifts.
- ask your child to plan or help you plan a party.
- provide your child with soft and interesting fabrics with which to play.
- provide your child with clothes and costumes for "dress up".
- hug your child often & make a big deal of the joy it give you when they hug you.
- encourage your child to have a pet & to take care of it. The best pets are those which can be touched & petted.

If you have a Frontal Right child:
- allow your child to be, act or dress differently.
- compliment him or her for his imaginative choices.
- remind your child that he or she does not have to join in.
- encourage him or her to explore.
- tell your child that daydreaming is ok and that some of the world's most creative people have been and are daydreamers.
- create a wall for your child's art.
- if at all possible be sure you child has a room or area of his or her own in which being neat is not necessary.
- read to your child about the lives of Nikkolaus Tessela and Edmond Halley.

If you have a Frontal Left child:
- help the child learn to reason.
- practice the art of critical analysis with the child.
- encourage the child to develop strong logical arguments for things he wants to have or do.
- create and play a debating game with your child.
- be sure he your child has machines & tools with which to play/work.
- be sure to comment positively on your child's skill in these areas.

An example of how an imaginative right brained parent helped validate his very left brained three-year old son was by going to the junk yard to find an old typewriter with which Adam could work and giving it to his son with a set of tools. For many months when his dad and mother would go to work or go out, Adam would "work" on his typewriter, which essentially meant he worked at taking it apart.

I understand that you believe in validating people. However, as a parent, I am also concerned that my children learn how to get along and become contributing, successful members of society. Based on all you've said, my son appears to be a Frontal right, internal image-generating thinker. He is also a real problem at home and in school. He doesn't do the things we ask him to and he doesn't do his homework. What do we do about this?

Typically, a child who resists as much as you are suggesting does so simply because he is having to <u>defend</u> who he is and because he is given no opportunities to succeed by doing what comes naturally for him. Your best bet in such a case is to study your child in order to determine what does come naturally for him and then give him plenty of opportunities to do it in contexts for which he will be rewarded (or at least complimented or praised by you). Once you are giving him a chance, consistently, to succeed at being himself, the dysfunctional behaviors will generally stop.

It is perhaps worth mentioning that the thinking pattern which most frequently causes the types of "antisocial behaviors" you have mentioned is the frontal right. Additionally, many of the things which come naturally for the Frontal Right, being a prankster, challenging the rules, experimenting, daydreaming and looking at internal, imaginary films--are not things which appear to be contributions desired by society. For this reason, it is important to keep in mind the research of Frank Farley at the University of Wisconsin. Farley's work demonstrates conclusively that such children, denied stimulation and frustrated, punished, rejected and invalidated for their thinking skills, become criminals; but, supported and stimulated, become the earth's creative geniuses.

One final question. I'm interested in the work of Jean Piaget whose work shows how children develop particular mental capacities as particular ages. What about this? Does this mean that at least a part of our "walking around the medicine wheel" and our attempts to develop all four functions may be physiologically based and stimulated?

That's an excellent question. Although there is certainly not enough evidence as yet to say you are 100% correct, there are scattered bits of information which taken together certainly point towards some such phenomenon. And although what we know is mostly about children, it is well worth reviewing.

According to Jean Piaget, there is a physiological window which can be observed in all children, from age two through age six, during which time the child is geared to acquire language. Although we are not certain whether that window involves only the Basal Left (vocabulary) or the Frontal Left (language structure) as well, what is certain is that during the time, the child can easily pick up one, two, three and possible more languages. The key is simply regular exposure and the opportunity to use. After this window closes, due to a shift in the biochemistry, the learning of a new language becomes markedly more difficult.

This dove-tails with other research that suggests that foreign languages learned in high school (when the window is closed) are not learned in the left where our native language(s) is learned, but rather in or by the Basal Right which learns by picking up and matching rhythms.

Another piece of this puzzle comes from Joseph Chilton Pierce (author of The Magical Child), who contends that reading should not be taught prior to the age of eleven or twelve. If he is correct, it may be because reading involves the ability to think conceptually, which requires both frontal lobes. This type of thinking cannot physiologically occur unless and until the child's corpus callosum has fully developed and its sheathing has hardened. For female children this may happen around the age of six or seven. For males children it occurs somewhat later, around the age of eight or nine.

Another tidbit comes from the studies of young babies who seem to recognize the human smile (and frown?) before they can see and recognize anything else. This ability is clearly located in the Basal Right region of the brain. Is this early recognition cued by physiology?

And, finally, there have been several studies, some done by the Institute for Creative Thinking in Buffalo, New York, which suggest that 90% of children under the age of five are highly creative, but only 2% of children over eight and adults are highly creative. Our reaction to this data is that although it is true that our society and schools tend to "kill creativity" in children, it is probably not quite as bad as these numbers make it seem. What is probably more true is that as infants we have another Piagetian "window" designed to enable us to learn about ourselves and our environment through direct, personal experimentation.

Taken together these facts begin to form a strong if not fully developed argument for a series of physiological triggers which might assist people in walking around their medicine wheel. What we would suggest is that it is highly likely some such system exists, as an overlay to the basic theory of brain dominance. Perhaps it exists so that we can all eventually grow. Perhaps it exists as a built in mechanism for insuring the survival of the species. A few years ago Katherine read (in a journal for mid-wives) about a new piece of research which shows that the human mother, when allowed to give birth unassisted by drugs or surgery, experiences a release of chemicals which seem to naturally increase her mothering instinct. Is that the same as a physiological boost to the Basal Right nurturing function? If so, it is an intriguing thought that we as humans are so well designed that even women for whom the Basal Right function is not a natural preference will at the crucial moment be given assistance. An amazing, perhaps for some, an incredible thought. But the human is an incredible animal.

An even more astounding possibility is suggested by the recent work of Michael Persinger in The Neurological Basis of God Experiences. His work suggests that many "spiritual experiences" occur in response to decreased levels of serotonin (brought on in some cases by stress and in others by deep meditation) which causes an increase in the rate of electron firings in the right parietal lobe as well as possibly the temporal lobe. If this were true, would it invalidate the truth of spiritual experiences? Perhaps. On the other hand, it might be the beginning of renewed faith for many. For indeed, is it not possible that the deep, life-altering experiences reported as "near death experiences" and the improbable but generally predictable sense of peace which "comes over" many people immediately prior to death are both the result of the same biochemical adjustment? And is it not also possible that this adjustment is triggered by another chemical which is released, possibly by the pituitary, when it receives signals that death is near? Certainly, it is possible, and, if so, it would be a marvelous example of what the Frontal Left engineer would call a "built-in safety mechanism" and the deeply religious Basal Right would label "divine grace".

SUMMARY:

Our mental preferences affect us throughout our lifetime. Most especially, they affect our self-esteem and success. When our natural mental preferences are rejected, our self-esteem is at risk. If and when this occurs, many of us have a tendency to adapt in order to fit in and receive the validation we need. Although this path promises immediate success and acceptance, if we become overly identified with an adaptive pattern, we run the additional risk of forgetting our true self--an occurrence which is likely to bring on two problems. We are likely to suffer from chronic low self-esteem, for the acceptance and validation we do receive are all for a "fake self." And we are likely to go through a mid-life crisis unless or until we re-embrace, use and validate our original and natural mental preferences. Thus, it would seem the principal rule for achieving happiness in the long haul is actually the one handed down the ages: **know thy self and to thy own self be true.**

Nonetheless, as important as it is for us to be true to ourself, the second rule of thumb for success and effectiveness reminds us that for long term survival and success we must learn to appreciate and use those modes which naturally we would probably rather forget or abandon. The key point in applying this rule, as it is described in the next part of this book, is to not forget your true preferences, while learning and using non-preferred competencies. This last point explains why so many problems which come up with adaption are problems which have begun early in our lives before we have fully developed and validated our natural self. For this reason, a further point of importance to keep in mind is this: **it is always wiser to learn about, develop and validate your natural strengths prior to developing competencies in other modes.**

With these pointers in mind, let's look together in the final section of this book at the two ways in which you can expand you abilities to use your whole brain: learning to speak and use the full range of mental languages to communicate effectively with others, and developing competencies in your nonpreferred modes.

PART IV.

THE ART
OF
USING YOUR WHOLE BRAIN

**Rule #2: To assure your survival, as well as guarantee your
long term effectiveness and success, manage activities and people
not matching your dominance by enlisting assistance from
complementary brains.**

CHAPTER 8

DEVELOPING COMPETENCIES & COMMUNICATING CLEARLY

Although both Jung and the Plains Indians believed that it was normal, natural
and probably necessary for a person to have one or two lead functions or modes,
both also believed that it is the task of life to expand beyond our innate
preferences to accept and develop all four modes to thinking.

While it is true that we cannot change our preferences, we can, nonetheless,
develop competencies even in our nonpreferred modes. This is because
competency in any mode develops naturally as a result of repeated usage. The
more you use a given mode, the more often you actually participate in activities
which require that kind of thinking, the more competency you are likely to
acquire. Unfortunately, this process takes time and, when working in an area of
nonpreference, may be more fatiguing and stressful than otherwise.
Consequently, you may be tempted to abandon the effort early on. If you want to
increase your ability to use and depend on a non-preferred mode, however, you

will have to resist the temptation to quit. Additionally, while you are working on developing a new competency, you should withhold judgment about how you are doing, give yourself permission to "feel dumb" and make mistakes, and give yourself plenty of time in which to succeed. For this reason, having a <u>tolerant and supportive attitude towards yourself</u> while working to develop a competency in a nonpreferred mode is the first and most important step towards achieving your goal.

Once you have adopted the appropriate attitude we suggest the following:

4-STEP PLAN FOR DEVELOPING A COMPETENCY:

1. **Find a role model or mentor** who has strength in and a preference for the quadrant you want to develop and begin hanging out with them. Ask them to talk about their thinking. Have them share with you their approach to problem solving and decision making. Get them to talk about their interests, values, and world view. Then **practice** seeing the world through their eyes. To the best of your ability, see things as they see them and gain as much familiarity as you can with that way of processing.

2. **Use the quadrant** you want to develop by involving yourself in a variety of activities which depend on it.

3. **Read** material that would interest someone with a natural preference in the mode you are seeking to develop. This means material that is about something which is generally of high interest to that mode. And it means material written in a way that the mode readily understands.

4. **Find a way to become a contributing member to a Whole Brain Team.** Your participation will enable you to fully see and appreciate the contribution of your non-preferent modes.

QUESTIONS AND ANSWERS:

The general strategy sounds great. But let's get specific. For example, how do I find a quadrant expert? How do I know the person actually has strength in the quadrant I am seeking to develop?

Finding a person who will be your mentor or advisor demands that you recognize the behaviors characteristic to the quadrant you are seeking to develop. In order to develop a clear picture of the person you want as a mentor, read the following **Perspectives Chart.** If you are still uncertain, reread the section in chapter three which describes your nonpreferred mode.

A PERSPECTIVES CHART
FOR RECOGNIZING THE BRAINS AROUND YOU

THE BASAL LEFT MODE

Descriptors: cautious, conservative, detailed, procedural, sequential

Skills: holding to deadlines and schedules, monitoring, performing routine or procedural tasks, whether operational or administrative, proof reading,

Typical Phrases: let's go by the book, look in the procedures manual, it's better to play it safe, law and order are important, we've done it this way, there's not reason to change, it's important to establish good habits, self-discipline, what's the right sequence or order?

Self-Perception: industrious, productive, reliable, thorough

As Seen By Others: boring, stuck in a rut or the mud, grinds out the task

THE BASAL RIGHT MODE

Descriptors: intuitive about people, musical, rhythmical, sensitive to nonverbal behaviors, spiritual

Skills: bridging, encouraging, harmonizing, nurturing, teaching, welcoming, writing personal notes & letters

Typical Phrases: caring, the family, human spirit, meaningful, participation, personal growth, sharing, team work

Self-Perception: a deeply caring and concerned person (if extraverted) a deep-feeling person (if introverted)

As Seen By Others: a non-stop talker, a soft-touch, touch-feely

THE FRONTAL RIGHT MODE

Descriptors: artistic, creative, expressive, holistic, intuitive, innovative, spatial, synthesizing, dreaming

Skills: creative problem solving, design, making change, seeing the big picture, seeing the trends and patterns

Typical Phrases: conceptual block-busting, being on the cutting edge, playing with an idea, finding something new, synergistic, all-encompassing

Self-Perception: a visionary leader (if extraverted)
a visionary thinker (if introverted)

As Seen By Others: a space cadet with his head in the clouds, a dreamer, unfocused

THE FRONTAL LEFT MODE

Descriptors: analytical, decisive, directing, evaluating, factual, logical, mathematical, quantitative

Skills: decision making, prioritizing, negotiating, financial problem solving, technical problem solving, using tools

Typical Phrases: understanding the key factors, doing a critical analysis, knowing the bottom line, breaking it down or taking it apart, using leverage, weighing all the variables

Self-Perception: a strong, decisive leader (if extraverted)
an expert (if introverted)

As seen by Others: critical, unemotional and uncaring, power-focused, calculating and manipulative
hard, cool, distant, intelligent (if introverted)

OK. Now, suppose I have found a mentor and have been hanging out with him or her, learning by "osmosis". What about the second step--Doing things which require me to use the mode I want to develop? This seems like the core of developing a competency to me, but I'm not sure what things to do for which mode. Could you give us some suggestions?

The following lists should provide you with some ideas:

ACTIVITIES FOR DEVELOPING COMPETENCIES

To develop the Basal Left: Begin valuing **form, structure, planning** and **organization**, then:

- Select an activity which you really want to do, then figure out how you could make time to do it regularly by doing something else which you have to do more efficiently. Then create a routine for doing the "have to," and do it regularly, using the time you save to enjoy the "want to".

- Identify a luxury, something under $100. which you want to buy but for which you do not have the "spare cash". Next, make a personal budget which will save you $5, $10 or $20 a week. Then follow the budget, being certain to spend the money you save on the luxury you selected.

- Strike a deal with your spouse or house-mate that if you do certain house work on a routine-basis (e.g., every Saturday a.m. you do laundry, or every evening you do dishes before relaxing for the evening) that you will get an extra long hug and cuddle from them each time.

- Make a list of your most frequently purchased groceries, toiletries and house-hold cleaning materials, xerox 20 copies of the list and keep one on your refrigerator at all times. Whenever something is almost out, go to the refrigerator and circle. Then, once a week or whenever you go shopping take the current list from the refrigerator door. After several weeks, notice whether you have fewer occurrences of

getting to the grocery store and wondering what else it was
you wanted.

The above entries are all opportunities to **use and appreciate routine**
as an efficient, resource saving mode. Learning to use routine is learning
to value one aspect of the Basal Left. The second major aspect is the
respect for and ability to focus on details. The following is an exercise in
that aspect:

-   Go through you home making a list of all the little repairs
    and or tasks you've been meaning to get around to (such as a
    broken latch, a squeaky door, a pile of papers needing to be
    sorted and filed). Then commit to taking care of one, and
    notice how it feels to have it taken care of (e.g., the relief,
    or sense of increased safety you feel).

To develop the Basal Right: Begin valuing **feeling, body
responses** and **intuitions about people,** then:

-   Keep a daily journal of your feelings.
-   Practice observing other's non-verbal communication.
-   Listen to rhythmic music & move your body with the
    beat.
-   Practice sharing your feelings regularly with a friend you
    trust.
-   Take an acting class.
-   Play with children and let them direct the play/game.
-   Take a Feldenkreis movement class.
-   Collect natural objects (shells, rocks, pinecones) and
    use them to remind you of special people & experiences.
-   Get and give regular massages.
-   Take a Reiki class and learn to heal with touch.
-   Ask yourself how you feel about the colors and textures
    in your environment.
-   Experience your spirituality through daily meditation or a
    prayer circle.
-   Get and give 10 hugs per day.

To develop the Frontal Right: Begin valuing **spontaneity,
creativity** and **intuitive thinking,** then:

-   Practice creating & using metaphoric descriptions of

people, things or ideas.
- Create a personal symbol, mask or logo using symbolic shapes, forms and materials. Then explain its meaning to someone else.
- Daydream.
- Take 300 photographs just to see what happens.
- Invent a "gourmet" dish and eat it!
- Go for an "adventure" in a part of the town you don't know, consciously entering at least two parks, streets, paths or alleys which apparently offer not promise & see if you can discover something thought provoking or idea generating in each.
- Keep a diary of your dreams and work with someone to interpret or analyze them.
- Read 3 pages each day from a new book outside your usual areas of interest or expertise.
- Take a Creative Problem Solving Workshop.[1]

To Develop the Frontal Left: Begin valuing **facts, analysis** and **rational thinking**, then:

- Take a logic or debate class.
- Practice prioritizing using rational reasons rather than feelings. Remember, you can prioritize anything, even your grocery list!
- Play logic games or chess.
- Find out how one of your home appliances works.
- Become active in an investment club.
- Take an auto repair class.
- Learn to program a personal computer.
- Play "devil's advocate" in the next group discussion.
- Analyze an intuitive decision for rational components.
- Write critical reviews of your favorite books, movies and radio or television shows.
- Describe an important project entirely in quantitative terms (using numbers).
- State your current goals and objectives in one short paragraph (1/2 page maximum).
- Learn how to use tools and measure precisely.

---

[1]For more information about where and how to enroll in one of these programs contact either Anne or Katherine at the address given in the Introduction.

In theory, what you're saying sounds wonderful. But I've tried developing competencies in areas outside my preference and all that happens is that I get upset, angry and frustrated. Can you give me some practical suggestions for how to succeed at developing the new skills I've selected?

Your concern is a valid one. Actually, almost everyone experiences these emotions when they begin to develop a weak mode. For this reason, we have developed a **7 Step Strategy for Success** which should be used whenever you begin step 2 of the **4 Step Competency Development Plan**.

7-STEP STRATEGY FOR SUCCESS

1. Select one or two activities which require the use of one of your non-preferred areas. The activities you select should both use the same non-preferred area. Pushing or pulling yourself in too many directions at once can be more confusing than growthful.

2. Spend time thinking about the activities you have selected. Why do you want to learn to do these things? Make a list of all the positive benefits. Then, make another list of all the difficulties you have had in the past few years because you have not known how to do these two things.

3. Determine what "stage props" you will need in order to learn or practice these activities.

4. Beg, borrow, steal or buy all the necessary "stage props" and don't scrimp when you do so. If you need something, buy it (even if it does cost more than you usually spend).

5. Create a space just for these activities and props which reflects the mode you have elected to develop and avoids stimulating other areas.

6. Practice the activities you've elected to develop. It is best if you practice daily and at the same time every day. It is also best not to schedule more than two hours on any given day.

7. Finally, remember that although you are learning to develop a new skill, you need to continue validating yourself for your natural strengths and, whenever possible, follow each competency practice session with an activity which uses your natural preference.

In your Strategy for Success, what do you mean by "stage props?"

Stage props are those objects or tools which stimulate the part of the brain you wish to strengthen, or alternatively turn down parts of the brain which might interfere with the area you are attempting to stimulate.

POSSIBLE STAGE PROPS

For the Basal Left: create a very organized space decorated in subdued tones, possibly a two-toned (white and brown) striped wall paper with:

> A filing cabinet with empty files to put thing in
> A word processor
> An accounts ledger
> A large calendar on the wall
> A Pert Chart
> A To do List
> A dictionary
> Procedures manuals
> Instructions manuals
> "How to" books
> A daily hour by hour schedule
> A desk set with containers for paper clips, pencils...
> Rectangular no-nonsense furniture
> Marching music.

For the Basal Right: create a sense of abundance or the "cluttered effect" decorating in bright "happy" colors possibly with a wall paper which has small flowers or hearts or circles on it with:

> Sea shells, pine cones, seed pods
> Green plants and fresh flowers
> Photographs of your family
> Photographs of smiling people
> Paper with Crayons or markers of many colors
> A fragrance source which stimulates positive feelings for you (incense, candles, scented potpourri.)

Comfortable chairs with an afghan or blanket
Inspirational books (with pictures) such as:
   Jonathan Livingston Seagull, the Bible,
    The Prophet, Gift From the Sea
A book of your favorite poetry
Clay with which you can play
Something connecting to children or infants
   (a child's drawing, their baby shoes)
A favorite, very soft stuffed animal
Ethnic or folk art, Native American, Mexican
Lots of personal mementoes your high school
   year book, gifts from loved ones
Rhythmical music as well as
Music of natural sounds such as waterfalls, the
   sea, rain falling, breezes blowing...

For the Frontal Right: create a spacious and airy area with high ceilings
decorated in light tones, off-white, like an artist's
studio, with natural lighting if possible and with:

Lots of flat available surfaces for stacking and
   working
A flip chart with lots of flip chart paper
Push pins to tack up things
Walls you can tack things onto
Lots of magic markers in many colors
Caricatures or line drawings
Photographs of abstract patterns & spirals
Geometric shapes to play with
Symbolic shapes or objects
A reading corner with magazines, reference
   books & articles
   on a wide range of topics
Lots of space with no structure
Pillows on the floor
Baroque music or jazz.

For the Frontal Left: create a space with minimal clutter, decorated in
black, white, grey or navy.

Photographs of Arrows
Machines and mechanical tools
Scales and or a gavel
A calculator
A statement of you goals and objectives
Charts with numbers and percentages
Framed awards, diplomas and certificates
A five year plan
Structured music such as Bach.

**I like the strategy for success you've just presented, but I'm afraid
that when I try to do Step 6 (in which I'm supposed to actually do
something) I'll feel bored, frustrated and uncomfortable and   I'll
find myself getting up and walking away. Do you have any
additional "helpful hints" for me?**

When working on developing a competency, it also may be necessary--as part of
setting the optimal climate--to shut off a competing part of your brain. For
example, many people find it easier to get in touch with their right brain if and
while they have turned down the volume and activity level of their left
hemisphere. They accomplish this by refraining from using words altogether
(since the speech centers are located on the left), and instead focus exclusively on
input and thinking processes native to the area they wish to access. If they are
working on developing a competency in the Frontal Right, this might mean
attending to shapes, patterns, line drawings, abstract forms and negative space.
If they are seeking to develop a competency in the Basal Right, this might mean
attending to rhythms, colors, feelings and the sense of their own body moving
through space. Additionally, when seeking to access either right mode, it is
helpful to refrain from left brained activities like sorting, prioritizing, analyzing
and clock-watching.

At first, structuring your thinking and awareness in this manner will be difficult.
As you already know, we are extremely susceptible to interruption and distraction
when we are functioning in our non-preferred modes. For this reason, it is best to
assume that any discomfort and resistance we experience when trying to develop

a new quadrant is just a normal reaction to operating in a non-preferred mode and should probably be ignored. This will be particularly true during the first **twenty minutes** of work in the nonpreferred area, during which time we will experience all kinds of impulses to abandon the task for something else. Generally, if we can hang in there through the first twenty minutes, the reactions will settle down and we can begin to develop our abilities in that area. Unfortunately, this twenty minutes of discomfort is not a one-time phenomenon; we are likely to feel this way each time we begin working in our nonpreferred mode and will have to make ourselves work "through" it again and again if we are to gain competency in that area.

I'm a reader, so Step 3 of your Competency Plan naturally interests me. Could you recommend books which are relevant for each of the four quadrants?

You might explore some of the following <u>books</u>:

For the **Basal Left:** Find and read three procedures manuals cover to cover. Read all the instruction manuals for your appliances.

For the **Basal Right:** <u>The Language of Feelings</u> by David Viscott, <u>The Angry Book</u> by Theodore Isaac Rubin, <u>Focusing</u> by Gedlin, <u>The Emotional Hostage</u> by Cameron-Bandler and Lebeau, any book on nonverbal communication.

For the **Frontal Right:** <u>Drawing on the Artist Within</u> by Betty Edwards, <u>Creative Dreaming</u> by Patricia Garfield, <u>The Right-Brain Experiences</u> by Marilee Zdenek, <u>Brainstorms and Thunderbolts</u> by Carol O. Madigan and Ann Elwood, <u>The Path of Least Resistance</u> by Robert Fritz, <u>The Intuitive Edge</u> by Philip Goldberg, <u>Higher Creativity</u> by Willis Harman.

For the **Frontal Left:** <u>The Prince</u> by Niccolo Machiavelli, <u>Thinking Physics</u> by Lewis Carroll Epstein, 'The Wall Street Journal', and any books on chess strategies.

Additionally, you might want to ask your **competency mentor** what he or she reads and read that.

What if you think you should be developing access in a particular mode, but don't really <u>want</u> to do it?

An individual's psychology can also have an impact on their ability to develop competency in a quadrant. This is particularly true when a person has a lot of anger, resentment, and invalidation built up around a particular area. For example, a strong Frontal Right who has been heavily invalidated by Basal Lefts and feels resentful at having to do left brain tasks at work all day, may very well need to release a lot of his pent-up rage before trying to acquire an appreciation for and competency in his own Basal Left. For such an individual, the first step to acquiring competency will be to make peace with the Basal Left quadrant and separate it from his negative past experiences.

For example, if you are a Basal Right who wants to access the Frontal Left (but who has many negative associations with that quadrant), one of the steps you can take to free yourself from your anger is to make a list of all the ways the Frontal Lefts in your life have used their analytic skill to put you down. After you have completed that list, ritually burn it while singing "We Shall Overcome". Alternatively, you may want to do some deep feeling work around those areas of personal invalidation with a competent therapist. And as a last step, you should work on increasing your validation of yourself as a Basal Right before you begin working on developing the competency.

No one should take on developing a competency from the position that "There's something wrong with me" or "I should be different". This is a form of adaption which will ultimately result in a loss in the individual's self esteem. It may also cause the area you are seeking to develop to be permanently "colored" with resentment and negative emotions. For this reason it is a good idea to very carefully consider what motivates you so that you want to change your pattern. In terms of dominance, there is no "good", "right", or "best" pattern. It is not better to be frontal or basal, right or left brained. If you are motivated to develop competencies out of dissatisfaction with who you are, you should instead devote your energies toward developing your preferences, validating your current pattern, and building your self-esteem. Only when you have completed that task should you move on to acquiring competencies.

That sounds like where I am. I don't want to develop a competency right now. But at the same time, I know I need to be able to communicate with people who see things differently from myself. What guidelines do you have for structuring communication so that someone with a different preference can understand you?

That's an excellent question. The first thing you need to remember is that to communicate effectively with a person who has a dominance different than your own, you must be willing and able to **speak their language**. For example, if you are a double left boss who is trying to work with a double basal employee, you should do beautifully as long as you are both relating from the Basal Left. Your problems will come when you move into your Frontal Left and your employee moves into his Basal Right. To effectively communicate then, you will both need to move back into the Basal Left <u>or</u> one (or both) of you will need to "take on" the language of the other (in this case, you would take on the Basal Right or they would take on the Frontal Left).

In theory, it doesn't matter who switches to match the other. In reality, however, many people are either **unwilling** to make the effort (since they believe the other person should be the one to do it) or they are **unable** to do so (since they are unaware of the problem and ignorant of how to solve it). For this reason, if communication is important to you, we recommend that you simply assume it is "your job" and take on the task of switching modes. Spending a lot of time trying to figure out whether it's a case of unwilling or incapable probably won't accomplish much. Furthermore, as you practice talking to the different "brains" you will increase your own personal power and ability as a communicator (which won't happen for the person who simply hangs out in their preference and demands that everyone else come to him).

To help you in this process of learning to relate, read through the following **Guidelines on dealing with employees, bosses, and personal relationships**. As you do so, remember that these guidelines are for dealing with quarter brains (which make up only 25% of the population) and that you will need to blend them when dealing with more complex patterns. Also remember that the stronger an individual's lead in a given mode, the more "quarter brained" they are likely to appear and the more these guidelines should specifically apply.

GUIDELINES ON HOW TO COMMUNICATE AT WORK

WHEN YOU'RE THE BOSS:

Since Employees come in all shapes, sizes, and dominance patterns, what guidelines can you give me as a boss to help me manage each of the modes effectively?

To manage an employee with a strong Basal Left:

- Give clear, specific, and <u>detailed, step-by-step instructions for each task</u> or project. If it is a complex project, be sure to break it into sub-routines and steps and teach each of those as a separate unit. Do not be afraid of being too specific during the learning phase.

- Provide your Basal Left employee with an <u>orderly workspace</u> in which they can have "a place for everything and everything in its place." It is important that they have files and other "devices" for organizing their working materials and minimizing clutter. Do not expect them to share space with a Frontal Right.

- Remember that your Basal Left employee wants <u>approval</u> for and gets satisfaction from matching established procedures. He/she will want to know if they did the "right" thing and if what they did was what they were"supposed" to do. You will need to give them that kind of feedback.

- Basal Lefts do not know how to improvise or deviate from <u>standard procedures</u> and feel extremely uncomfortable doing so. If you want them to make "exceptions to the rule" you will have to design <u>a procedure</u> for handling it.

For example, a close friend of Anne's, who owns and operates a gardening business, came to her for advice on how to handle a problem with a Basal Left worker. It seems that this young man would do fine on all "standard" tasks but would become resistant and unhappy when asked to do "special" things for a client (and often would "forget" to do them altogether). When asked what was going on with him, he would simply say that he didn't know why anyone should get "special treatment" and that it wasn't "part of the standard procedure". In order to get him to do these tasks, his boss had to redefine and restructure his concept of what was "standard procedure". To do so, she worked up a "standard procedure" checklist for each client (which made the "extras" simply part of the standard procedure for that client instead of "extras"). She also defined a new overall standing procedure; namely, that it is "standing procedure" to check and follow the "standing procedures" for each separate client. Once she did this (and her worker had time to adjust to this new arrangement), everything went fine. He no longer had to deal with exceptions; he had a standard procedure for everything (even if those procedures varied from client to client) and he completed all the tasks.

- Basal Lefts want to work <u>regular</u> and <u>predictable hours</u> (and take their breaks and lunch at predictable times). If you ask them to deviate too much from their routine, they will become frustrated and difficult. Do not expect this employee to work much voluntary overtime unless you have and use a clear <u>procedure</u> to request it. Even then, don't push it.

- Basal Lefts work at a <u>slow</u> and <u>thorough pace</u> and will not respond well to being pressured or hurried up. They need to know what their deadlines are in advance and be able to be sure they have time to meet them. They also need to work with <u>a minimum of interruptions</u> (since interruptions break down their routines).

- Do not ask Basal Lefts to handle <u>crisis situations</u> unless there is a <u>prearranged procedure</u> for dealing with that particular crisis (these are the people who actually paid enough attention during the fire drills to know where they are supposed to go and what they are supposed to do). When managing Basal Lefts be sure to have specific procedures for all the "emergencies" they are likely to encounter and cover those procedures with them in advance.

To manage an employee with a strong Basal Right:

- Give them work which uses their <u>interpersonal expertise</u> (counseling, teaching, encouraging, nurturing). Do not expect them to be highly attentive to repetitive tasks, statistics, or work which takes analysis.

- Understand that the Basal Right needs to "<u>like</u>" the people he works with and will often stay on a job they otherwise <u>dislike</u> or are not suited for because they "like the people". Interpersonal problems on the job are a major source of stress and dysfunction for the Basal Right and should be "taken seriously" by their manager (since the Basal Right is not likely to get much productive work done until the problem is handled).

- Provide your Basal Right employee with a <u>warm and friendly work environment</u>. Harmonious colors, plants, a comfortable chair, their own coffee mug and space for personal mementoes (pictures, sentimental objects) on their desk are necessary for their sense of emotional well-being.

- The Basal Right seeks to belong and needs to feel they are a <u>part of the team.</u> Activities which encourage <u>group sharing</u> and which include everyone are important to keeping the Basal Right worker happy and productive. Basal Rights do not respond well to hierarchies or to the idea that some people are more important than others. They need to feel that they can have a <u>dialogue</u> (in which their feelings/opinions are valued/respected) with their supervisors and managers.

- You <u>can</u> get your Basal Right employee to work overtime personally asking him to do so (preferably "as a favor") and by emphasizing either how much he/she is <u>needed</u> or that it's part of being a good "team player" (which to a Basal Right means filling in when and where they're needed).

- Basal Rights rarely work for a long time at a stretch and they need to take frequent "relationship breaks" (which means that they need to stop what they're doing to chat/relate for awhile). To effectively manage a Basal Right, you will need to see these breaks as normal and natural. Trying to stop a Basal Right from taking his/her "relationship breaks" will only result in less productivity during the time when they are doing other things. Gently steering them "back to work" (without criticism) after such a break is probably the best approach.

- If you're going to manage Basal Rights you should realize that they use "feeling comfortable and connected" as their standard for evaluating the success of their day and the way their job is going. If they feel good and connected with their co-workers, "work is going well"; if they feel badly or there is a lot of stress and tension in the office (which they will notice more readily than others), "work is going badly". Thus, it is important to check in with them regularly to find out not only what they've been doing but also how they feel about it. You should take those feelings into account when adjusting their work.

- Basal Rights tend to have trouble staying on a production schedule and being punctual since they will always prefer interpersonal activities over impersonal tasks and will readily interrupt work to deal with people problems. To help them stay on task you will need to connect their timeliness or the deadlines (whatever you want them to attend to better) with its effect on other people. Most Basal Rights will try to be more timely when they can see that by doing so they make another person's life easier and by not doing so they make it more stressful.

- Basal Rights work for approval and appreciation (positive strokes, compliments, "hugs", tokens of appreciation, recognition of their contribution) rather than just for money or promotion. In fact, many Basal Rights have talked themselves out of promotions because they wanted to stay with the "people they liked". You will bring out the best in your Basal Right worker by being generous with your praise and your attention.

To manage an employee with a strong Frontal Right:

- This employee is best used in a creative, research and development or trouble shooting capacity. He will become bored quickly doing repetitive tasks (like processing forms) or working with details. He is best used in the innovation phase of any project and then moved on once the project is up and running. If you leave him with a project that has become "routine", he will begin to tinker inappropriately with the procedures and make a lot of unnecessary work for you (and everyone else).

- Whenever possible allow the Frontal Right employee to <u>work alone</u> and to <u>set his or her own hours</u>. He/she will tend to work for long periods of time and then need to take long periods of time off. Do not under any circumstances expect him to fit himself into a standard 9 to 5 schedule.

- While at work, the Frontal Right employee may appear to be <u>doing nothing</u> (as he sits staring out a window or resting his head on his typewriter). In actuality, this "daydreaming" is the Frontal Right's way of <u>incubating</u> and processing the information he is working on. As a manager, you will have to allow him his "doing nothing" (incubation) time or give him two or more projects to work on simultaneously (so he can incubate one while working on the other) if you want his brain to work the way it's designed to.

- With his passion for innovation, the Frontal Right employee spends a lot of his time trying to find ways to alter and improve work procedures (even if nobody has asked him to or is in the least bit interested). You may want to exploit this natural tendency of his and have him put his ideas in writing, turning them in to you as he writes them. Some of them are likely to be quite good.

- Provide the Frontal Right employee with a <u>large work space</u> in which there is plenty of room to stack and spatially arrange things and many surfaces available for displaying visual cues (walls, boards, shelves, and counters).

- Realize that the Frontal Right employee is terrible at meeting operational deadlines and at estimating the amount of time necessary to complete a task and adjust all his time projections accordingly. Remember that as a strong Frontal Right, his mind sees the project already done: it also neglects to notice all the steps needed to get there. Everything takes longer than he thinks (sometimes much longer).

- Frontal Rights prefer to work <u>unsupervised</u> and with as little intervention in their process as possible. The best thing you can do for them is give them a problem to solve and then leave them alone while they solve it. You may want to check in with them every once in a while to see "how it's going". When you do so, they may not tell you (because they don't exactly know how it's going). You need to remember that a great deal of Frontal Right work is "unconscious" and try not to worry.

- Frontal Rights prefer to be given instructions which leave a lot of the details open and up to their own discretion. This is the kind of person who will appreciate it if you tell them to just "Wing it" and figure it out anyway they can.

- Frontal Rights (particularly those with very little Basal Rights) tend to offend others without knowing they are doing so. As their manager, you will probably need to explain that they aren't being rude when they doodle in meetings (a moving pencil helps them to think) and they aren't being "disrespectful" when they don't follow the rules (they just don't follow rules) and they weren't "making fun of you" when they laughed inappropriately during the budget review (they were just looking at their own off- the-wall internal pictures). Don't expect the Frontal Right to handle these interpersonal disputes. His strategy will be to withdraw to avoid the conflict altogether. Besides, he isn't known for his ability articulate why he does things anyway. Of course, you could also introduce your Frontal Right to the Whole Brain thinking model, and while validating his identity and your appreciation of his creative abilities, help him to understand how his behavior affects others.

- When giving your Frontal Right employee a task or project, be sure to provide him with an overview of how the work you're giving him fits in to the whole system. He needs to see <u>The Big Picture</u> and will not be satisfied with just doing his "part" because you tell him to.

- Your Frontal Right employee may want money or special equipment for some project he is working on but don't expect him to be able to "sell" it to frontal left management. He's counting on you to do that for him. A good manager (to an Frontal Right) is one who gives him the space in which to be creative, sees he has the equipment he needs, and makes sure nobody bothers him while he's working. (When you're managing an Frontal Right it's sometimes difficult to remember exactly which one of you is "the boss" - since they certainly don't treat you that way. Try not to take it personally, they don't follow rules either.)

To manage an employee with a strong Frontal Left:

- Give directions and present information in a <u>brief, direct and logical</u> manner. Stress <u>salient facts</u> and <u>highlight key points.</u> Remember this individual is interested in knowing the bottom line, not the process you used to get there or how you feel about it.

- Provide them with a <u>functional workspace</u> in which they have access to all the tools they need to do their job. Whenever possible give them exclusive use of those tools (Frontal Lefts dislike sharing their tools with anyone else). If you don't know what such a workspace would look like, ask your employee.

- Give them specific goals to meet but allow them to decide what process to use

-    Give them specific goals to meet but allow them to decide what process to use to accomplish the goals. Don't be surprised if they delegate part of the task to someone else. They will not necessarily do all the work themselves, but they will consider themselves ultimately "responsible" for seeing the goal are met.

-    Expect them to be competitive and to jockey for position in the organizational hierarchy. Frontal Lefts believe in the "fast track" and will do whatever they can to leverage their way "up" the organization. If it looks like one of your Frontal Left employees is going to be promoted <u>over</u> you, do whatever you can to help him. By furthering their success instead of resisting it, you make it likely they'll take you with them.

-    Do not expect them to participate in "social functions" unless it increases their chances of promotion or advancement. They tend to be social only for <u>political</u> reasons.

-    Plan to give them specific <u>rewards</u> (money, promotion, increased power) for "a job well done". Frontal Lefts work to get ahead. They do not work for approval, belonging, or emotional strokes.

-    Give them work which uses their strong <u>evaluation</u> and <u>decision-making</u> skills. Do not give them work which is highly repetitive or which requires strong interpersonal skills.

-    Your Frontal Left employee values effectiveness and rationality. He will have extreme difficulty dealing with anything that looks like "incompetence", "redundancy", or "emotionality" and will probably manifest that difficulty by becoming critical and contemptuous. It is also important to remember that Frontal Lefts are generally totally oblivious to the "messages" conveyed in their non-verbals and their tone of voice. They often sound like they're giving orders and may be perceived by others as "cold, critical, and uncaring". It will probably be necessary to get the Frontal Left's co-workers to "come to terms" with him, since he is not interested in (or skilled at) working out interpersonal differences. This does not mean you let him walk on or abuse his co-workers. Only that they need to learn that his non-verbals don't mean the same things as theirs.

———

And finally, for all employees, introduce them to the whole brain model so they can learn to "work smart" as well as to value the function, style, needs and contribution of each of the other modes.

WHEN YOU'RE THE EMPLOYEE:

I've had a lot of different Bosses over the years (some of whom I got along with better than others) and I'm beginning to think that many of my problems with them had something to do with brain dominance. Will you give me some tips for dealing with each of the different dominances?

How well we get along with a particular boss largely depends on **6 distinct factors**:
- our own dominance pattern (strengths and weaknesses),
- our boss's dominance pattern (strengths and weaknesses),
- how well our pattern matches the job we are being asked to do,
- how well our boss's pattern matches the job he or she has to do,
- our own level of emotional maturity,
- our boss' level of emotional maturity.

All these factors need to be taken into consideration when trying to understand the dynamic relationship between boss and employee. Obviously, it is important for you to know your own pattern and to see how well it matches your job. It is also important for you to consider your boss's pattern not only in relationship to your own but in relationship to his job as manager/supervisor. If there is a poor fit between his job and his pattern, he may be frustrated or angry and as such he will be more likely to procrastinate (or avoid altogether) many of the tasks you need him to do as your manager.

What we want in a manager largely depends on who we are and what we expect. Before we go into the specifics of dealing with each of the different brains as bosses, take a minute to look at how some other people defined their "best" and "worst" managers.

In the first example, Paul, an engineer working for a large international oil company with a quarter brain Frontal Left pattern (shown in black), considers his best manager (solid line) a quarter brain Frontal Left like himself, and his worst manager (dotted line) a quarter brain Basal Right. When asked why the Frontal Left manager was the best his response was: "He was like myself, logical and methodical. He liked numbers and he left me alone." When asked why the Basal Right manager was the worst, Paul's response was that "He wasn't interested in numbers".

Paul
Paul's Best Manager

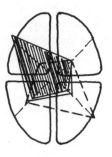

Paul's
Worst Manager

AN ENGINEER, HIS BEST AND HIS WORST MANAGER

Another example shows how differently employees identify what they need in a good manager. Jill, a double right works in Marketing. Her best manager was a Triple Translator (double left and Frontal Right) who was best because, as she put it, "He had more of my semi-strengths. We complemented each other." In contrast, her worst manager was a quarter brained Frontal Right. Her explanation of this was that "He offered less than I did in all three areas. He was very creative, but that didn't wash in a work environment".

Jill's Best Manager

Jill's Worst Manager

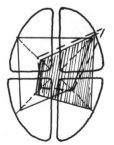

Jill

A MARKETING SPECIALIST, HER BEST AND HER WORST MANAGER

Our final example illustrates how we can dislike a manager even if we both share the same lead function. For George, a Double Left, his worst manager was a quarter brained Frontal Left (even though that was George's own lead mode). His explanation: "He was difficult to work with, very financial and detailed and constantly checking. He refused to listen and he had the interpersonal skills of a rock---not even a pet rock."

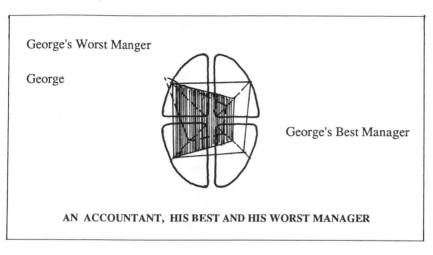

George's Worst Manger

George

George's Best Manager

AN ACCOUNTANT, HIS BEST AND HIS WORST MANAGER

For George, his best manager was Whole Brained. In describing this manager, George told us, "He was a combination of a lot of things. He also had an ability to operate in all areas."

As you can see, everyone has a way they prefer to be managed, and it is <u>not necessarily by a boss with a matching brain profile</u>. Before you go any further, you may want to think about how you like to be managed and what you expect from a boss. As well, if you are or have been a manager, think about how you like to manage others. Then compare your personal preferences with the information that follows on how each of the different "brains" likes to manage.

These charts on "Getting Along with Your Boss," cover each of the four modes in two different ways: first, by giving you an **overview of that particular type** of boss and then by giving you some **guidelines for dealing with them.**

Please remember that these are quarter brain descriptions and must be blended for the more complex patterns. Also, remember that **a boss's area of weakness will be almost as important as his area of strength.** A double left with an avoidance in the Basal Right and a double left able to used the Basal Right at will may manage very differently indeed.

GETTING ALONG WITH YOUR BOSS

THE BASAL LEFT BOSS

General Characteristics of the Basal Left Boss:

- Most highly values <u>consistency, loyalty and reliability</u> in an employee.
- Actively dislikes change and resists innovation. He prefers to stick with the established procedures and "the way things are done around here".
- Expects staff to be punctual.
- Expects staff to meet all deadlines.
- Expects you to be familiar with the procedures manual, the dress code, & "the rules" and to follow them.
- Takes a long time to make a decision and generally makes his decisions based on precedent (Has this been done before? What happened then? Who else has already done this? etc.)
- Is most amenable to answering informational questions ("how-to's") or explaining procedures.
- Has difficulty understanding functions such as Research and Development and Organizational Development.
- Expects workers to stay on schedule and complete all their tasks in a neat and orderly manner.
- Is poor at handling crisis, doing troubleshooting, or revising procedures that no longer work.
- Evaluates his personnel using a standard form and by checking to see if they have completed all their assigned tasks in a thorough and timely manner.

Guidelines for getting along with the Basal Left Boss:

- Be punctual. Be neat. Be "appropriate".
- When you have something to discuss, schedule a formal meeting.
- Whenever possible, send a memo and an agenda in advance of your meeting or presentation.
- Talk slowly.
- Use words carefully.
- Emphasize security, guarantees, safe-keeping, and ways to limit risk.
- When using audio-visual aids in making a presentation: show a lengthy, step-by-step action plan which indicates who will be affected and how they will

be affected by this change or project.

- When making a project proposal, provide lists of other companies who have done similar work or used a comparable system. List all the research which backs up your proposal (a lengthy bibliography) and the names and positions of those who support this type of work, system, or approach. Come up with as much supportive and historical documentation as possible.
- Play by the rules. You may think a dress code is ridiculous; your boss probably doesn't.
- Don't hurry him through decision making. He needs time to review all the historical data before he will be willing to decide.
- Going through "correct channels" is very important to Basal Lefts. Find out the "correct procedure" for asking for a raise, getting time off, making a complaint and do it that way first. (Many people don't get what they want from Basal Lefts because they don't approach them the "right way".)
- Pay attention to details. When you work for this person, how you do something (and in what order) matters as much as the final result.

THE BASAL RIGHT BOSS

General Characteristics of the Basal Right Boss:

- Uses the consensus method for decision making and will need to know how everyone feels about it before proceeding further.
- Actively avoids making unpleasant or unpopular decisions (which is why many Basal Right managers are known as "country club" managers)
- Has difficulty requesting or creating schedules.
- Is supportive of "personal growth" and activities which improve employee morale or develop their skill at "team building".
- Resists the notions of hierarchy and authority. Wants everyone to be "part of the team" and wants the department to be "one big happy family".
- Puts people's needs ahead of production schedules, often making exceptions to the rule.
- Will be supportive of your need for personal time and understand that your moods can effect your job performance.
- Expects personal loyalty and has personal relationships with their staff.
- Is not particularly effective lobbying for change or money.
- May play favorites on the basis of who he or she likes best.
- Is highly sensitive to interpersonal conflict. Will try to resolve it and, if that is unsuccessful, suppress it.
- Evaluates personnel by how well they "fit in", how enthusiastically they participate, and whether or not they have a good "attitude".

Guidelines for getting along with the Basal Right Boss:

- "Get to know them" before doing anything else.
- Listen to and reflect their feelings back to them.
- Respond to their feelings and the feelings of others (You must always remember to address the feeling concerns. With a Basal Right, feelings are actually more important than "the facts".)
- Talk in terms of "WE".
- Use symbolic metaphors, especially ones which deal with life-cycles, family, and spiritual truths (i.e. birth, seeds, parenting).
- Talk in terms of the contribution you, this project or the department can make.
- Express your concern for others and your desire to be of help/service to them.
- Present ideas and make requests in personal, informal conversations.
- When using audio-visuals in a presentation: make them up as you go along, use pictures (especially of people smiling), and avoid references to numbers, percentages, or money.
- When doing handouts, use color (especially rose, light blue, light yellow, light green, or pink). If you include a bibliography, be sure to include some information on the people (who they are, where they are, etc.)
- To sell them on an idea, show them how they can use it to build morale, facilitate "personal growth" or help others.
- When you want something, ask for their help in getting it.
- Relate personally. Take the time to build rapport.
- Be social and participate fully in group processes and events (potlucks, retirement and birthday celebrations).
- Be enthusiastic.
- Use plenty of eye contact.
- Be physically expressive. Use touch to "make your point" or establish connection (if the situation permits it).

THE FRONTAL RIGHT BOSS

General Characteristics of the Frontal Right Boss:

- Wants his/her employees to supervise themselves
- Prefers to give his staff an overview (the "big picture") and have them take care of filling in and handling the details.
- Make his decisions intuitively and becomes confused when asked to justify the decision logically.
- Often uses metaphors to describe what he wants to accomplish or how he wants someone to act.
- Likes innovation, novelty, & ideas that are on the "cutting edge"

- Is far more interested in concepts than in things or people.
- Actively avoids conflict and will not get involved in personality problems or interpersonal disputes. Will give the impression of being oblivious to what's going on. Telling him what's going on will not change the situation in the least (he'll still refuse to get involved).
- Often changes things (procedures, the office layout) just for the sake of novelty.
- Actively dislikes paperwork and may be chronically late in getting it completed even when it has to do with promotion or his own budget.
- May be extremely vague when giving directions or explaining what he wants. He sees his own internal pictures but tends to forget <u>his staff can't see them.</u>
- Will have difficulty lobbying with Frontal management for budget, equipment, extra staff even when he is extremely excited about a project.
- Hates doing personnel evaluation (he dislikes both the form and the procedure) so you may not know where you stand with him (or the job) for months on end. When he gets around to it he usually evaluates by considering whether or not the person has interesting ideas and makes a creative contribution to the department.

Guidelines for getting along with the Frontal Right Boss:

- If you are not a strong Frontal Left yourself, find a strong Frontal Left to help your boss lobby for your project with management.
- Handle all personnel disputes yourself.
- Communicate ideas in informal, personal conversations (don't expect him to sit through meetings).
- Talk more rapidly than you usually do.
- Show how your ideas relate to the "cutting edge", the "latest research", etc.
- Create word pictures when presenting information to him (remember this is a highly <u>spatial, visual, pattern sensitive</u> mode).
- Show how your idea parallels theories in other, non-related fields.
- Use words and phrases like: vision, perspective, the "big picture".
- Use humor and play with ideas.
- When trying to present a concept, use metaphors. A few examples are:

concept	metaphor
value of diversity	most card games use more than one suit
people united by shared values	aligned, they're stronger even magnetic
people acting without questioning	lemmings

- Do use audio-visuals for a presentation: draw pictures emphasizing symbols and shapes (circles, spirals, squares, wings, pyramids, wheels...), draw on a flip chart as you talk , or on a napkin or scrap of paper.

- Encourage your Frontal Right boss to doodle or draw with you as you talk.
- In preparing handouts, cite references to connecting concepts and ideas, list book titles (with authors' names) that relate and may be of interest.
- Be prepared to handle all the details yourself and paperwork for proposals yourself. Your Frontal Right boss just wants the overview. If you need something signed, hand carry it in to your boss and watch while he signs it. He may have a visual filing system but it's only for papers he considers important and your forms probably won't be important to him. Under no circumstances should you just "leave" the papers on his desk.
- Don't move his stacks or "clean up" his workspace. You will destroy his whole "filing system" and he'll hate you forever.
- Be amused. It will endear you to your boss & it's better than the alternative.

THE FRONTAL LEFT BOSS

General Characteristics of the Frontal Left Boss:

- Most highly values effectiveness and productivity.
- Likes making decisions and tends to do so quickly.
- Makes decisions on the basis of "the effect such a change would have on the entire system" or by using a cost-benefit analysis.
- Is results oriented. Evaluates "success" by the bottom line.
- Is goal oriented
- Is interested in moving up the organizational ladder.
- Tends to delegate well and often.
- Likes being on top of a hierarchy.
- Will probably be possessive of his territory and/or authority.
- Dislikes handling personal or personnel problems.
- Uses his employees' and division's performance as a way of moving ahead personally.
- Respects a competent "arguer" and a strategic negotiator
- Expects his workers to make logical presentations when they present information or ask questions.
- Tends to "give orders" rather than "make requests".
- Is often perceived as cold, critical, and uncaring due to his lack of awareness of his own non-verbal signals and his tone of voice.
- Prefers to have information presented in a concise manner with the key points expressed in ratios or percentages and emphasized by the use of "bullets".
- Evaluates his personnel by: cost-benefit, their personal effectiveness, their productivity, and their promise/potential for long-term gain to him and the organization.

Guidelines for dealing with the Frontal Left Boss:

- Be brief. Know what you're going to say before you say it. Stress the <u>key points</u> and provide half-page written summaries when possible.
- Learn to do "critical analysis" and present material in that form.
- Use precise numbers (42.5), percentages (15%), and dollar amounts ($150,000) whenever possible.
- Cite recent research when making your case for a project.
- To score points, show how the policy or product you are endorsing will give the organization or a key person "leverage".
- Prepare handouts which are: precise, concise, in black and white.
- When using audio-visual aids in making a presentation: use pre-prepared charts showing bottom line numbers or numerical research, restrict data to the key points, use straight lines and angles, use black and white, and make sure the charts and diagrams are <u>precisely</u> drawn. You should also check to be sure that the <u>technical</u> aspects of your presentation come off without a hitch.
- When requesting something, be specific & state logically its functional value.
- Don't take his tone of voice or his "order giving" personally.
- Realize he actively dislikes "incompetence", "inefficiency", "redundancy" and "emotionality". Don't waste his time and don't let him catch you wasting yours. Also keep your personal life out of the workplace.

———

I've read through the information on how to relate to my boss and my employees and I understand that it can be generalized to non-work situations. Still, I would like some additional information on what to expect from and how to cope with each of the modes on a personal basis. Are there any "tips" you can give me?

There are **five general tips** which we suggest you consider when dealing with someone **at home** whose preference pattern differs from your own. As well, we have created quadrant-specific guidelines similar to those provided for your work life, but specifically geared to one's domestic and social life.

First, the tips:

Tip #1: Remember that variety is the spice of life and that even though we are all created equal, we are not all the same. Learn to **appreciate the differences** between yourself and others as not merely amusing, but necessary. And, give up any ideas you have that your way of doing things is the only way or the "right" way. Your preferred way is just one of the ways.

Tip #2:   Be **patient** with yourself and others. Relating is hard work and you're not going to do it perfectly (no matter how much you know).

Tip #3:   **Practice**, practice, practice. Then practice some more.

Tip #4:   Realize that disappointment usually comes when we expect a particular behavior and get another behavior instead. It is important to **learn not to expect** an Frontal Left to behave like a Basal Right (and vice versa).

Tip #5:   Have **fun** reading through these guidelines and associating them with the people you know. Just because this is important doesn't mean it has to be serious.

Now, with these tips in mind, consider using the following guidelines in your personal or home life.

GUIDELINES ON HOW TO COMMUNICATE AT HOME

About the Basal Lefts in your life:

-    Basal Lefts prefer to plan and schedule activities and outings in advance. If you are dating a Basal Left, he or she will be happiest if your "date"always falls on the same day of the week so they can predict what will "happen" on that day and plan for it. On the other hand, Basal Lefts dislike surprises and resist doing anything "spontaneously" or on "the spur of the moment". They will often decline to go on an outing (which might have   been fun) because they didn't "plan" for it or know about it far enough in advance.

-    Basal Lefts prefer to have <u>every day filled and scheduled</u> so they can predict what will happen and build routines around it. So, arranging to meet a friend who has a strong Basal Left can   sometimes be difficult because they have no "free time" (Wednesday is my dance lesson, Thursday I have to clean my house, Friday I do my grocery shopping, and so forth). Furthermore,they won't feel comfortable deviating from their routine in order to "fit you in".

-    Basal Lefts value consistency and predictability in their friends. If you want to get along with a Basal Left, you'd better do exactly what you said you would exactly when you said you'd do it. You'd also better be on time (for everything).

-    Basal Lefts usually have and stay on a budget. Don't expect them to be comfortable deviating from that budget even if something is a "good buy" or a "wonderful opportunity" (unless they have a procedure for handling such a situation). They like to plan their spending, keep their checkbook balanced, and know   where their money goes (down to the last penny).

-    Basal Lefts value tradition and the way things have been done in the past. Your Basal Left will probably want to observe the same holidays every year in exactly the same way (and eating exactly the same food). A friend of Anne's discovered this fact (to her great dismay) when she tried to introduce a new way of preparing green beans into the Thanksgiving dinner. Her Basal Left husband became extremely upset by this alteration and promptly explained to her at length that "this is NOT the way green beans are prepared." If you're trying to change a Basal   Left's habits or routines, do so gradually and be prepared for resistance and some emotional upset along the way.

-    Basal Lefts often have difficulty making friends so they often get involved in structured group activities, like dance classes or bridge clubs, that have the social element built in. If you want to meet a Basal Left, those are good ways to do so.

-    If you're going to live with a Basal Left (as a lover or a roommate you would better learn to be neat, orderly and regular in your routines. Basal Lefts have a "place for everything" (and they want everything in its place). They also tend to have "right" ways for doing just about everything and they adhere to them faithfully. For many Basal Lefts, there is one and only one way to bake a cake, make a bed, decorate a Christmas tree, clean a bathtub, etc. and if you don't do it their way, you're wrong. If you need to live in a less structured way, try arranging it so you each have **private space** and that should make it easier to keep the **communal space** "his way." Alternatively, you can try a scheduled rotation of how the space is going to be kept; 1 month in your companion's Basal Left way 1 month in your way.

-    Since Basal Lefts need to build everything into habitual patterns and they are anxious about change and the unknown, they tend to date for a long time before they marry. If the Basal Left in your life is taking a long time to pop the question, it's probably because he's not "used" to you yet. Be patient and emphasize the ways being married is going to be just like what you're already doing.

-    For a Basal Left, half the fun of going on a vacation is planning it in advance. When they sit down and work out a detailed,   step-by-step itinerary of where they're going and what they're going to see (preferably minute by minute) what they're doing is loading their routine. Next, during the weeks (or months) before they leave,they get the pleasure of anticipating the successful execution of that routine. And finally, on the vacation, they have the pleasure of actually running their pre-loaded routine (and the closer they are to being perfectly on schedule the happier they are. Basal Lefts like planned, scheduled, and organized vacations; they like packaged tours, they like using guidebooks, and they like going all the way through the museum or the chateau (or whatever they happen to be touring), making sure they see what they are "supposed" to see. Those who prefer a more spontaneous approach should vacation with someone else.

About the Basal Rights in your life:

- Basal Rights like to have "favorites" - their favorite food, favorite song, favorite color, favorite restaurant, etc. - and they will probably want to know what your favorites are (so they can give them to you). If you are not the kind of person who has "favorites", it will probably suffice to give them a list of things you "really like" (but don't be surprised if they ask you which of those things you like most).

-    The Basal Rights in your life will want to share and process feelings. Consequently, they will always want to know more than just "what happened"; they will also want to know how you feel about what happened and what it means to you. Then they will want to tell you how they feel about it and what it means and so forth. Conversations which only give information are not considered "real talking" by Basal Rights.

-    Basal Rights are sentimental about holidays and anniversaries and they expect to observe and celebrate them. (Forgetting a Basal Right's birthday is practically a mortal sin). If you're trying to come up with a present to give them, remember that it doesn't have to be large or costly but it does have to be personal, something that "reminds you of them". You can also them give flowers since most Basal Rights are extremely fond of them and like to have them around.

-    One of the things that often amazes non-Basal Rights is the sheer number of friends, acquaintances, and "people to relate to" many Basal Rights have in their life. What amazes them even more is how much of their time Basal Rights devote to "staying in touch", whether chatting on the phone or by sending cards and writing notes. If you're going to be in a relationship with a Basal Right you better get used to all the people and not feel jealous because you don't get all of their attention.

- Remember that Basal Rights value touch and are therefore likely to want to give and receive lots of hugs. Hug them often (and not just in a sexual context).

- Basal Rights prefer to live in a warm, cozy and harmonious environment, usually filled with plants, sentimental objects (pinecones, shells, a dried corsage), and pictures of places they've been or people they love. They need to have their "things" around them - it's what makes it feel like "home".

- For a Basal Right, a vacation is an opportunity to visit friends or family or to have the time to "re-connect" with significant others. Once again, people are the primary focus rather than places or activities.

- Many Basal Rights are hyper-sensitive to tone of voice and nonverbals.Since their brain monitors for dis-harmony, they tend to interpret any movement to increase the physical distance between you and them as a kind of rejection and any sharp, curt, or abrupt tone of voice as criticism. Remember, with Basal Rights, how you say something is probably more important than what you actually say.

- Basal Rights tend to spend money impulsively and emotionally, particularly when they are buying things for other people. Don't expect them to manage their money (or even to be clear where it went).

- Basal Rights value homemade gifts and are likely to give presents they have made themselves (a pie they baked, a sweater they knitted). They also like to do "potluck dinners" because, at a potluck, everyone gets to contribute something they've made. If you want to be disapproved of by a Basal Right, bring "store bought" stuff to a potluck. (Obviously your life must be terribly out of balance for you to need to do such a thing.)

- Basal Rights who have children may bring them along to social events whether or not it is appropriate for the children to be there. They seem to do this because they are more worried about leaving their children in someone else's care (who may not treat them as the Basal Right wants them to be treated) than they are about inconveniencing others by the children's presence.

- Lastly, many Basal Rights want to believe that it is possible for people to get along all of the time. This notion causes them a lot of disappointment and tends to lead to rather unrealistic expectations about their own and other people's behavior. Not "liking" someone (or not being liked) is hard on a Basal Right and is likely to upset them emotionally.

About the Frontal Rights in your life:

- Frontal Rights <u>don't attend (graciously) to mundane details</u> like paying bills or remembering to buy groceries. For many Frontal Rights, these things only come to mind at the last minute and so they often have to scurry around trying to get the "problem" handled. If you're in a relationship with a strong Frontal Right and having bills paid on time is important to you, you probably better plan on handling them yourself. Alternatively, you can try putting up signs all over the house that say "Pay the Bills!!!" This will probably get them to pay them (but it still won't make it matter to them).

- Frontal Rights avoid conflict in relationships and tend to handle it by <u>withdrawing physically and emotionally</u>. They also tend to actively resist wanting to "talk about it" (unless they have a strong Basal Right as well). If they are going to express hostility, they are most likely to do so through passive aggressive acts. If you push an Frontal Right long enough, his strategy of withdrawal and avoidance will ultimately break   down. At that time he will go into one of his back-up modes (Frontal Left, Basal Left or Basal Right) and do his fighting from there, which can surprise you if you aren't prepared.

- When an Frontal Right becomes preoccupied with a creative problem his environment tends to become messy, cluttered and completely disorganized. Then, all of a sudden his spatial sensitivity will kick in and he will rush about straightening   things and restoring visual order. You should not confuse this Frontal Right penchant for visually pleasing space with a desire to keep a clean house (they're not into cleaning). You must also learn not to move their stacks or try to clean up their mess when they're working on something. Those stacks are part of their thinking process and need to stay where they put them until they're done working.

- Frontal Rights like to do things spontaneously; they like "impromptu", "spur of the moment" activities and outings and their favorite approach to a trip is just to "pick up and go". They want their friends to take as much pleasure in this approach as they do and will be hurt if you don't want to drop everything and pursue this new idea they have.

- Because play, entertainment and humor are important to them, they are likely to eliminate anyone who is boring from their circle of acquaintances. Although this may not seem like a good reason to "cut" someone, for a Frontal Right, not being interesting is a serious character defect.

- Many Frontal Rights tend to resist formal commitments and may date or even live with someone for years without taking steps to more specifically (or legally) define the relationship. They may also date a number of people simultaneously without feeling any conflict about doing so. One very Frontal Right research and development engineer of our acquaintance found that when he first started to date someone and that relationship was in the innovation phase he wanted to spend quite a lot of time "working on that project". Once the relationship was established and had become more routine, although he was still interested in continuing to relate, he would tend to pull back and find another "project" to give his attention to. This was very hard for his partners to handle, since they interpreted his shift of attention as rejection. In actuality, he was just behaving like a typical Frontal Right "innovation" junkie.

- Frontal Rights like to be alone and tend to require lots of physical and emotional space. They need the time to think their own thoughts and look at their internal pictures, especially when they are working on a project. At such times, give them a wide berth.

- Frontal Rights don't like to spend too much time doing any one activity. For them, variety is the spice of life and a little of something goes a long way. Expect them to need to get up and move around after they've been talking for awhile. Expect them to want to vary their activities. And expect them to always have more than one book going at the same time. Don't necessarily expect them to finish any of these things.

- Frontal Rights see vacations as opportunities to explore and adventure. They may go white water rafting or off to explore some culture that intrigues them. In either case they will do the minimum amount of planning necessary to get them there. While on vacation they will want to keep their days open and unscheduled so they can go off in any direction that intrigues them. They should never vacation with a Basal Left.

- Frontal Rights spend money impulsively and may not necessarily know where it went. They manage money by a kind of gestalt "awareness" of "about" how much they have and "about" how much they owe and "about" how much is coming in. Unlike Basal Rights who tend to spend lots of money on others, Frontal Rights tend to spend money on other people only when they are actually with them and they are feeling good about the themselves and the interaction. The key phrases for their style of gift giving are spontaneous and unplanned.

- When dealing with a Frontal Left you need to remember that feelings are not something they want to deal with. So, don't expect them to "pay attention" to your feelings. (They won't.)   Don't expect them to notice their own feelings. (They won't). And don't expect them to willingly spend any of their time "sharing" feelings, "processing" feelings, or "relating on a feeling level". (They won't). Also remember that Frontal Lefts actively dislike emotional scenes and will go out of their way to avoid them. So, if you're thinking of throwing a fit or telling them how you "really" feel (in order to clear the air or convince them to do something), give it up. It will only convince them that you are someone to be avoided.

-     Frontal Lefts see vacations as a time to unwind, relax, be alone, or do nothing. Going fishing is a perfect Frontal Left vacation activity. If you require more fun, socializing, excitement, or variety, you probably should not vacation with a Frontal Left.

-     Frontal Lefts tend to be workaholics and may only participate in social activities that somehow advance their careers. To get them to go to social functions you will have to demonstrate how doing so will help them get ahead. Telling them that "It'll be fun!" is not a recommended strategy.

-     Frontal Lefts tend to decide that they are ready to marry (and then very systematically go about finding a partner). They also tend to choose their partners for functional reasons, based on   their assessment that the person they have selected will handle certain tasks well (like, raising the children) or fulfill certain roles (being a hostess). Romantic "love" is not a necessary prerequisite. Please remember that when an Frontal Left marries he is not doing so in order to have someone "to share his deepest feelings with". It is more likely that he is marrying in order to have someone to handle all the feeling functions so he won't ever have to be bothered with them.

-     Frontal Lefts see their homes as private places where they can have peace and quiet and relax and unwind. They do not necessarily see them as "places to relate". Many a Frontal Left   husband prefers his evening paper to a friendly "chat" with his wife. If you're going to be married to a Frontal Left, you're going to need to remember he doesn't particularly like to talk. Leave him alone, he's not intentionally rejecting you.

-     Frontal Lefts want to be the prime decision makers and have control of the major purchasing decisions for the household. They also tend to delegate certain "areas" of responsibility to their partner (like managing the grocery budget, making the food buying decisions). The areas they delegate tend to be either things they don't want to handle (like dealing with social situations) or things they consider too "unimportant" for them to waste their time on (remember the 80/20 rule).

-   When subjected to chronic stress Frontal Lefts often have "Vesuvius tempers" (which means they unexpectedly "blow up") since they don't vent their feelings easily or on a regular basis. When this happens, the best thing to do is notice the anger but don't react to it. The Frontal Left is frightened that his anger will be dangerous and destructive. If you attend to it without reaction, it will pass more quickly and will probably soon be forgotten. (note: this pattern actually occurs due to a weakness in the Basal Right, and as such may occur as well in strong Frontal Rights and occasionally Basal Lefts.)

-   Remember Frontal Lefts "argue' and play "devil's advocate" for the pleasure it gives them (and because it sharpens their analytic brain). Try not to take it personally if they are curt and abrupt and don't get your feelings hurt because they are "badgering" you or "ordering" you about. They don't do it to hurt other's feelings. They are just oblivious to the effect it has on other people's feelings.

-   Frontal Lefts want to live in a functional environment. They want their tools and appliances to be well maintained and in good working order and, if they have time, will gladly do home improvements and repairs. They also like to spend their time "tinkering" around in their workshops. If you want to have someone help you fix your plumbing, ask a Frontal Left.

-   Frontal Lefts tend to buy quality products using the rationale that when you amortize their cost over time they are the best value for the money. Since Frontal Lefts are so critical of "poor workmanship," they tend to inspect the things they buy carefully and at length. Let them buy their own tools, clothes, etc unless you are absolutely certain you know exactly what they want.

-   Lastly, Frontal Lefts tend to become unreasonably annoyed at anyone who "wastes resources." They expect you to turn off the lights when leaving a room. They expect you to regularly attend to the maintenance of your automobile so that it performs well and lasts as long as it should. They are appalled if they think you are wasting your money or are doing a poor job of managing it. These may not seem like "big deals" to you, but they are to a Frontal Left and you can expect to be criticized when you "fail to act responsibly" in these areas.

In the preceding pages, we have detailed two tools which you can use to enhance your ability to survive over time. These tools are: the **Four Step Competency Development Plan** to be used to strengthen your nonpreferred modes and the **Guidelines on How to Communicate** to be used at work and at home to insure the effectiveness and success of your efforts to communicate with those around you whose preference patterns differ from your own. Because of its detailed and specific nature, you may have found yourself skimming over much of this chapter. Indeed, it contains too much information for most people. Nonetheless, it is excellent reference material. When you have a specific problem at work or at home, turn to the appropriate set of guidelines and read the relevant material to see what light its contents shed on your problem.

Moreover, keep in mind that these guidelines for competency development and communication are for situations in which the second Rule of Thumb for long term success and survival applies. To be happy and healthy you will need to continually seek a **balance** between these long term strategies and your personal needs for immediate success and satisfaction--as achieved by the first Rule of Thumb through the validation and use of your natural strengths. Keeping in mind this need for balance, we can begin to develop a vision of how and where the growing understanding and use of models such as this will affect our future.

CHAPTER 9
MANAGING PREFERENCES TO MAXIMIZE EFFECTIVENESS

There are two basis approaches to managing our preferences - each of which can contribute significantly to enhance our personal effectiveness. Both are discussed below. Maximum benefits come from using the two approaches in combination.

LEVERAGING YOUR STRENGTHS

From the perspective of brain dominance know thy self and to thine own self be true can be translated as: leverage your natural strengths. The best and surest way to do this is to energize or "charge" yourself by starting each day over center using your natural lead, in a context that suits your extraversion/introversion.[1]

---

[1] Physiologically, extraversion equates with a low internal level of arousal that drives a person to seek stimulation so they will wake up enough to enjoy life. Introversion equates with a high internal level of arousal that causes them to function best in quieter environments. To learn more about how our arousal level affects our lives, listen to KBA's audio taped series on Increasing High Performance [To identify your natural arousal level (i.e. your extraversion/introversion)] take the BTSA and read your own Feedback.

Not surprisingly, different people need to engage in very different, highly specific activities to insure this self-charging.

- A person with a natural preference in the Basal Left mode will be energized by attending to something that allows him to think/act in a proceduralized manner sequencing, organizing things that lend themselves to being sequenced; or by using well organized materials.
- A person with a natural preference in the Basal Right mode will be energized by attending to something that allows him to focus on the presence or absence of harmony and act to maximize the harmony between people and voices, instruments, colors in the environment.
- A person with a natural preference in the Frontal Right mode will be energized by attending to something that allows him to use his visual-spatial imagination in combination with metaphoric thinking to be creative; generate a positive vision for the future; invent a new solution, strategy or product.
- A person with a natural preference in the Frontal Left mode will be energized by attending to something that allows him to use his logical skills to evaluate and prioritize options; or make decisions concerning complex but known problems.
- Highly extraverted person's will be energized by doing an over center task in a noisy, crowded, fast paced or competitive environment.
- Highly introverted person's will be energized by doing an over center task in a quiet, out of the way, or slower environment with fewer distractions.

Significantly, individuals and teams who start their day over center, using their natural preference for at least an hour, report their whole day goes better. There is no doubt about it, starting each day with activities that use our natural lead makes a critical difference in the quality of our life.

For best results structure your time so that for the first 1 to 2 hours each day or work period you do only those tasks which allow you to use your gifts in a context suited to your arousal level, without interruptions.

MANAGING YOUR WEAKNESSES

Our only completely natural strength is in our area of preference. All other modes are relative weaknesses, even if we have developed significant competencies in applying them. This is most true of our greatest natural weakness - the mode diagonally opposite our natural preference. Regardless of how much we develop a mode if it is not a natural preference it does not enjoy the same natural energetic advantages.

For this reason, consciously managing when and how we attend to people and tasks that engage our weaker modes is important. Fortunately, six strategies have been shown to be highly effective when managing tasks or persons that draw heavily on a non-preferred mode of thinking. Not all are equally appropriate or even possible in a given situation. However, taken together as a set of tools, they provide us with an empowering alternative to being frustrated and exhausted; and/or doing a less than an optimal job. Significantly, these six strategies fall into two very different categories or approaches: redesigning the task or job and requesting help. Some of you may be more comfortable with one approach than the other. However, to optimize your options and effectiveness, we suggest you read and become familiar with both approaches.

REDESIGNING TASKS

Generally speaking there are two types of redesign possible: <u>formal</u> and <u>informal</u>. When your evaluation has revealed that the fit between your preferences and the tasks you are expected to perform is poor, it is often a good idea to consider a <u>formal</u> redesign such as a job or career change.

The technical wizard (Introverted Double Frontal) who finds he has been promoted into administration (a Double Left job) as a reward for being an excellent researcher may well determine that he wishes to request a demotion back to research. The entrepreneur (extraverted Frontal Right) whose company has been successful may find she is doing more administrative and operational work (Basal Left and Double Left) to keep pace with the demand for her product and decide to restructure or sell out in order to be "free to pursue new interests" compatible with her Frontal Right lead. The Basal Right Nurse who entered nursing to help people and has moved up the career ladder to a supervisory position (Double Left) may request a demotion to staff nursing or switch to a career in Human Resources or Public Relations.

When the degree of fit is moderate or better, the necessary redesigning may be accomplished through one or more <u>less formal</u> means. These strategies, along with the four for requesting help are the strategies we recommend people use to manage their weaknesses on a day in-day out basis.

When you have a degree of competency in the required non-preferred task, such informal redesigning may be accomplished by **Sandwiching** the task which uses your non-preferred competency between two tasks each of which draw upon your true preferences.

The power of this highly effective approach is based on energy management. Using your natural preferences energizes you. Using your non-preferred, developed competencies exhausts or fatigues you. Assuming your system begins the day in neutral, by first doing something you prefer, you energize the system. By using a nonpreference immediately afterwards, when the system is "charged" you will tend to experience the fatigue or drain as simply taking you back to neutral. If you follow this step with a naturally preferred task, you will again move "up" -- to a positively charged position.

By contrast, engaging in non-preferred tasks randomly, without charging the system before and after, can result in much of the day being spent between a "down" or negatively charged position and neutral. Indeed, this conscious ordering of tasks allows you to conserve a valuable resource -- you.

Strategies for Managing Your Weaknesses
First, Accept Your Weakness, then **Redesign the Task** 1   sandwich it between two strengths 2   schedule it at a peak energy time **Request Help** 3   select and use a modal mentor 4   trade the task to a modal expert 5   delegate the task to a modal expert 6   hire a modal expert

Another informal strategy involves conscious **Scheduling**. Two effective Scheduling techniques are:

- Scheduling the non-preferred tasks at times of the day when you are generally, naturally "up"; and
- Never scheduling important non-preferred tasks at times of the day when you are generally "low";

Other informal techniques that you can implement alone; without help from another person include:

- Remind yourself just before starting the task that it is something you don't prefer, but are <u>choosing</u> to do as part of a total package for which you have accepted responsibility;

- Do a deep breathing exercise immediately prior to doing the non-preferred task in order to energize your brain.

When the above techniques are inappropriate or insufficient, your best step is to request help.

REQUESTING HELP

Requesting help is generally the best solution when the task or person requires you to:

- use your greatest weakness (e.g. your achilles heel); or
- perform in a context in which doesn't suit your arousal level is challenged.

Moreover, requesting and using help is not something to be ashamed of. Most jobs, especially problem-solving or management jobs, are whole brained. To do them completely or well, one needs to use every mode, which we now understand, means use 4 different persons with complimentary preferences. For this reason, highly successful companies today formally sanction executives and employees helping each other through team leadership, self-managing teams, and whole-brain team building.

Generally speaking, there are four ways to enlist the help you need:

- you can find a **mentor** whose natural strengths, extraversion or introversion match the task facing you;
- you can **trade** the task to a co-worker whose natural strengths, extraversion or introversion match the task facing you;

or, <u>if you are a manager or supervisor,</u>

- you can **delegate** the task to someone who already works for you and whose natural preferences and arousal level include those required; or
- you can **hire a new employee** whose preferential pattern includes the mode or arousal level in which you need help.

One advantage of using a <u>mentor</u> is that, with their help, you may develop a reasonable degree of competency and thereby become more self-sufficient. The disadvantage of using a mentor is that for some time you will need to devote more, rather than less, time to your non-preferred mode, listening to and observing your mentor in action as well as practicing your new non-preferred language and skills.

By contrast, <u>trading</u>, <u>delegating</u>, and <u>hiring an expert</u> to do your non-preferred tasks, frees your time and energy to do what you do best.

When deciding which strategy to use, consider both the immediate and long term implications of each option. Generally speaking, if the task required is "generic", one which you will need and can use to your advantage almost everywhere, such as negotiation, you may want to use a mentor so that you can learn to do it for yourself and have it in your personal "tool kit". If the task is less generic then it may well be wiser to trade or delegate it to an existing staff person with the appropriate preference/arousal level; or hire someone who can do it well.

In summary, managing your own preferences involves:

*   designing your job so that at least 50% of what you are expected to do utilizes your personal mental preferences in contexts that match your arousal needs for high, moderate or low stimulation, and
*   managing those tasks which require the use of your non-preferred modes or arousal levels through redesigning how and when you do them, or requesting help from someone with the necessary mental preferences.

These latter actions are critical. They make it possible for you to do your job well while not pushing you mental achilles heel. Moreover, used in combination with the guidelines for communicating clearly at work (Chapter 8), these strategies allow you to transform uncomfortable or unpleasant situations into rewarding and energizing ones.

APPENDICES

THE TRADITION OF THINKING ABOUT THINKING

Like most new ideas and inventions, the Benziger Model was not created in a vacuum. It is just one more evolutionary step in a long tradition of interlinked models, all of which seek to explain conscious human thinking and decision-making.[1] Two of the principal the models in this historic tradition are the Native American Medicine Wheel, which is thousands of years old and held in high regard principally by native cultures, sociologists and anthropologists; and Carl Gustav Jung's 4-function model, developed by him in the 1920's and 30's to explain how people obtain and process information.

Interestingly enough, these two 4-modal models, developed centuries and continents apart, are very similar. The Indians' cold, unfeeling but <u>wise</u> "Buffalo" is much like Jung's cool analytic "Thinking" type. The introspection of their "Bear" is like the "Sensation" type's tendency to look within to find how he has done something before and/or <u>"what worked" before.</u> The innocent, trusting "Mouse" offers at least one description of the ever-hopeful, "Feeling" type. And,

---

[1] The lists of words used to describe many of these models in this essay are awkward combinations of nouns and adjectives. They are, however, the actual words used by the credited authors.

the far-sighted <u>vision</u> of the "Eagle" is an apt description of many "Intuitives". Moreover, both of these models include information which says each person is born with one or two natural preferences, but must over his or her life-time grow in the ability to use his or her non-preferred or "shadow" functions.

The Native American Medicine Wheel[2]

NORTH: Buffalo, Wisdom, cold without feeling.
WEST: Bear, Introspection and Looks-within Place.
SOUTH: Mouse, Innocence and Trust, Touching.
EAST: Eagle, Illumination, clear far-sighted vision, but
        close to nothing, always above & separated from life.

Carl Gustav Jung's Four Functions[3]
(1920's-30's)

Jungian based models: Myers-Briggs (1962),
Drake-Beam-Morin (1972), Keirsey-Bates (1978)

THINKING: objective, analytic, principles, criteria, critiques
SENSATION: focus on past, realistic, down-to-earth, practical, sensible
FEELING: subjective, personal, values intimacy, sympathetic &
            sensitive to harmony & to extenuating circumstances,
            humane
INTUITION: hunches, futures, speculative, fantasy, imaginative

---

[2] Infomation about the Medicine Wheel is from conversations with Shirley Barclay, a Native American who is also a practicing therapist, and the book <u>Seven Arrows</u> by Hyemeyohsts Storm, 1972.

[3] Information about Jung's model comes from Katherine's mother, a practicing therapist who was raised by a student of Jung's, and from several books by and about Jung, including:

<u>Contributions to Analytical Psychology</u>, C.G. Jung. Harcourt, Brace & Company, 1928.

<u>Psychic Energy: It's Source & It's Transformation</u> with foreward by C.G. Jung, by M. Esther Harding. Random House, 1963.

<u>Psychological Types</u>, C.G. Jung. Princeton University Press 1971.

<u>The Psychology of the Unconscious: A Study in Transformation & Symbolism of the Psyche: A Contribution to the History of the Evolution of Thought</u>, C.G. Jung. Dodd Mead & Company, 1931.

Moreover, it is not surprising that both of these models have commanded reverence among those who have lived and worked with them, for both have a timeless, universal quality. In fact, were it not for three considerations, each of which limits their utility, it would be easy to identify these two models the Alpha and Omega of the tradition. These limiting considerations are:

1) neither model includes an easy diagnostic tool whereby individuals can objectively identify their preferred style;
2) the generalized, "archetypal" nature of both makes it difficult for most people to rationally apply them to specific life concerns; and
3) the lack of hard, scientific evidence linking either model to the brain has made it difficult for "non-believers" to accept that there are, in fact, real and innate differences in thinking styles, "which we cannot help," and that these differences play an important role in our lives.

Nor is it surprising that since Jung's time most of the models developed have attempted to address one or more of these limiting factors.[4]

For example, from the 1930's until well into the 1970's, many efforts were made to make Jung's model itself more available and useful to the average person by designing easy to use diagnostic tools to accompany it. Principle among these Jungian-based models are: the Myers-Briggs Type Indicator (1962), Drake Beam Morin's I-SPEAK Survey (1972) and the Keirsey-Bates' Inventory in Please Understand Me (1978). Popular with many, these models are used by therapists, management consultants, trainers and church groups to help clients understand and accept the general differences between people in the hopes that it will improve their ability to accept these differences and to communicate effectively.

As far as they go, these models are successful. They do not however go far enough to assist people in career decisions, nor do they offer any scientific basis for the four styles. As such, people are asked to accept that four modes exist and to appreciate all four modes without really understanding the value or contribution each makes.

By contrast, many other models from this period, developed to explore and explain specific social behaviors, are highly specific. Within this category of "more specific models" there are three subcategories: those developed by educators to distinguish one "type" of student from another (often called "learning style inventories"); those developed by organizational theorists to distinguish

---

4 For a partial listing of the models we have examined see the chart, Highlights in the Tradition, following this discussion.

categories of employees (followers) and/or categories of leaders; and those developed by social scientists to explain specific problematic behaviors, such as criminality, conflict patterns, resistance to change and creativity. What is significant is that a close study and logical analysis of these behavioral models reveals a tremendous amount of support for Jung's original four "functions." Nine of the ten models reviewed directly or indirectly identify logical analysis as a distinctive mode. Four of the ten pull out the ability to attend to details in a thorough manner (which is part and parcel of the sensation function). Eight of the ten directly or indirectly identify the personal feeling mode. And, four of the ten identify a future-oriented, speculative competency.

That this behavioral research identifies what on the surface appears to be some new as well as some of the same styles of thinking, should not be surprising. Nor is it invalidating to Jung and the Medicine Wheel, both of which recognized that although each person had a lead function, each person also had to varying degrees access to all four modes. It is simply a reflection of the differing ways in which the research was conducted.

Suppose I asked you to identify the three "primary" colors on earth. If you sought to answer my question by going out into the world and observing the colors you found in the sky, the water, the grass, the leaves of trees, and the soil and sand of the earth itself, you would probably conclude that the three primary colors are blue, green and brown-- because they are the three colors which are most frequently seen. If on the other hand, you were to structure your research such that you looked deeply into the true nature of color itself, you would discover that the true primary colors are: red, yellow and blue, and that although they do not all occur in their pure form with equal or great frequency, they are nonetheless the elements or units from which all colors are made.

Just so, one might say the Native Americans and Jung going deeply into human nature identified the true "primary" or universal units of human thinking, while the behavioral researchers, looking at external manifestations of our thinking, saw not the primary modes, but rather those patterns or combinations of modes which occur most frequently in human beings.

Thus, for a time it seemed that either one used a generalized model which described all the core modes but was not readily meaningful or useful to people in their day to day living; or one used a specific model which identified only the most frequent patterns as they related to a particular concern. Only some breakthrough, some specific knowledge about what is really happening in the brain could resolve the confusion.

In the late 1950's and 1960's, the science and technology of brain research finally became sufficiently developed to make it possible for the adherents of this long intellectual tradition to address the third principle limitation--the tradition's lack of scientific substantiation. As might have been expected, the first attempts, which simply categorized people as either right- or left-brained, were sadly inadequate. And, although some people were excited by this bi-modal dichotomous choice, many rejected the model, knowing it was far too simplistic. Yet, due to the limited capabilities of neurology's fledgling technology, it was not until the mid-1970's that the next link in the chain was added by Ned Herrmann. At that time Paul MacLean's Tri-Une or three-in-one Brain Model, identifying the brain as a unified system with three sub-systems, the Cerebral Cortex, the Limbic System and the Reptilian Core, was en vogue.

Herrmann's model identified four modes of thinking and assigned each to one of four physical sites within the brain:

> the left cerebral cortex
> the left limbic brain
> the right limbic brain
> the right cerebral cortex.

The similarity between Herrmann's four modes and Jung's functions is striking.

Jung	Herrmann[5]
Analytical Thinking	Analytic Facts
Practical Sensation	Organized, sequential Form
Personal Feeling	Interpersonal Feeling
Intuitive Futures	Intuitive Futures

In fact, it would be largely accurate to say that what Herrmann did in the 1970's in terms of describing the contents of the four modes was to ground Jung's theory in what was then known and hypothesized about the actual workings of the brain. As such, it was a major breakthrough and, perhaps because of its scientific aspect, was well received by American and European businesses who use it to identify innovative and "creative types," as well as to help employees understand their co-workers and identify the types of tasks they each do best.

---

5 Categories and adjectives listed to describe the Herrmann Model are taken from 'The Creative Brain'--an interview with Ned Herrmann, in ASTD's *Training & Development Journal*, 'Oct 1981.

By the mid-1980's, however, as an evolving technology enabled medical researchers to more accurately identify the actual specialized functions of much of the cerebral and limbic brain areas, it became clear that the Herrmann model was technically inaccurate, particularly with respect to the role it assigned the limbic brain. Today we know that the limbic brain does not actually think--not even in a sensitive, interpersonal way. All actual thinking goes on in the cortex supported and enabled by the activity of both the limbic and reptilian brains. The limbic system, for example, supports our thinking in the following manner:

The LIMBIC SYSTEM enables or affects our THINKING by

- <u>enabling</u> us to form and store new memories in the cortex
- <u>accessing</u> existing memories from the cortex
- <u>focussing</u> our attention
- <u>energizing</u> our thinking
- <u>directing</u> our thinking by engaging us emotionally
- <u>fogging</u> our thinking by engaging us emotionally
- <u>signaling</u> us to provide maternal care for our young
- <u>shifting our cerebral activity</u> under stress to the basal
  portion of the cerebral cortex.

And, the reptilian brain supports our thinking as follows:

The REPTILIAN CORE enables and affects our THINKING by

- bringing in <u>new information</u> from the environment
- providing us with <u>energy and "drive"</u>
- helping <u>focus</u> and direct our attention
- instinctively sensing and asserting <u>territoriality</u>

In conjunction with the more in-depth research which has been carried out on the cortex itself since the mid-1970's (for more detailed information about the physiology underlying the Benziger Model see: Appendix B), these scientific findings offer important insights into the structure of thinking. For one thing they suggest an important distinction which has never really been clarified by psychologists and psychiatrists, namely, the difference between feeling (a cortex ability) and emotion (a limbic activity).   For another, they suggest a natural explanation for why analytic and imaginative thinkers tend to appear more self-motivated and energetic than other persons--an observation which may as well explain why you can train a person to be competent, but not to be an expert, an issue of critical concern to American business today. As a next step in the tradition of thinking about thinking, therefore, the Benziger Model seeks to draw on the most current neurological information, as well as the best historic information about thinking styles. In particular, it acknowledges its debt to the work of Carl Jung, whose insights have influenced the work of virtually all who have followed him as well as the work of Karl Pribrim whose comprehensive and innovative understanding of the human brain gave our own thinking direction.

For those already familiar with another model of human thinking, several of the more popular models in this tradition are summarized in the following chart. Where a mode described appears to be markedly similar to one of the four modes comprising the Benziger model the appropriate mode or combination of modes is noted using a two-letter abbreviation (BL, BR, FR, FL, DR, DL, DF, DB).

HIGHLIGHTS IN THE TRADITION[6]

I. GENERIC MODELS

THE FOUR HUMOURS: Galen 200 A.D.
(Used to understand human differences, as well as diagnose and treat illness)

MELANCHOLIC:	sad, moody, anxious, reserved, rigid, quiet, sober, pessimistic, unsociable. (descriptive of many introverts who have had difficult lives or been invalidated for being introverted)
PHLEGMATIC:	cool & self-possessed, passive, carefree, thoughtful, peaceful, controlled, reliable, even-tempered, calm. BL
SANGUINE:	cheerful, sociable, out-going, talkative, responsive, easy-going, lively, carefree, willing and eager to lead. (Generally descriptive of extraverted persons.)
CHOLERIC:	hot-tempered or angry, touchy, restless, aggressive, excitable, changeable, impulsive, optimistic, active. FR

NATIVE AMERICAN MEDICINE WHEEL: "As old as the Native American"
(Used to convey a symbolic, metaphoric understanding of life.)

NORTH:	Buffalo, Wisdom, cold without feeling.	FL
WEST:	Bear, Introspection and Looks-within Place.	BL
SOUTH:	Mouse, Innocence and Trust, Touching.	BR
EAST:	Eagle, Illumination, clear far-sighted vision, but close to nothing, always above and separated from life.	FR

---

6 Note: This is not an exhaustive listing of the tradition, which contains literally hundreds of models, including other traditional models, not unlike the Medicine Wheel.

II. PSYCHOLOGICAL MODELS

CARL GUSTAV JUNG's FOUR FUNCTIONS: 1930's
Jung's model was designed to assist an individual identify and understand his
or her conscious and unconscious motivations and needs. (Many models have
been developed from Jung's original work. These include: Myers-Briggs
(1962), Drake-Beam-Morin (1972), Keirsey-Bates (1978).)

THINKING:	analytic, objective, principles, standards, criteria, critiques.	FL
SENSING:	past, realistic, down-to-earth, practical, sensible.	BL
FEELING:	subjective, personal, valuing intimacy, extenuating	
	circumstances, humane, harmony.	BR
INTUITION:	hunches, futures, speculative, fantasy, imaginative.	FR
EXTRAVERSION:	an outwardly directed life-orientation which seeks	
	to influence or control its environment.	E
INTROVERSION:	an inwardly directly life-orientation which seeks to	
	inner understanding or experience.	I

JEAN SHINODA BOLEN's GODDESSES IN EVERY WOMAN: 1984
(Identifies dominant archetypes guiding female growth and development)

ARTEMIS:	independent hunter, prefers wilderness, competitive	FR,E
ATHENA:	wise, decisive, warrior, tool maker	FL,E
DEMETER:	nurturer and spiritual guide,	BR,E
HESTIA:	spiritual, centered, meditative	BR,I
HERA:	traditional, status & role conscious,	BL,E
PERSEPHONE:	compliant, passive, chameleonlike	BL, I

ROBERT MOORE & DOUGLAS GILLETTE's MASCULINE TYPES: 1990
(Identifies four dominant archetypes guiding male growth and development)

KING:	stability, order, fecundity	BL
WARRIOR:	goal-focussed, aggressive, alert, flexible, strategic,	
	acts decisively, skilled with weapons.	FL
LOVER:	feeling, connected, spiritual, nature lover	BR
MAGICIAN:	mystical, pattern-sensitive, insightful	FR

III. EDUCATIONAL LEARNING STYLE MODELS

DAVID A. KOLB's LEARNING STYLES: circa 1974
(Useful in assisting teachers to understand and communicate with students.)

ABSTRACT		
CONCEPTUALIZATION:	analytical, evaluative, logical, rational.	FL
REFLECTIVE	tentative, watching, reserved, reflecting,	
OBSERVATION:	observing, conservation.	BL
CONCRETE	receptive, feeling, accepting, intuitive,	
EXPERIENCE:	present-oriented, experiential.	BR
ACTIVE	practical, doing, active, pragmatic,	
EXPERIMENTATION:	experimentation, responsible.	FR

ANTHONY F. GREGORC'S LEARNING STYLES: circa 1977
(Useful in assisting teachers to understand and communicate with students.)

ABSTRACT SEQUENTIAL:	analytical and auditory, reads and thinks.	FL
CONCRETE SEQUENTIAL:	programmed by step-by-step demonstration	
	needs well-organized, hands-on learning.	BL
CONCRETE RANDOM:	needs games, simultaneous, interpersonal	
	and experiential learning opportunities.	BR
ABSTRACT RANDOM:	visual and questioning, discusses.	FR

IV. ORGANIZATIONAL EMPLOYEE & LEADERSHIP MODELS

IRWIN THOMPSON'S: ARCHETYPES IN HISTORY: circa 1970
(Focus on theoretical insights)

HUNTER:	military general.	FL
LEADER:	administrative leader.	BL
SHAMAN:	spiritual leader.	BR
FOOL:	leader in impossible situations.	FR

WILSON LEARNING SYSTEM'S SOCIAL STYLES circa 1975
(Focus on increasing selling and influencing skills with bias towards perceived extraversion.)

ANALYTIC:	technical doer, provides detail and accuracy, needs to be told how.	BL,I
DRIVER:	efficient, results-oriented, builds structure, wants to know goal.	FL,E
AMIABLE:	feeling, agreeable, supportive, interpersonal.	BR,I
EXPRESSIVE:	intuitive, stimulating, dreams.	FR,E

IRV RUBIN's INFLUENCE STYLES: circa 1980
(Focus on helping leaders to be more effective by expanding choice of options.)

REASON	with logic.	FL
ASSERT	established goals.	BL
BRIDGE	with other people.	BR
ATTRACT	with visions.	FR

PERFORMAX'S DISC: circa 1985

DOMINANCE:	authoritative, decision-making, gets results in difficult circumstances.	DF,E
COMPLIANCE:	critical thinking, attention to standards & key details.	DL,I
STEADINESS:	patient, calming, follows accepted work pattern, good listener.	DB,I
INFLUENCING OTHERS:	motivating, enthusing, expressive, group-oriented.	DR,E

BRIAN H. KLEINER: TUNING INTO TEMPERAMENTS: circa 1986

SCIENCE ORIENTED THINKING:	logical & visionary combined.	DF
RESPONSIBLE JUDGING:	loyal, thorough, industrious, stabilizer.	BL
SELF-ACTUALIZING-INTUITION-FEELING:	personal, sensitive to others.	BR
ARTISTIC-SENSATION-PERCEIVING:	creative, loner, risk-taker.	FR

HAROLD LEAVITT's EXECUTIVE STYLES In Praise of Pathfinders©1986
(Focus on identifying excellent leaders.)

IMPLEMENTER:	commanding and persuasive action.	DL
PROBLEM SOLVER:	logical and analytical.	FL
PATHFINDER:	impulsive and impractical visionary.	FR

V. SOCIAL SCIENCE MODELS

THOMAS-KILMAN's CONFLICT STYLES INVENTORY: circa 1965
(Focus on enabling people to collaborate more effectively to resolve conflicts.)

COMPETITION:	manipulates and negotiates to win, not lose.	FL, E
	(This could also describe any extreme extravert)	
COMPROMISE:	adjusts goals according to a "fair" formula.	BL
COLLABORATION:	explores to find a win-win.	BR or DR
AVOIDANCE:	goes within, leaves, turns away from conflict.	FR, I
	(This could also describe any extreme introvert.)	
ACCOMMODATION:	gives over to the other party gracefully.	BR

FRANK FARLEY's THRILL-SEEKING MODEL: circa 1970
(Explores connection between creativity and criminality among other things.)

BIG "T":	thrill-seeking, high stimulation needs, novelty, risk.	FR, E
	(This pattern is most true for extraverted FRs.)	
LITTLE "T":	thrill avoiding, predictable, clarity, rigidity.	BL,I
	(This pattern is most true for introverted BLs.)	

VI. PHYSIOLOGICALLY BASED MODELS

NED HERRMANN'S WHOLE BRAIN MODEL c 1976
(Focus on understanding and enabling creative thinking)

CEREBRAL LEFT:	FACTS, analytical, mathematical, logical, technical, problem-solver.	FL
LIMBIC LEFT:	FORM, sequential, controlled, conservative, planner, organizer, administrative.	BL
LIMBIC RIGHT:	FEELING, interpersonal, emotional, musical, spiritual, talker.	BR
CEREBRAL RIGHT:	FUTURES, creative, imaginative, synthesizer, artistic, holistic, conceptualizer.	FR

KATHERINE BENZIGER's WHOLE BRAIN MODEL c 1987
(Focus on validating and making effective use of all modes and patterns.)

FRONTAL LEFT	DIRECTION & DECISION-MAKING, analytical, logical.
BASAL LEFT	STABLE FOUNDATIONS & ROUTINE, sequential, orderly, procedural.
BASAL RIGHT	PEACEFUL, HARMONIOUS FOUNDATIONS & FEELING, rhythmic, sensitive to nonverbals.
FRONTAL RIGHT	ADAPTION & INTERNAL-IMAGING, abstract, imaginative, sensitive to patterns.
EXTRAVERSION:	A basic life-orientation in which the person seeks continually seeks a hightened level of stimulation
INTROVERSION:	A basic life-orientation in which the person naturally lives at such a heightened level of arousal that high levels of stimulation cause the individual to "back off" and "go within" .

The model presented in this book has two key theoretical components: **functional specialization** and **dominance.** The first of these, functional specialization, states that the brain is subdivided into discrete areas each of which has things it does best. The second, dominance, states that given functional specialization, most people are born with a natural physiological preference for one or more modes. In order to fully appreciate the neuro-scientific bases for the model, we will look at both of these components in three different essays:

Part I: Functional Specialization:

An Historic Overview:

Functional specialization was first suggested in the 1860's by a French surgeon who noticed damage to a particular region of the left frontal lobe predictably resulted in a type of speech difficulty known as aphasia. The area, now long accepted as the region of our brain naturally "encoded with the structure of language," is known today as Broca's area in honor of its discoverer. From today's perspective the next piece of significant work in the area of functional specialization was done by Roger Sperry, a biologist working with epileptics who had undergone "split-brain surgery" in an effort to isolate and limit their seizures.

Today, although it would appear that more neurosurgeons and neurophysiologists subscribe to functional specialization than reject it, the theory still has some missing and/or unclear pieces. The first has to do with language. Subsequent to the work of Broca, Werneke established that in addition to the area dealing with structure, there was an area which he called "the language lump" in the temporal lobe of the left hemisphere. The fact that two discrete areas were involved in processing language was startling to functional specialists. Even more problematic were EEG read- outs which suggested that high activity levels in the basal right occurred in some people.

The second key problem with the theory of functional specialization is that it has been referred to and popularized as "hemispheric specialization." The principle objection to that model is simply that it is too simple. For if, as appears to be true, a high degree of functional specialization does occur naturally in our brains, then it is definitely more complex and specific than the gross right/left division. Much of this resistance has come from neurologists who, working in tandem with psychiatrists, diagnose and treat illnesses which result from damage to or the malfunction of very specific, discrete areas of the brain. In other words, those who rejected the hemispheric specialization model seemed to be doing so because they needed a similar, but more specific tool. Their reaction, then, is not unlike a carpenter who asks for a "1/4" phillips" and is handed a straight-edge screwdriver. What he wanted was a screwdriver, and what he was given was a screwdriver, he simply needed a different one from the one he was given.

In contrast, those who have been most taken with the concept of hemispheric specialization are those for whom a generalized tool is probably just right. These are the people seeking to link intelligence, thinking and learning styles, psychology, and management styles to some structural "truth" about the brain; people for whom such a model made sense if it could be shown that the key operational rule of functional specialization is dominance. Hence, the wave of right/left brain mini-tests in magazine after magazine and right/left brain self-help books. The only problem was that reality simply does not conform to the idea that most people were only one or the other. So, for every person who took such a test and felt that this explained their life-long sense of confusion, there were at least two for whom the bi-polar model made no sense whatsoever. Typically if asked about it, these dissatisfied parties would observe that: "I'm some of what's called left and some of what's called right, but there are a lot of things in both categories which don't fit me at all."

In the mid to late 1970's, Ned Herrmann, working at General Electric, combined what was then state of the art EEG data on the functioning of the cortex with Paul MacLean's Tri-une Model and his own data on thinking styles. The result was a refined, 4-modal version of the right-left brain model.

In 1981, Katherine began to explore the connections between her own work in change management and conflict resolution with that of Herrmann. She became convinced that the model had validity due to, among other things, its striking resemblance to the work of Jung, Thomas and Kilman (see Appendix A). Subsequently, Katherine attended one of Herrmann's certification workshops and began to collaborate with Herrmann and his associates. For the next few years she used Herrmann's model as well as his assessment, the HBDI, to work with many groups of clients across the United States.

In 1984, however, after teaching several workshops for the American Academy of Medical Directors, Katherine became convinced that there was no functional basis for believing the two "lower" modes were limbic in nature. Quite to the contrary, there was substantial physiological evidence to indicate that the various components of the limbic brain, invaluable as they were, had little to do with thinking styles.

Finally, in 1985, Katherine sought advice and guidance from one of the nation's foremost experts on the human brain, Dr. Karl Pribram. Pribram, who had been a practicing neuorsurgeon prior to obtaining a PhD in Psychology and heading up Stanford's Behavioral Research Labs, is one of those rare individuals whose areas of expertise crossover generally segmented specialities. An expert in brain structure and the known neurochemical bases of mental activity, as well as the various psychological models used to predict behavior, Pribram was able to make sense of the data in a way no one else had.

His observation was quite simply, that the four modes identified by the model most probably reflected the four cerebral chunks: the right and left frontal lobes, and the right and left basal areas (the occipital, parietal and temporal lobes) of the cerebral cortex, In establishing these locations, he assigned Herrmann's four modes as follows: the cerebral left to the frontal left lobe, the limbic left to the basal or posterior section of the left hemisphere, the limbic right to the basal region of the right hemisphere and the cerebral right to the frontal lobe of the right hemisphere. He went on to add that the central fissure which separates the frontal lobe of each hemisphere from the basal regions was already known to be one of the most significant divisions in our brain and that many scientists thought it was actually more significant than the hemispheric separation.   An intriguing point which he also commented on was that there are strong connections between the limbic brain (which among other things is the energetic brain) and each frontal lobe. His point was that some people are very energetic or active, while others appear to be more tranquil--along the lines of the Type A and Type B personalities--and that it would appear that those people who are naturally more frontal are also naturally more active. As a final note, almost of verification, Pribram added that Herrmann's description of the left limbic mode did indeed fit some of what he himself was discovering about the structure of stored memories in the basal left.

A final point worth adding is that, although Pribram's locational restructuring of the model appeared to be in conflict with the existing EEG evidence from the 60's and 70's, two contributing explanations can be found. The one offered by Pribram is technical: EEG measurements done during those years, when the technology was new and unrefined, did not always manage to pick up or measure the functioning of the basal lobes. particularly its deeper regions. The second reason is that when people were tested for thinking skills the testers did not think to take a reading while they were doing a routine function or following instructions. In other words, until the Herrmann research spotlighted the left limbic mode, no one bothered to separated it out as a discrete mode of thinking.

Subsequent to discussions with Pribram, Katherine began to seek further evidence. Certainly what was known about the brain's processing of language was consistent with Pribram's proposal. Broca's area processed structure and it was true that those who Herrmann identified as having strong access to what we now called the frontal left (where Broca's is located) were generally more articulate than a person with a weakness in this area. In contrast, a person with a strong basal left access, the region in which the Werneke's language lump is located, although not articulate, was generally adept at using the "form" of language--speaking in full sentences, using commas and periods etc.   What's more, the area Pribram suggested as the location for the basal right explains some confusing EEG evidence (that some people appeared to be using portions of their right parietal and temporal lobes in connection with language). If this is where the basal right mode is located, then what the tests were probably registering was the nonverbal processing which is part of language and which tends to be well developed in people with strong basal rights.

Since 1985, Benziger (and later Sohn) have continued to look for substantive physiological data to corroborate Pribram's hypothesis and build "neurologically sound" model of thinking.

What we now know about the physiology of the brain that supports the concept of functional specialization:

The **reptilian core** consists of the basal ganglia, the pons, the reticular formation, the medulla, and the cerbellum (to name the most significant parts). The **basal ganglia**, which themselves consist of the globus pallidus (the source of displaying behavior), the caudate nucleus, and the putamen, are the oldest part of the brain. Because the basal ganglia are concerned with psychomotor coordination, damage to them causes slowed movement, rigid muscles, and a loss of facial expression.

The **pons**, with the help of the **medulla**, controls the slow-wave and paradoxical sleep cycles while the **reticular formation** controls wakefulness. Another "duty" of the reticular formation is to arouse the cerebral hemisphere by generating "expectancy waves", which energize the system and bring it to attention. The reticular formation sends these waves to the cortex via the thalamus (the control center for all sensory input into the cortex). From the thalamus, they then go directly to the frontal lobes through special nerve cables or to the basal lobes through the auditory, visual, and sensory cortexes. Conversely, an idea generated in the cortex (say of getting a nice, hot cup of tea) will send impulses to the reticular formation which, in turn, will excite the motor cortex into action and send you on your way to the kitchen.

The other important pieces of the reptilian complex are the **medulla**, which controls heart rate, swallowing, vomiting, and respiration as well as the sleep cycles, and the **cerebellum**, which appears to have three different, albeit related, functions. First, it controls posture, equilibrium, and balance. Second, it coordinates your movement into a smooth sequence (so you don't spill that cup of tea you just got all over the table). Lastly, through its connection to the limbic system, it serves as a kind of "master regulator" for sensory, motor, and emotional processes and is part of the "pleasure system". This cerebellum-limbic connection is particularly evident in the delighted reactions most young children have to being rocked, tossed in the air, "flown" around the room, and bounced on grandpa's knee, all of which stimulate the cerebellum and, in turn, the limbic pleasure centers.

Moving up the evolutionary ladder as well as upward in the brain, we come to the **limbic system**, which is the part of the brain most concerned with **emotion**. The component "parts" of this system are: the thalamus, the hypothalamus, the hippocampus, the amygdala, the septal area, the mammilary bodies, and the cingulate gyrus.

The **thalamus** is the control center which directs sensory information from the environment (which comes in through the brain stem) to the auditory, visual, and sensory cortexes in the right and left basal lobes. It is also the conduit for sending "expectancy waves" to and from the reticular formation and the cerebral brain (both frontal and basal lobes).

The **hypothalamus,** which lies just below the thalamus, appears to be the master regulator of the autonomic nervous system. It controls body temperature, blood pressure, water levels, sex, appetite/food intake, and endocrine levels (through its control over the **pituitary**). Additionally, the hypothalamus is part of pleasure/punishment system, depending on which half of it is stimulated. Lesions in the posterior hypothalamus produce an increase in aggressiveness and electrical stimulation of this area generates a rage reaction and attack behaviors. Conversely, stimulation of the anterior hypothalamus produces pleasure reactions. Lastly, and perhaps most importantly when considered in relation to human thinking, the hypothalamus appears to function not only as the central control for the limbic system, but also as the liaison between the limbic system and the cerebral cortex.

The **Hippocampus** (or rather, "hippocampi" since there are two of them) lies tucked within the basal (temporal) lobes of the cerebral cortex. It appears to have two rather different functions, being responsible for adjusting moods and emotions to incoming information from the environment as well as playing a critical role in the process of memory formation. In this latter role (memory), the hippocampus is responsible for forming a memory of the part of the environment which has already been explored so that it may be distinguished from unexplored areas. Therefore, what activates this memory formation sequence (and turns on the hippocampus) is "novelty" in the environment. In addition, the hippocampus is involved in the laying down and retrieving of long term memories (though the specifics of this process are not, as yet, fully understood) and if the hippocampus and the amygdala are both damaged global anterograde amnesia results and no information can be committed to or retrieved from memory.

In its other capacity as mood adjuster, the hippocampus is usually inhibited by the neurotransmitter seratonin. When it is deprived of seratonin, which can be caused by temporal lobe epilepsy, hallucinagens, repetitive chanting, meditation, or marathon running among other things, the hippocampus fires wildly and loses its connection to "external reality". The result is the same kind of experience that characterizes right temporal lobe epilepsy: dream states, feelings of deja- and jamais-vu, a sense of "significance" and meaningfulness", cosmic insights, and the re-living of past experiences in vivid sensory detail. If such experiences appeal to you but have eluded you in the past, the solution to your problems may simply be to find ways of depriving your brain of seratonin.

The **amygdala** (of which there are also two) are involved in associative memory and, with the hippocampus, in long-term memory storage and retrieval. Like the hypothalamus, they are part of both the pleasure and pain systems, though the "pain" component is by far the more significant. The amygdala is connected to aggression and electrical stimulation of this area will produce displays of excitement, rage, and fear. And, although removal of the amygdala does cause a reduction in aggression, it also produces excessive sexual displaying and a loss of status in the social hierarchy.

The **septal area** lies in front of the hypothalamus and is the major pleasure center in the limbic system. Stimulation of this region produces heightened alertness, feelings of pleasure, and sexual orgasm (in fact, if you inject this area with acetycholine the result will be multiple orgasms lasting up to 30 minutes). Conversely, destruction of this area causes a reduction in awareness and emotional expressiveness. The septal area is the part of the brain that is excited (temporarily) by the use of marijuana, cocaine, or heroin. However, research has shown that long-term use of these substance ultimately produces the opposite effects---withdrawal, apathy, and depression.

The **mammilary bodies** and the **cingulate gyrus** are the last two notable parts of the limbic system. The mammilary bodies are involved with the memory process and can be destroyed by alcohol (Korsakov's Syndrome). The cingulate gyrus, which is the newest part of the limbic system (evolutionarily speaking), control three instinctual behaviors found in all mammals but not found in reptiles: the desire to play, maternal caring for the young, and audiovocal communication. If the cingulate gyrus is destroyed, these three behaviors stop.

Obviously, the limbic system is an important "brain" that has a significant impact on our thinking--which is not to say that it is a brain that thinks. Like the reptilian, the limbic system is a "primitive" brain, largely hardwired and incapable of reading, writing or any form of reasoning, evaluation, or judgment whatsoever. Furthermore, the emotions it generates may or may not have any basis in reality. So it's perfectly possible for your limbic brain to convince you that something is "real, true, and significant" or "the right thing to do" or something "really worth believing" when what it is telling you is dead wrong. Nevertheless, given the power emotions have to affect our lives, it is probably reasonable to say that "wherever mankind may be, and wherever we may be going, depends to an as yet incalculable degree on the workings of the limbic system." (quoted from The Brain:The Last Frontier, p.76)

Last, but certainly not least, we come to the **cerebral cortex,** the "newest" of our three brains. As most of you are undoubtably aware, this brain is bisected front to back by the **longitudinal fissure** which divides it into the left and right hemispheres. These hemispheres, although separate, are able to communicate with each other by way of the **corpus collosum,** a neural network which runs between them. Next, each of these hemispheres is divided by the **central** or **rondalic fissure** into the **frontal** lobes (which are sometimes called the pre-frontal lobes) and the **basal** lobes (which are actually three lobes grouped together).

The basal lobes (both right and left) are made up of the temporal, parietal, and occipital lobes. The **temporal lobes,** which run along the sides of the head, contain the auditory cortex (whose primary job is the analysis of sound) and some parts of the visual cortex. Also contained within these lobes (in the transverse convolutions of Heschl) are the musical centers.

Although both right and left temporal lobes process sound, they do not attend to the same things. Research has shown that the left temporal lobe is most sensitive to words and verbal communication, while the right temporal lobe is more aware of non-verbal sounds (rain falling, a car honking its horn, fingernails scraping a chalkboard) and emotional utterances (crying, screaming, laughing). In the same vein, Damasio and Wyke's studies on music (referenced in The Mind) suggest that we naturally sing, play, and listen to music with the right hemisphere but that the left hemisphere takes over this function in those who are formally trained or who make it their profession.

The temporal lobes are also deeply involved with memory storage and damage to these lobes not only makes it impossible for information or experience to be filed in long-term memory, it may also cause the loss of all existing memories (as is the case in dementia). However, memories do not appear to be distributed randomly between right and left. In a recent study, experimental subjects were asked two different kinds of questions and monitored to see which hemisphere they accessed to come up with the answer. The subjects uniformly accessed the right hemisphere to answer "emotionally charged" questions ("Is your mother-in-law an interfering person?) and the left hemisphere to answer general information ones ("How many s's are there in Mississippi?"). Additional studies have substantiated these findings and strongly suggest that emotionally charged memories are stored on the right, whereas formal information is stored on the left.

Also known as the "interpretive cortex", the temporal lobes are closely connection to the limbic system and, when stimulated, they produce the same kind of "cosmic/ spiritual experiences" detailed in the section on the hippocampus. According to Karl Pribram, "A lesion in the temporal lobe near the amygdala can produce something akin to mysticism. There is a disruption in self awareness, a kind of consciousness without content, like the oceanic consciousness of the mystic state. The distinction between self and other disappears." (quoted from The 3-Pound Universe, p. 330) Unfortunately, the temporal lobes can be involved in negative experiences too. For example, "panic attacks" are the result of a temporal-hippocampal malfunction (incoming sensory information is misinterpreted and this generates an intense fear response).

The **parietal lobes**, which are located on the top of the head, contain the somatic sensory cortexes which collect "feeling" (not emotional) information from receptors in the skin, joints, muscles, and tendons. They also deal with "body awareness" and damage to these lobes can literally cause us to lose awareness of our own bodies, in part or whole. The **occipital lobes** contain the visual cortex and damage to the back of the head, where these lobes are located, can result in blindness (even if your eyes themselves are undamaged).

In trying to understand the basal lobes, it is important to remember that the Basal Left is the site of the Wernicke's area, one of the two speech centers. If this area is damaged, we lose the ability to understand word meanings and to manage spoken and written grammar or syntax. We do not, however, lose our ability to articulate or to speak easily and fluently (which is governed by the Broca's area in the Frontal Left lobe). In other words, if we damage this area we can still talk well enough but nothing we say will make any sense. This condition, which is called aphasia, can have the interesting side effect of expanding our skill at reading non-verbals (a basal right ability) to the point where we may be able to "understand" what someone "means" even if we cannot comprehend a single word they say. (For more information on this phenomenum, read "The President's Speech" chapter in Oliver Sack's book, The Man Who Mistook His Wife For A Hat).

Finally, before going on to discuss the frontal lobes, there is an additional point of information specifically about the Basal Left which is worthy of inclusion. In a study by Kimura (referenced in Two Sides of the Brain), it was found that damage to the Basal Left produces apraxia, which is the inability to coordinate movement into a sequence (e.e. setting a table or performing any other routine incorporating multiple discrete acts.) and it is also known that lesions on the left parietal and temporal lobes disturb planning and sequencing skills.

If the cerebral cortex is the "new brain", then the **frontal lobes** are the "newest of the new" and, as such, they represent the most evolutionarily advanced part of us. Yet well into this century many neurologists believed they served no function whatsoever beyond being the site of the motor cortex. As it turns out, the frontal lobes are the part of the brain that generates goal-directed behavior and individuals who have damaged frontal lobes cannot create plans or choose actions to carry them out. Furthermore, such individuals are easily distracted by irrelevant stimuli and inclined to randomly change actions for no reason.

The rash of pre-frontal lobotomies performed during the 1940's and 50's has given us ample opportunity to see what the loss of the frontal lobes costs the system. After this surgery, the lobotomized individual tends to be:
- Limited in his thoughts and actions to sequences he has
  already learned
- Unable to grasp the "key points" of a situation
- Prone to tantrums and fits of childish behavior
- Unable to focus his attention
- Lacking in verbal expressiveness and trivial and uninspired
  in his verbal contributions
- Easily distracted by irrelevant external stimuli
- Slow and deliberate in his movements
- Lacking in initiative and purpose
- Unable to consider and plan for the future
- Lacking in judgment
- Unable to defer immediate gratification
- Disturbed by changes in the environment and desirous
  of keeping everything "the same"

All of which reinforce the idea that the frontal lobes function as the seat of will, intention, and future-oriented behavior.

The Left Frontal lobe, as we have already mentioned, is the site of the other speech center (Broca's area) and is responsible for articulation. Damage to this area results in "telegraphic" speech (where the words come out one by one in a labored fashion). Studies have also shown that this is the part of the brain that excels at mathematics, at analysis, and at processing information in a logical (linear) way.

Conversely, the Right Frontal lobe has been shown to process information in a visual-spatial way (there is a visual-spatial complex on the right corresponding to the Broca's area on the left). Individuals who have damaged this area misjudge the size, direction, and distance of objects, they cannot copy simple shapes or arrange blocks or sticks to form a pattern, and they lose their ability to describe even well known routes. The frontal right is also the "expressive" part of the brain and a stroke or lesion in this part of the brain can cause a loss of all emotional inflection in the voice and an inability to laugh, cry, or express any other emotion. It is significant to note, however, that the ability to experience emotion is not impaired, only its outward expression. Additionally, there is no impairment in perceiving other people's emotions (the basal right skills remain intact).

Anecdotal Support for Functional Specialization

Additional corroborating evidence can be found everywhere. Two recent examples are in Oliver Sacks book, The Man Who Mistook His Wife for a Hat, and in the forthcoming book by Michael Persinger, The Neuropsychological Bases of God Experiences.

In his lead story about Dr. P, Sacks observes that Mr. P was able to recognize some types of visual input but not others. Among those things which were not recognizable to Dr. P were the faces of his wife and friends, his shoe, and much of his environment. Among the things which he found recognizable were: abstract forms and shapes, stylized designs and caricatures, and on occasion a single human face or photograph with such strong lines so as to appear almost a caricature of itself. Although at first this seems confusing, the mystery dissolves as soon as the data is viewed through the lens of the Benziger model. Those things which are not recognizable to Dr. P are things processed by the right and left occipital lobes, located within the basal modes. We know specifically, for example, that faces in all their uniqueness are processed in the right occipital. Those things which are see-able, however, are distinctly part of the pattern sensitive frontal right mode. What is most interesting is that it is quite possible for another person suffering from the exact same condition not to see the things Dr. P could, simply because that other person might not have Dr. P's strong preference for the frontal right mode (an access strongly suggested by Dr. Sack's references to Dr. P's quirky and bizarre sense of humor.

In a pre-publication article on Michael Persinger's book, at least four different research projects are referred to, all of which suggest that spiritual experiences can be correlated with a heightened amount of electrical firing in the right temporal and parietal lobes. The suggested causes are stress, such as oxygen deprivation or a near-death experience, and meditation practices, such as Transcendental

Meditation, both of which can affect the serotonin level in the brain. According to Persinger, increased nerve firing in the temporal regions produce feelings of intense "meaningfulness." It would be interesting to know whether those who have a distinct preference for the basal right region also have a rate of nerve firing in this region which exceeds that of other people. If so, it would explain their generally heightened sensitivity to "spiritual values" and "meaning".

Another interesting point which Persinger's work brings up is that under stress, particularly life-threatening stress, the neural firing increases in both basal regions. Although we do not know why this happens, it may well be part of an evolutionary "survival mechanism" since, when we are subjected to severe stress, we need two things to survive: hope (which is perhaps what the spiritual experience offered by right temporal and parietal lobes is really all about) and the ability (as Churchill said) to "carry on." This latter ability is apparently encouraged by the increased firing of the basal left (procedures and routines) and is consistent with the fact that, under stress, people tend to revert to old, routine ways of doing things.

Part II: Dominance

The model's second key theoretical component is dominance. Some of the evidence for this has already been cited: the enthusiastic support for the right/left brain bi-polar model by those who were either clearly right or left and for whom the other half of their brain seemed in no way naturally or easily available to them. Additionally, since the successful completion of the paper and pencil test, known as the HBDI or HPSF (Herrmann Brain Dominance Instrument or Herrmann Participant Survey Form), approximately 150,000 persons have been profiled and had an opportunity to respond to their "scores." The evidence is overwhelming that people feel sudden affirmation, relief, and acceptance at having someone tell them that something they have known, but not been able to explain about themselves, is ok and true.

The verification is not, however, all anecdotal. According to an unpublished paper, "Cognitive Styles, EEG Waves and Brain Levels," by Drs. Lawrence L Schkade and Alfred R Potvin chairpersons respectively of Systems Analysis and Biomedical Engineering, a study was done at the University of Texas, in which EEG evidence was gathered correlating Herrmann's Cerebral Right and Cerebral Left modes (i.e. they did not seek to establish or measure what Herrmann was calling "limbic" activity) with actual brain activity. Only persons whose brain dominance pattern showed a clear preference for the left (selected not surprisingly from the accounting department) or the right (selected from the art department) were used. What happened was this. A list of activities were compiled which would use analytic and visual thinking in an alternating pattern. Although it is generally accepted that the left frontal lobe does math, analysis and logical processing and that the right frontal lobe does spatial thinking including geometry and artistic activities such as sketching, when these select subjects were asked to perform the selected list of activities an intriguing thing happened. When those who had an been identified by Herrmann's testing as strong analytic thinkers performed the list of "to do's" they tended to use a significant amount of frontal left thinking, even when the task could not benefit from it. And, when those who had tested out as strong internal image-oriented thinkers performed the list of "to do's" they tended to use a significant amount of frontal right thinking, even when the task could not benefit from it. In other words, they were trying to use their natural preference even if it couldn't do the task easily or well.

According to a story told to one of the authors by Herrmann, a double frontal, equally strong in both analytic thinking and internal imaging, additional illuminating data was discovered when he performed a similar list of to-do's while being monitored with EEG equipment. While performing an analytical or mathematical task his frontal lobes showed prominent activity in the frontal left and a quieting in the frontal right. Then, when he would shift to an activity best handled by spatial, pattern and image skills, his frontal left would show a marked decrease in the quantity of beta waves, sometimes shutting off almost entirely, while his frontal right was registering 100% beta. Thus, the study not only served to demonstrate the existence of dominance, but also spot-lighted another of Herrmann's theoretical contributions: the principle of situationalness. Otherwise stated: if a person has access to two modes, he or she will naturally use the mode best suited to the task.

More recently, with the assistance of state of the art technologies including PET Scanners, research is being conducted which suggests even more strongly that what we and others have been labelling brain dominance has its physiological roots in the chemistry of the brain that impacts both the speed at which neurons fire as well as how much energy they consume. Preeminent among the researchers in this area is Dr. Richard Haier whose findings on the glucose metabolic rate in the brain under differing circumstances have been reported at several national conferences.

Summary of the Physiological Bases for the Model:

There is a sufficient body of evidence to assert that the two key theoretical components of the Benziger Model---functional specialization and dominance---are neurologically valid.   Other theories suggested in the book, such as the neurochemical basis for dominance, remain unproven as yet (though they probably will not be for long). The field of brain research is a dynamic, growing one and it is hard to stay "current" when new discoveries are being made daily. Nonetheless, we look forward to the challenge.

If this brief physiological overview has whetted your appetite for more "hardcore" information about the brain, we can recommend the following books to you:

RECOMMENDED READINGS
on
FUNCTIONAL SPECIALIZATION AND DOMINANCE

'BERGSON AND THE BRAIN: A BIOLOGICAL ANALYSIS OF CERTAIN
    INTUITIONS, by Karl Pribram. an unpublished paper from Feb 1983.
'BRAIN MECHANISM IN MUSIC: PROLEGOMENA FOR A THEORY OF THE
    MEANING OF MEANING,' by Karl Pribram.
'BRAIN SYSTEMS AND COGNITIVE LEARNING PROCESSES,' by Karl Pribram
    in Proceedings from the Harry Frank Guggenheim Conference, 1982.
'CORTICAL GLUCOSE METABOLIC RATE CORRELATES OF ABSTRACT
    REASONING & INTELLIGENCE, STUDIED WITH POSITRON EMISSION
    TOMOGRAPHY ', by Richard Haier et al. unpublished paper from January 1988.
DECIPHERING THE SENSES by Robert Rivlin and Karen Gravelle, 1984.
'EMOTION: A NEUROBEHAVIORAL ANALYSIS, by Karl Pribram. In Approaches
    to Emotion, 1984.
'FREQUENCY ENCODING IN THE MOTOR SYSTEM, by Karl Pribram et. al. in
    Human Motor Actions - Bernstein Reassessed, 1984.
'IMAGING' BY Karl Pribram and E. H. Carlton. unpublished paper July 1984.
'LOCALIZATION AND DISTRIBUTION OF FUNCTION IN THE BRAIN', by Karl
    Pribram. In Neurology After Lashley, 1982.
MECHANICS OF THE MIND by Colin Blakemore, 1976.
'OBJECT PERCEPTION,' by Karl Pribram, E.H.Carlton. unpublished paper July 1984
'PSYCHOANALYSIS AND THE NATURAL SCIENCES: THE BRAIN-
    BEHAVIOR CONNECTION FROM FREUD TO THE PRESENT, by Karl
    Pribram, an unpublished paper May 1981.

'PSYCHOLOGY AS A SCIENCE,' by Karl Pribram. In <u>Psychology's Second Century: Enduring Issues</u>. 1981.

SCIENCE AND THE MIND-BRAIN ISSUE, by Karl Pribram.

'TEMPORAL VARIABLES IN SPEECH' by Karl Pribram, from an unpublished paper presented at The Hague, 1980.

<u>THE BRAIN</u> by Richard Restak, M.D. , 1984.

<u>THE BRAIN: THE LAST FRONTIER</u> (also by Restak), 1979.

<u>THE MAN WHO MISTOOK HIS WIFE FOR A HAT</u> by Oliver Sacks, 1985.

<u>THE MIND</u> by Anthony Smith, 1984.

<u>THE NEUROPSYCHOLOGICAL BASIS OF GOD EXPERIENCES</u> by Michael Persinger, 1987.

'THE ORIGINS OF SENSORY BIAS IN THE DEVELOPMENT OF GENDER DIFFERENCES IN PERCEPTION AND COGNITION', By Diane McGuinness and Karl Pribram. In <u>Cognitive Growth and Development</u>, ed. by Morton Bortner. Brunner Mazel Publishers, 1979.

'THE ROLE OF CORTICOCORTICAL CONNECTIONS, BY Karl Pribram. an unpublished paper Nov 1984.

<u>THE SPHINX AND THE RAINBOW</u> by David Loye, 1983.

'THE STUDY OF PERSONALITY WITH POSITRON EMISSION TOMOGRAPHY' by Richard Haier et. al. in <u>Personality Dimensions & Arousal</u>, ed. by Jan Stvelan & Hans J. Eyesenck. Plenum Publishing Company, 1987.

<u>THE TANGLED WING</u> by Melvin Konner, 1982.

<u>THE 3-POUND UNIVERSE</u> by Judith Hooper and Dick Teresi, 1986.

<u>TWO SIDES OF THE BRAIN</u> by Sid Segalowitz, 1983.

APPENDIX C
LIMBIC & REPTILIAN ACTIVATION INDICATORS

I: Limbic/Reptilian states that are experienced as positive and "good":

Happy	Passionate	Enthusiastic	Proud
Seductive	Ecstatic	Adoring	Certain
Loving/Loved	Eager	Safe/Secure	Reverent
Loyal	Nostalgic	Peaceful	Sentimental
Nurturing	Delighted	Playful	Playful
Joyous	Cheerful	Patriotic	Trusting
Content	Impressed	Excited	Calm
Pleased	Sleepy	Amused	Satisfied
	Sexually aroused = "in the mood"		

II: Limbic/Reptilian states that are experienced as negative and "bad":

Angry	Resentful	Irritated	Ambivalent
Furious	Smug	Hostile	Uncomfortable
Belligerent	Grief-stricken	Annoyed	Embarrassed
Controlling	Insecure	Arrogant	Fearful
Dominating	Judgmental	Critical	Invalidating
Dogmatic	Absolute	Antagonistic	Domineering

Contemptuous	Argumentative	Hateful	Willful
Defensive	Jealous	Possessive	Guilty
Bored	Apathetic	"Shutdown"	Frightened
Envious	Hurt	Worried	Anxious
Emotional	Needy	Timid	Intimidated
Subservient	Sad	Invalidated	Desperate
Suspicious	Nervous		

III: Intense Reptilian/Limbic states, usually held as "Very Bad":

Paranoid	Obsessive	Delusional	Addicted[1]
Hallucinating	Ritualistic	Territorial	Aggressive
Punitive	Submissive	Masochistic	Sadistic
Violent	Superior	Inferior	Repulsed
Disgusted	Glutonous	Reactive	Degraded
	Humiliated	Horrified	

Obviously there are a lot more words that could have been added (just as there are hundreds of shades, nuances, and variations on emotional states). If you think of additional words, please feel free to add them to this appendix.

---

[1]In conjunction with chemical changes in the cerebral cortex.

ADDITIVE ADAPTION:

> An adaptive pattern of behavior in which the person selectively increases the range of his or her access to include another mode.

ATROPHY:

> The inability to use an area or mode which develops as a result of avoidance, neglect or abstinence. This most often happens to a person's non-preferred mode when they marry someone whose strength in the mode enables them to "take care of those things" for their spouse. Since their non-preferred mode gets used less and less, what little strength the person originally had tends to "wither" away.

AVOIDANCE PATTERN:

> A behavioral pattern in which someone consciously avoids all activities which would engage a particular mode.

BASAL:

> Tending to be very concrete, visceral or earthy, having a preference for both the right and left basal areas or modes with little or no skill in either frontal mode.

BASAL LOBES:

> The posterior three lobes of each of the cerebral hemispheres. The occipital, parietal, and temporal lobes.

BASAL LEFT:

> The three basal lobes of the left cerebral hemisphere and the skills at which they are adept. Generally speaking: the mode of thinking which establishes and performs routine functions through adhering to sequence, order and schedule.

BASAL RIGHT:

> The three basal lobes of the right cerebral hemisphere and the skills at which they are adept. Generally speaking: the mode of thinking which establishes harmony and connections through a sensitivity to rhythm, movement, feelings, and color.

CEREBRAL CORTEX:

> The newest part of the triune brain. The seat of conscious thinking.

COMPETENCY:

> The ability to perform a skill in any of the four quadrants which exists as the result of usage and practice. Competencies may exists in area of preference or areas of non-preference. Key life issues such as finding satisfaction and meaning often arise when an individual identifies strongly with a competency which is not also a preference.

CREEPING DOMINANCE:

> The tendency to slip in your own thinking style when trying to communicate in a non-preferred mode. Creeping dominance may occur in your word choice, your speed of speech, your grammar, your perception of humor or your choice of examples.

DOMINANCE:

> The natural preference for one of the four key areas of your brain which seems to occur as the result of your brain's unique chemical make-up.

EXTRAVERTED:

> Having a naturally low level of arousal which causes the individual to seek higher than normal levels of stimulation in order to "feel alive". Typical ways in which the extravert seeks stimulation include: trying to influence or control his or her environment, confronting others, engaging in competiton, attending crowded parties or events "where the action is."

FIRST LAW OF CYBERNETICS:

> "The unit within the system with the most behavioral responses controls the system," is the first law of the science of cybernetics, otherwise known as the science of systems. It is used in brain dominance to explain why the multidominant individual tends to control and lead his environment as well as to rise to the top of many organizations. It is also used as an argument for developing whole brain access.

FRONTAL:

> Very conceptual, having a preference for both of the frontal lobes or modes with little or no skill in either of the basal modes.

FRONTAL LOBES:

> The foremost lobe of both the right and left hemisphere, located immediately behind the forehead.

FRONTAL LEFT:

> The foremost lobe of the left cerebral hemisphere, adept at logical and analytical thinking, as well as the seat of grammar and the laws governing the structure of language.

FRONTAL RIGHT:

> The foremost lobe of the right cerebral hemisphere, adept at imaginative, adaptive and metaphoric thinking. This lobe generally processes internally generated images.

HALF-BRAINED:

> Someone with a natural preference for any two of the four modes.

INTROVERTED:

> Having a naturally high level of arousal which causes the individual to seek lower than normal levels of stimulation in order to not feel overwhelmed. Over a period of years this need to not be overhelmed

by external stimulation develops into an internally focussed thinking style which may seem withdrawn, meditative, quiet or even reclusive to more extraverted persons. Typical ways in which the introvert seeks to control the level of stimulation include: spending time reading, reflecting or otherwise alone, avoiding or accomodating to others, competing mostly with oneself or self image, going to small parties or out of the way places.

LIKES ATTRACT:

The rule for friendships, also known as the "mirror rule", which says that people are most likely to choose friends who think the way they do and who have the same mental preferences.

LIMBIC BRAIN:

The middle brain as identified in Paul McLean's tri-une brain model. It is generally believed and to be involved with emotions, body temperature and sex as well as with the memory storage and retrieval.. (For a detailed description of this portion of the brain see Appendix B.)

MID-LIFE CRISIS:

A personal, internal emotional disturbance most frequently experienced in mid-life by those persons who abandoned their birth dominance in order to "fit in" and were most probably motivated by the need to find one's true "self."

MID-LIFE SPREAD:

A tendency to explore activities outside of one's dominance in mid-life. It is motivated primarily by curiosity.

MISFIT:

Any person who lives or works in a situation in which they are different from everyone else. Often used to identify a child whose lead area is one in which neither of his parents has a strength.

OCCIPITAL LOBES:

The most posterior lobe of each hemisphere responsible for processing the visual input from the eyes. Included in this model as a portion of the basal right and left.

OPPOSITES ATTRACT:

>   The rule for marriage which suggests that most people,   particularly in an early or first marriage will marry a person whose strongest area is the same as their weakest.

PARIETAL LOBES:

>   Otherwise called the sensory lobes. Found immediately behind the frontal lobes and separated from them by the central or rondalic fissure. Included in this model as a portion of the basal right and left. Recent research substantiates that the right parietal lobes is the seat of what people call the "spiritual experience," which may be another reason why basal rights are so very interested in love and caring.

PREFERENCE:

>   The same as dominance.

REPLACEMENT ADAPTION:

>   The adaptive behavior pattern in which a person abandons one preferred mode of thinking, usually because it is rejected by their environment, while picking up or adding another which they believe to be more acceptable.

REPTILIAN BRAIN:

>   The inner or core area of the human brain. Popularized by Paul MacLean in his tri-une model and described by people working with stress reactions as the seat of the fight or flight response, which when out of control can harm a person's biochemistry. This area of the brain oversees and monitors the autonomic nervous system including the regulation of the heart rate and the pumping of the lungs. (See Appendix B for more detailed information)

REQUISITE VARIETY:

>   Same as the First Law of Cybernetics. Strictly translated, the variety needed in order to gain control.

QUARTER-BRAINED:

>   Someone with a preference for only one of the four modes.

SECONDARY ACCESS:

>   Access which is neither strong enough to be rated as a preference nor weak enough to be called an area of avoidance. Typically, one can use a secondary area through consciously focusing one's will.

TEMPORAL LOBES:
>   Included in this model as a portion of the basal right and left.   These
>   lobes are lower down than the parietal lobes and nestled under the
>   sylvian fissure on each side. One specialty of the left temporal appears
>   to be the acquisition of words or a vocabulary.   Both right and left
>   temporal lobes process sound input.

THE SMART-DUMB RULE:
>   The rule which governs most people's choice of career as well as
>   their patterns of procrastination. It states that we tend to choose to do
>   what comes most naturally and to select tasks and careers which can
>   be done by our most preferred mode.

THE MIRROR RULE:
>   Same as: "Likes attract."

TRANSLATORS:
>   People whose access to three or four of the modes is so <u>fully and</u>
>   <u>equally</u> developed that they can easily translate between speakers
>   of those different modes and thereby facilitate communication.

TRIPLE BRAINED:
>   Having access to three of the four modes.

WHOLE BRAINED:
>   The natural ability to access all four modes, <u>or</u> more commonly,
>   having sufficient competency to access and use each of the four
>   modes situationally, as required by an environment or event.

This workbook has been specifically designed to accompany <u>The Art of Using Your Whole Brain</u>. In order to gain the maximum from the exercises, work chapter by chapter, doing those exercises which relate to a specific chapter as soon as possible after reading the chapter. Some of the exercises are like a self-test. Others seek to assist you in applying what you have learned in your reading to you own life.

Also, although you can benefit tremendously from doing the exercises on your own, experience suggests that you will learn more and faster if a friend of family who has read the book does the exercises at the same time. In this way, once you have both completed an exercised you can discuss what you have noticed or discovered.

CHAPTER ONE:

EXERCISE 1: Drawing Your Own Kite

A "kite" is a visual representation of someone's dominance pattern. It is a particularly useful way to represent the data (your scores) when communicating with a frontal right person.

To draw your own kite, transfer your actual scores from the self-assessment in Chapter One to the space provided below so that they are available to work with.

My Scores from the Assessment: <u> 3 </u> <u> 12 </u> <u> 13 </u> <u> 3 </u>

                                                  FL   BL   BR   FR

Now, you need to "scale" each of your 4 scores individually by converting each to a percentage. If you are inherently analytical, you will already have done this step. If not, you may accomplish this step by multiplying each of your scores by five, or if you are really right-brained, with "no brian for numbers," you can use the following conversion chart. Simply, find one of your scores in a left-hand column, follow the dots to its corresponding scaled value, and then write the scaled value in the appropriate place at the top of the next page.

1.......5	6.....30	11.....55	16.....80
2.....10	7.....35	12.....60	17.....85
3.....15	8.....40	13.....65	18.....90
4.....20	9.....45	14.....70	19.....95
5......25	10.....50	15.....75	20...100

Now, take a minute to study the graph below. You will notice that it is divided into four quadrants and that the axis of each of the quadrants is numbered. Find the place on the frontal Left axis that corresponds numerically to your converted frontal Left score and put a "dot" there. Repeat this procedure for each of your scores by finding and marking each score on the appropriate axis (BL score and basal Left axis, BR score and basal Right axis, and so on). When you have placed a dot in each of the four quadrants, draw your "kite" by connecting those dots.

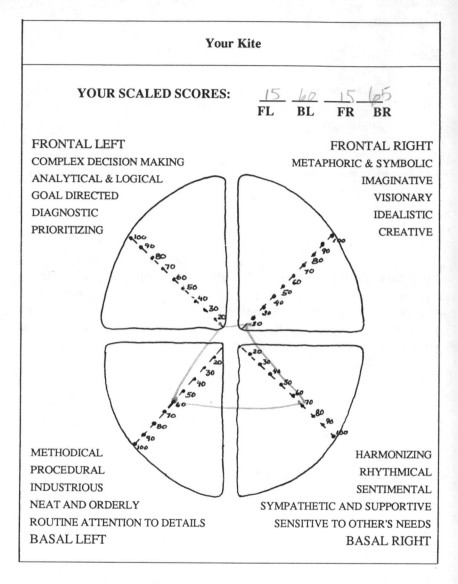

After you have completed your "kite", take a minute to study it. Does its shape remind you of anything? Is it square or pointed or tilted or slanted? What feeling, if any, does it convey? Is it "grounded" or "uplifting"? If you were going to give your kite a "nickname" what would it be and why?

CHAPTER TWO:

EXERCISE 1: Determining Your "Eyedness"

As we have already pointed out, **dominance** is a principle which governs much of your physiology. In these exercises you'll learn to identify some of the physiologically based dominances which affect your life. To find out which **eye** is your dominant eye, do the following exercise:

Step 1:   With each hand, make a circle by joining the tip of your thumb to the tip of your index finger. Keep the rest of your fingers pointing straight out and move each hand so it is directly in front of you with your thumbs pointing up. If you have done this correctly, you will be making the sign for "okay" with each hand.

Step 2:   Place one circle over the other circle so you have a single circle.

Step 3:   Now, extend your arms straight out in front of you <u>as far as you can</u> and look through the circle formed by your fingers.

Step 4:   Looking through that circle, find an object to focus on and center it in the middle of your circle.

Step 5:   Close both eyes, making sure you keep your arms and hands still. Then, open <u>only</u> one eye. Is the object that you were focusing on still in the center of the circle? Now, close that eye and open <u>only</u> the other eye. Once again check to see whether the object is still in the center of the circle. If it's not, notice where it is.

When your **dominant eye** is open, you will see the object in the circle. When your non-dominant eye is the open eye, the object will appear to have "moved" to the circle's edge or even to outside the circle. The reason this shift occurs is that you do 95% of your focusing with your dominant eye. The other eye contributes only about 5% and is used primarily to bring things into 3 dimensions.

EXERCISE 2: Determining Your "Armedness"

Step 1:   Cross your arms in front of your chest (the way you normally would if you were listening to someone or standing around waiting).

Step 2:   Notice which **arm is on top**. That is your dominant arm.

Step 3: Now, without moving your elbows away from the sides of your body, uncross your arms by opening or rotating them 90 degrees in front of you, such that your hands point forward.

Step 4: Recross your arms with your <u>non-dominant</u> arm on top.

What was it like to put your non-dominant arm on top? Awkward? Uncomfortable? When you did it were both of your hands are hanging down? What most people discover is that, when the dominant arm is on top, the position is comfortable and easy to maintain because the hands are in a "locked" position. Whereas, when the non-dominant arm is on top the position is uncomfortable and takes effort to hold.

One last thing you may want to notice is whether your dominant hand and your dominant arm are on the same side of your body. If they are not, you would need to do some kind of compensatory muscle development should you decide to take up a sport like rock climbing, in which you have to be able to leverage yourself up cliffs.

EXERCISE 3: Determining Your "Footedness"

To determine your dominant foot, answer the following question:

> "When you put on pants or stockings or shoes, which leg or shoe do you put on first? "

Whichever one it is is your dominant foot. It is also the foot you use as your lead when you step off curbs and climb stairs.

So, now you know your dominant hand, arm, eye, and foot. So what? Well, if you've ever wondered why some people can hit "home runs" and others can't, this may provide you with an answer. You see, in order to be a good hitter, you must have your dominant hand, arm, leg, and foot all on the same side of your body. But you must have your dominant eye on the opposite side. If your physiology is ordered differently than this, you simply won't do as well. (So, now you can stop beating yourself up for not being the Babe Ruth of the sandlot. It was the fault of your lousy dominance!)

CHAPTER THREE:

EXERCISE 1: Name that Brain Dominance

Below are 10 quotes from famous people. For fun and practice, try to figure out which of the brain's four modes is speaking in each of the following quotations. In order to do this, pay attention to word choice, length of sentences, style of speech, and subject matter. Ask yourself the question, "Which of the four brains would be most likely to talk like this and about these subjects?" You may also want to use the charts from Chapter 3 as references.

As a second step, you may also want to guess the name or occupation of each speaker.

1. "Religion is an **illusion**."
    "Analogies prove nothing."
    "If one wants to form a true estimate of the full grandeur of religion,
    one must keep in mind what it undertakes to do for men. It gives
    them information...it assures them of protection...amid the changing
    vicissitudes of life..."

    The LEAD MODE of this speaker is _____.
    The speaker's name or occupation _____.

2. "The Republic is a **dream**. Nothing happens unless first a dream."

    The LEAD MODE of this speaker is _____.
    The speaker's name or occupation _____.

3. "I like strawberries----but when I go fishing I use worms."

    The LEAD MODE of this speaker is _____.
    The speaker's name or occupation _____.

4. "The business of America is business."
    "There is no right to strike against public safety."
    "One with the law is **a majority**."

    The LEAD MODE of this speaker is _____.

The speaker's name or occupation _____.

5.   "Well, if I called the wrong number, why did you answer the phone?"
      "It's better to know some of the **questions** than all of the answers."

      The LEAD MODE of this speaker is _____.
      The speaker's name or occupation _____.

6   "The Fifth Amendment is **an old friend**---a good friend. It is one of
      the **great landmark**s in man's struggle to be free of tyranny, to be
      decent and civilized."

      The LEAD MODE of this speaker is _____.
      The speaker's name or occupation _____.

7.   "They always talk who never **think**."

      The LEAD MODE of this speaker is _____.
      The speaker's name or occupation _____.

8.   "I cannot forecast...it is a riddle
      "I have nothing to offer but blood, toil, tears, and sweat."
      "The watchword should be **'carry on.'**"

      The LEAD MODE of this speaker is _____.
      The speaker's name or occupation _____.

9.   "Industry in art is a necessity---not a virtue---and any evidence of
      the same, in the production, is a blemish, not a quality; a proof, not
      of achievement, but of absolutely insufficient work, for work done
      well will efface the footsteps of work."

      The LEAD MODE of this speaker is _____.
      The speaker's name or occupation _____.

10. "The responsibility of great states is to **serve** and not to dominate the world."
    "We must build a new world, a far better world--one in which the **eternal dignity of man is respected**."

    The LEAD MODE of this speaker is _____.
    The speaker's name or occupation _____.

ANSWERS

1. Double Frontal with a strong tilt to the Frontal Left, Sigmund Freud, psychiatrist.
2. Frontal Right, Carl Sandburg, poet.
3. Double Frontal tilted strongly to the Frontal Right, Dale Carnegie, entrepreneur
4. Basal Left, Calvin Coolidge, president
5. Frontal Right, James Thurber, author and cartoonist
6. Frontal Right, William O. Douglas, jurist
7. Frontal Left, John Donne, poet
8. Basal Left, Winston Churchill, a visionary Frontal Right leader speaking to the Basal Left people. British culture and choosing his language in order to influence them. Churchill was a notoriously eccentric frontal Right who had an ongoing "love-hate" relationship with the British people. He did not learn to match their dominance in his speeches until well into his career.
9. Double Frontal tilted to the frontal Left, James Whistler, painter.
10. Double Right, Harry S. Truman, president.

EXERCISE 2: Owning the Model

This exercise is a wonderful one suggested by a friend of ours, Elizabeth Myers. It's special benefit is that it allows you to describe the model using your own words symbols. Simply read through each of the following questions, and then write or draw your answers in the appropriate quadrant or mode of the blank model which follows. For fun, we've included Elizabeth's model at the end of this exercise. If you're having difficulty getting started, read over hers first.

1. In your own mind, what color best describes each mode?
2. If you were to close your eyes and imagine touching each mode, what texture would each be? How would each feel to you?
3. If each mode were a shape, how would you draw or diagram each?
4. What words would you use to describe each shape?

Your Model
FRONTAL LEFT   FRONTAL RIGHT
BASAL LEFT   BASAL RIGHT

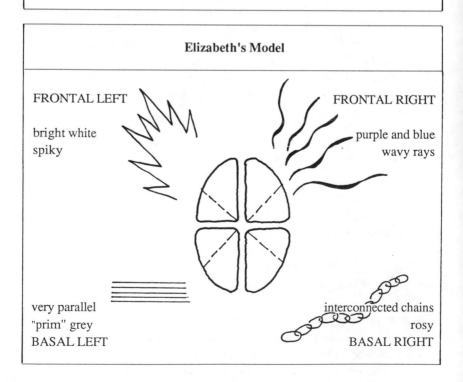

Elizabeth's Model
FRONTAL LEFT   FRONTAL RIGHT
bright white   purple and blue
spiky   wavy rays
very parallel   interconnected chains
"prim" grey   rosy
BASAL LEFT   BASAL RIGHT

EXERCISE 3: Dominance Metaphor

Metaphors are a good way of checking to see what you understand about a subject. They also generate pictures which can be processed by the Frontal Right brain. To do this, fill in the blank in the first part of the sentence and then come up with as many ways to complete the sentence as you can.

Life with my dominance pattern is like: _____

Because: _____

_____

As an example, here is a metaphor that one of Anne's students (with a double right preference pattern) generated:

Life with my dominance is like: <u>riding a carousel.</u>
Because:
- it's colorful and musical and a work of art.
- it's magical and populated by strange and exotic creatures.
- my dreams are like the brass ring and every time I go around I get a new dream.
- it's fun and exciting and brings out the child in me.
- I'm always getting to see a new point of view (as I go around)
- My basal Left stays happy because even though I go up and down & around in circles, I am still going on the same, predictable path.

From reading her metaphor, would you have guessed she's a double right?

Now it's your turn.

Life with my brain dominance is like _____

_____,

because...

continue

Now, re-read what you have just written. What did you learn about the way you see your dominance pattern and the effect it has on your life? Is it generally positive? Generally negative? In between?

If your perception was generally **positive**, then you have completed the exercises for Chapter 3. On the other hand, if your perception is that it was generally **negative**, use this space to generate a list of at least 10 positive skills and abilities that come with having your particular dominance pattern.

1.

2.

3.

4.

5.

6.

7.

8.

9.

10.

Then, when you have completed the list of 10 positive aspects to your pattern, see if you can generate another metaphor which expresses those positive traits.

Life with my brain dominance is like _____

_____,

because...

CHAPTER FOUR:

EXERCISE 1: Your Job -- A Match or Mismatch

Although most jobs have a clear slant or dominance, most of them are also, to some degree, whole brained. Because of this, we can sometimes tie the comfort or discomfort, ease or frustration, we have with certain parts of our job to our dominance.

Instructions:
1   On the profile chart below, <u>draw your kite</u>

2. Next, list at least 15 specific aspects of your job, especially those that regularly (daily or weekly) consume time, those that consume large amounts of time whether or not regular, those you like a lot, those you don't like and those you notice you procrastinate.

3. Then, take a stab at placing each of these job aspects in the quadrant which actually does that kind of stuff. If you like, use the following coded questions.

- Is this analytical (FL)?
- Is this technical (FL)?
- Is sequential or procedural if done properly (BL)?
- Does this involve respecting schedules and rules (BL)?
- Do I teach when I do this (BR)?
- Do I need to be empathetic (BR)?
- Do I need to tolerate ambiguity (FR)?
- Do I need to be innovative (FR)?

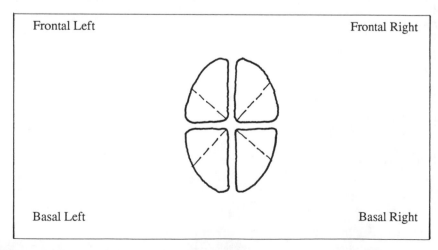

Frontal Left   Frontal Right

Basal Left   Basal Right

4. Now, look back at the job profile you created for your current job considering each of the following questions as you do so:
- How well does it match your dominance pattern?
- Is a large amount of your work in areas outside your areas of strength?
- How might you handle this?
- Is there anyone you could delegate those tasks to?
- Is there anyone who could assist you in completing them?
(Who do you know who does have strength in those areas?)

Jot down any ideas you have for aligning your job to your dominance in the space below.

```
Ways in which I could tailor my job to my dominance:




```

EXERCISE 2: Here Come the **Tribes**

Many people hire others who think like themselves match their own thinking style (as with the ICU nurses described in Chapter 4). This vastly increases the probability that specific departments or specialties within an organization will become separate, identifiable tribes.

Step 1: Identify at least two groups, committees, or departments within your organization which you believe to be "tribes".

Step 2: In the blank space below, describe the "tribal pattern" or mind set of each. Include any specific behaviors, dress codes, benefits, or languages people in your organization associate with those "tribes."

Step 3: Now, review the data you've generated and speculate as to each tribe's Brain Dominance. What is their most preferred mode? What is their least preferred mode? How does each tribe's dominance affect its general effectiveness in your organization? Who do they interact with well? Who do they interact with poorly?

Finally, based on what you've just learned, what are the advantages and disadvantages of "tribes"?

```
Tribal Data & Observations:




```

CHAPTER FIVE:

EXERCISE 1: Avoiding the "Big Dumb"

In this exercise you are going to have an opportunity to see how your dominance determines the work you avoid or procrastinate.

Instructions:

1. Looking back over your life, identify 3 times you've used avoidance strategies to manage an uncomfortable situation: when you quit a job or project, transferred jobs, chose to not join a group, or did not volunteer to do a particular work task. List these 3 situations in the box below.

2. Now, look to see if those situations would have required (or were requiring) the use of one or more of your non-preferred modes.

To do this, you may want to ask yourself some of the following questions:

What are my non-preferred modes?

What modes would I have needed to do those projects, that job?

What was the dominant mode used by members of that group?

What tasks would I have had to do in those situations that I feel "dumb" and incompetent trying to handle? What mode handles these tasks best?

Which modes (that I like) did I get to stay with by turning down that other work?

```
┌─────────────────────────────────────────────────────────┐
│                                                         │
│  Situations in which I avoided being "Big Dumb":        │
│                                                         │
│                                                         │
│                                                         │
│                                                         │
│                                                         │
│                                                         │
│                                                         │
└─────────────────────────────────────────────────────────┘
```

3. As a final step to this exercise, you may want to remind yourself that there is nothing inherently wrong with choosing not to work in your non-preferred modes. It is simply useful to understand why you make the choices you do and how your dominance influences those choices.

EXERCISE 2: Your Best - Worst Manager

How a person thinks often influences how they want to be managed. This exercise is designed to show you how you prefer to be managed.

Step 1: Take a minute to identify the two people you recall as your Best Manager and Worst Manager. In the space below, explain why you selected these two people.

What did each do or not do?
What did you value or find disturbing in each?
Why?

My Best Manager:

My Worst Manager:

Step 2: Now, on the graph below, draw your own kite and a kite for your Best Manager, based on the information you've just written. (You may want to use contrasting pens in order to delineate which is which)

Me and My Best Manager:

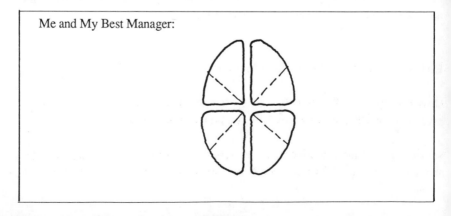

Step 3: Notice what, if any, connection there is between your brain dominance and your selection of your Best Manager.

> What about his or her profile made this person a good manager of you?
> What about your profile made you a receptive and responsive employee?

Write your observations in the space below.

Insights about my Best Manager & how and why I liked him or her:

Step 4: Next, draw your kite and the kite of your Worst Manager, once again using the information you wrote earlier to predict his dominance pattern. Remember to use contrasting pens and to identify which kite is which.

Me and My Worst Manger:

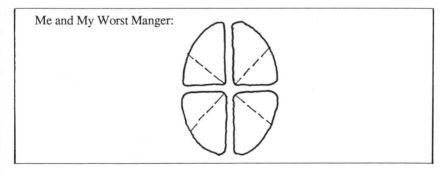

Step 5: Take a few minutes to notice the connection between your brain dominance and your choice of Worst Manager.

> What made this such a counter-productive, stressful relationship?
> What about this person's dominance made him or her such a bad manager for you?
> What about your profile made you a hostile, non-receptive subordinate to that manager?

Jot down your observations in the space below.

Observations about me and my Worst Manager and how & why I did not like him or her:

As a final step, take a moment to consider what you have learned from this exercise. Are there any conclusions you can come to about how you like to be managed? And what dominance patterns work the best for you and why?

EXERCISE 3: Your Best - Worst Employee

How a person thinks may also influence how they manage. This exercise is designed to put you in touch with how you like to manage and how that connects to your dominance and the dominance of those who work for you.

Step 1: Identify the two people you recall as your Best and Worst employees. Then explain why you selected these two people.

   What did each do or not do?
   What did you value or find disturbing in each? Why?

Write down this information in the space provided below.

My Best Employee:

My Worst Employee:

Step 2: Now, on the graph provided below, draw your own kite and then, based on what you have written, a kite which shows the dominance profile of your Best Employee. Use contrasting pens for each and identify which is which.

Me and My Best Employee:

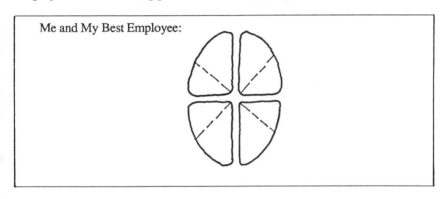

Step 3: Notice what connection there is, if any, between your brain dominance and the brain dominance of your Best Employee.

What about this person's brain dominance made them such a "good employee" for you?

Jot down your observations in the space provided below.

Insights about my Best Employee:

Step 4: Now, draw your kite and the kite of your Worst Employee, once again using contrasting pens.

Me and My Worst Employee:

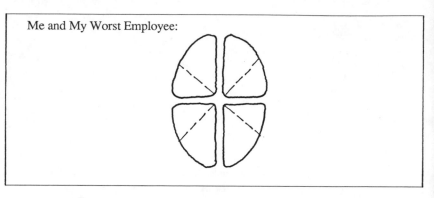

Step 5: What, if any, connections do you see between your brain dominance and your selection of your Worst Employee?

What about this person's brain dominance made them such a "bad employee" for you?

You may use the space below to record your thoughts.

Observations about my Worst Employee:

Looking at this exercise as a whole, what conclusions can you draw about the relationship between your brain dominance and your preference in employees? What patterns work well for you and which don't? Why?

Conclusions:

EXERCISE 4: Your Best - Worst Co-Worker

As you can imagine, how a person thinks also influences how they work with their peers. This exercise is designed to put you in touch with what you prefer in a co-worker. Some of you will find your preferences in a co-worker are very stable, others will find that how you feel about your co-workers and their dominance patterns varies with the nature of the task.

Step 1: Identify the two people you recall as your Best Co-Worker and your Worst Co-Worker. Then explain why you selected these two people.

> What did each do or not do?
> What did you value or find irritating in each? Why?

Jot your observations in the spaces below.

Best Co-Worker:

Worst Co-Worker

Step 2: From the notes you have written, create a kite for your Best Co-Worker and draw it on the graph which follows. Then, using a contrasting pen, draw your own kite.

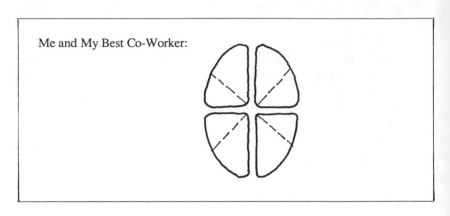

Me and My Best Co-Worker:

Step 3: Notice if there is a connection between your brain dominance and your selection of a Best Co-Worker.

What made that person such a "good person" for you to work with?

How did your dominance patterns fit together?

Insights about my Best Co-Worker:

Step 4: Now, draw your kite and the kite of your Worst Co-Worker. Remember to use contrasting pens and identify which is which.

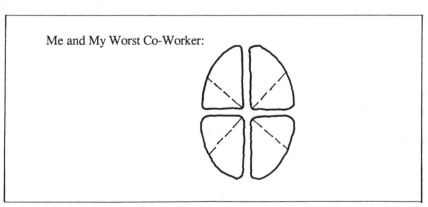

Me and My Worst Co-Worker:

Step 5: Notice what the connection is between your brain dominance and the brain dominance of your Worst Co-Worker.

What made this person such an undesirable person to work with?

What if any conclusions can you draw from this exercise?

Observations about my Worst Co-Worker:

Looking back at the last 3 exercises (Best & Worst Managers, Employees, and Co-Workers)

What general patterns can you see in your behavior?

Is it easier for you to work with someone who thinks just like you?

Or, someone who has complementary thinking?

Does who you're comfortable with depend on the nature of the task?

Or, on their organizational relationship to you?

What conclusions can you draw?

How might you use this information to improve your life on the job?

General Patterns, Tendencies and Ideas:

CHAPTER SIX:

EXERCISE 1: Sorting Out the "Brains" in your family

Step 1: Based on what you've read so far, we'd like you to take some time to consider the brain dominance patterns of the people in your family. Work at your own speed but be sure to consider each person individually. If they have a strong preference for an area, put an "X" in the corresponding column. If they have an avoidance of an area, put a "0" in the corresponding column. And if they use the mode on occasion if necessary, leave the box blank.

FAMILY MEMBER	B. LEFT liking routines	B. RIGHT liking feelings	F.RIGHT liking creativity	F.LEFT liking analysis
Your Mother:				
Your Father:				
Your Step Parents: (if applicable)				
Your Siblings:				
Your Spouse:				
Former Spouses: (if applicable)				
Your Children:				

FAMILY MEMBER	B. LEFT liking routines	B. RIGHT liking feelings	F.RIGHT liking creativity	F.LEFT liking analysis
Other Significant Family Members:				

Step 2: Now, look at the data you've collected to see if you can find any patterns.

Who do you get along with particularly well?
What is their dominance pattern? And, how does their pattern relate to yours?
Who do you have difficulty with (and in what way) and what is their pattern? How does their pattern relate to yours?
Which of your family members have brain patterns similar to your own? How well do you get along?
Which have complementary patterns and are strong in your area(s) of weakness?
How did your parents' dominance affect your home life and your upbringing?
How does your dominance and your spouse's dominance affect your marriage?

Before leaving this exercise, review your family once again, identifying what you enjoy doing with each person. As you do this, notice which modes you are choosing to use.

Insights about dominance and my family:

EXERCISE 2: "Sorting Out" Your Friends

Step 1: In this exercise we'd like you to consider the dominance patterns of your friends, past and present. You can begin by filling in this chart according to the instructions given earlier.

FRIENDS	B. LEFT liking routines	B. RIGHT liking feelings	F.RIGHT liking creativity	F.LEFT liking analysis
Your "Best Friend" from childhood:				
Your "Best Friend" during your teen years:				
Your "Best Friend" in college:				
Your current "Best Friend":				
3 of your closest female friends:				
3 of your closest male friends:				

Step 2: Once again: What patterns, if any, can you find?
What part(s) of your friends do you get along with and what part(s) do you have difficulty with?

Which and how many of the modes do you have in common?
What dominance patterns seem to work best for you and why?
How does your dominance affect your choice of friends?

Write your answers to these questions and any other observations you may have in the box on the next page.

```
┌─────────────────────────────────────────────────────────────┐
│  Insights about dominance and my friends:                   │
│                                                              │
│                                                              │
│                                                              │
│                                                              │
└─────────────────────────────────────────────────────────────┘
```

EXERCISE 3: Other Significant "Brains" in Your Life

Step 1: As with the preceding two exercise, we would like you to use your understanding of the four modes to speculate about the dominance patterns of:

SIGNIFICANT PEOPLE	B. LEFT liking routines	B. RIGHT liking feelings	F. RIGHT liking creativity	F. LEFT liking analysis
Your Mentors (if applicable):				
A Role Model or Inspirational Hero:				

Step 2: What do you notice about the relationship between their dominance patterns and your dominance pattern?

Why were these people "good choices" to mentor or inspire you?
What conclusions can you draw from this exercise?

```
┌─────────────────────────────────────────────────────────────┐
│  Insights about dominance and my mentors:                   │
│                                                              │
│                                                              │
│                                                              │
│                                                              │
└─────────────────────────────────────────────────────────────┘
```

CHAPTER SEVEN:

EXERCISE 1: Discovering Your Original Dominance

Follow the steps outlined in Chapter 8 to discover your dominance as a child.
After following those steps, consider these questions:
>   What do you think your original dominance was?
>   What if any, adaptive pattern did you take on?

Spend some time considering the circumstances and experiences that led you to
adapt away from your original pattern. Finally, consider the steps you can take to
re-own your original pattern and re-build competency in those quadrants (see
Chapter 9 for suggestions).

```
┌─────────────────────────────────────────────────────────────┐
│  Observations about my original dominance                     │
│  & my adaptive patterns:                                      │
│                                                               │
│                                                               │
│                                                               │
│                                                               │
│                                                               │
│                                                               │
│                                                               │
│                                                               │
└─────────────────────────────────────────────────────────────┘
```

EXERCISE 2: Looking at Mid-Life Crisis

Part A: Identify someone you know who has gone through a major career shift or
a mid-life crisis. Write their name here and hold a picture of them in your mind as
you answer the following questions._____

>   Based on what you know about them and the model, what would
>   you say is their brain dominance?
>   Looking at how they resolved their "crisis", what might you guess
>   about their original pattern?
>   Which modes did they use most heavily before their crisis?
>   What "new" modes did they take on afterward?
>   How did that crisis change their pattern?

Jot your observations in the box on the top of the following page.

```
┌─────────────────────────────────────────────────────────┐
│                                                         │
│   Dominance and Mid-Life Crisis:                        │
│                                                         │
│                                                         │
│                                                         │
│                                                         │
│                                                         │
│                                                         │
│                                                         │
│                                                         │
└─────────────────────────────────────────────────────────┘
```

Part B: Based on what you've learned so far about brain dominance, yourself, and patterns of growth, do you think you are likely to experience a mid-life crisis or a mid-life spread? Why?

```
┌─────────────────────────────────────────────────────────┐
│                                                         │
│   Predictions for my Future:                            │
│                                                         │
│                                                         │
│                                                         │
│                                                         │
│                                                         │
│                                                         │
│                                                         │
│                                                         │
│                                                         │
│                                                         │
└─────────────────────────────────────────────────────────┘
```

CHAPTER EIGHT:

EXERCISE 1: Dealing With Differences

The value of learning to speak and write in each of the four brain languages is that it enables you to communicate effectively with others. After reading the suggestions made in Chapter 9, you should have some specific ideas on how to approach each of the "brains" as well as a clearer understanding of what each of them wants from you. This exercise will give you an opportunity to apply and practice that learning.

Step 1: Select a "problem person" or a "problem tribe" which you would like to influence more effectively. Create a typical problem or use one you are currently facing. Then, in the space below, define the problem in terms of:

Who's involved in this problem?

What's their brain dominance?

What's your brain dominance?

What's at issue?

What hasn't worked in the past?

continued

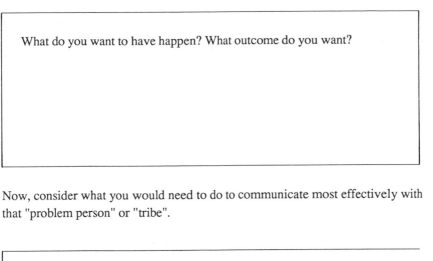

What do you want to have happen? What outcome do you want?

Now, consider what you would need to do to communicate most effectively with that "problem person" or "tribe".

IDEAS FOR RESOLVING THE PROBLEM

What would be the best climate, setting or location? (formal,casual)

What would be the best time/timing? (pre-scheduled, in the elevator, in another meeting, etc.) (brief, long)

What would be the best medium (written, verbal,visual)?

What would be the best line of "argument"? It's new, it's an improvement which will double our net income? It's safe and tested--it's the way G.E., Shell, IBM, Apple are doing it? I think it will be good for morale?

continued

Who and how many should meet with "them"? (Why?)

Should anyone else be present? Why? (Do you need a translator?)

After you have finished this exercise, review your strategy. Is it consistent with what you have learned about communicating with each of the modes? Is there anything else you should include? What and why?

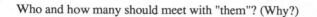

You have now completed all the exercises we have developed to assist you in mastering The Art of Using Your Whole Brain. From here on, you'll be creating your own opportunities to develop, use and benefit from the information in this book. If you're like most of our clients, you'll begin to integrate what we have offered you with what you already know from your own experience and training. That's an excellent next step. In fact, only once you and others who are experts in other fields have tested and mastered this information by applying it both at work and at home, and subsequently taken this information into your own areas of expertise will it be possible for the vision described in Chapter 9 to become an empowering, vitalizing reality. And so, as we move forward together, dreaming and creating our futures,

---

**WALK IN PEACE AND LOVE
AND ENJOY**

KBA'S LIFE-BUILDING TOOLS

KBA's life-building tools are all based on the synthesis of state of the art knowledge from neurophysiology and psychology. The most significant and central tool is the BTSA. All other tools have been designed to facilitate the effective application of this tool to a wide range of life situations. For this reason, the BTSA is explained in detail below. Following that description is a comprehensive list of available products, along with ordering instructions.

THE BENZIGER THINKING STYLES ASSESSMENT

People are more productive, as well as happier and healthier when they use and are rewarded for using their natural mental preferences. This is even truer when their natural extraverted or introverted needs are simultaneously understood, valued and rewarded.

Although these statements seem self-evident, they are not as easy to apply as you might think. Many people adapt early in life, developing and using one or more non-preferred modes as a result of environmental pressure and/or opportunities. Such early adaption may even result in an individual identifying so strongly with such skills and competencies that they forget their natural or true identity. When this occurs, a person is apt to suffer from chronic self-esteem problems, low-grade depression and/or burn-out.

For this reason, we recommend the BTSA be used in conjunction with <u>The Art of Using Your Whole Brain</u> by anyone seriously interested in using the model to help themselves and others. The 8-page assessment, which is lengthier and more complex than the self-assessment at the beginning of this book, is designed to help you sort out your true natural preferences from any developed but non-preferred competencies. Upon completing the assessment you will receive a 20-page feedback packet including a personal analysis of your thinking style, your strongest and weakest modes, your extraverted or/and introverted needs and your life patterns of adaption.

Everyone can benefit from knowing more about themselves. The insights and self knowledge provided by the BTSA can help us select more appropriate jobs, set more appropriate personal and professional goals or expectations as well as understand, accept and work more effectively with others whose preferences differ from our own.

KBA's Life-building Tools	
<u>**Item**</u>	<u>**Contribution**</u>
• The BTSA Assessment and Feedback	Gathers data about you or another person. The Feedback explains the data in a manner that allows you to learn about yourself or another person in a positive affirming way.
• <u>The Art of Using Your Whole Brain</u>	Presents guidelines for communicating effectively. Exercises which allow you to apply the model to your worklife while gaining insights into: • which jobs are best for you and why; • which jobs are a problem for you and why; • why you have difficulty communicating or working with certain colleagues. Stories and exercises relating the model to your home life: • sheds light on problems between family members; • offers ideas for improving the quality of your home life; and • offers ideas for living with and helping your children.

KBA's Life-building Tools (continued)

Item	Contribution
• The BTSA User Manual	Presents a comprehensive discussion covering: • the construction and properties of the BTSA; • the theory behind the BTSA; • details for administering the BTSA; • applications for the BTSA; • technical and statistical information on the BTSA's reliability and validity.
• Falsification of Type	Groundbreaking. Presents an in-depth analysis of this problem from a psychological and physiological perspective, especially its role in weakening the immune system and self-esteem of the individual.
• Increasing Your Own and Others High Performance (a set of 4 audio tapes)	Presents strategies for improving performance and effectiveness. Includes strategies for managing individual and group weaknesses.
• Maximizing Individual and Team Effectiveness	Presents specific guidelines for applying the model to your own and other's lives. Functions as a useful **concordance**, assisting it's reader-user to find pertinent material in other KBA publications and tapes.
• Developing Positive Self-Esteem	Introduces an empowering approach to helping yourself, for those wanting to increase their self-esteem.
• Overcoming Depression	Provides powerful, healing insights into the physiological basis of depression. A set of life skills which have been shown to be successful in overcoming depression.

For a current price list and order form call or write:

KBA • *The Human Resource Technology Company*
P.O. Box 116 • Rockwall, Texas 75087

(214) 771-3991

Notes: